PIRATES

of the 21st Century

Marshall County Public Library
1003 Poplar Street
Benton, KY 42025

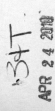

NIGEL CAWTHORNE

PIRATES

of the 21st Century

JB

JOHN BLAKE

Published by John Blake Publishing Ltd,
3 Bramber Court, 2 Bramber Road,
London W14 9PB, England

www.johnblakepublishing.co.uk

First published in paperback in 2009

ISBN: 978-1-84454-807-1

All rights reserved. No part of this publication may be reproduced,
stored in a retrieval system, or in any form or by any means, without
the prior permission in writing of the publisher, nor be otherwise
circulated in any form of binding or cover other than that in which it
is published and without a similar condition including this condition
being imposed on the subsequent publisher.

British Library Cataloguing-in-Publication Data:

A catalogue record for this book is available from the British Library.

Design by www.envydesign.co.uk

Printed in the UK by CPI William Clowes
Beccles NR34 7TL

1 3 5 7 9 10 8 6 4 2

© Text copyright Nigel Cawhtorne
Photographs © Getty Images

Papers used by John Blake Publishing are natural,
recyclable products made from wood grown in sustainable forests.
The manufacturing processes conform to the environmental
regulations of the country of origin.

CONTENTS

INTRODUCTION

CHAPTER 1   THE SEIZING OF THE *SIRIUS STAR*   1

CHAPTER 2   THE HOSTAGES' TALE   23

CHAPTER 3   SOMALI STANDOFF   35

CHAPTER 4   THE PRISONERS OF *LE PONANT*   55

CHAPTER 5   THE *SEABOURN SPIRIT*   65

CHAPTER 6   THE SOMALI SEA   75

CHAPTER 7   THE GULF OF ADEN   99

CHAPTER 8   THE NAVY STRIKES BACK   113

CHAPTER 9   PORTRAIT OF THE PIRATES   143

CHAPTER 10   THE STRAITS OF MALACCA   161

CHAPTER 11   THE SOUTH CHINA SEA   197

CHAPTER 12   BRAZILIAN BRIGANDS   215

CHAPTER 13   PIRATES OF THE CARIBBEAN   227

CHAPTER 14   BACK TO THE SPANISH MAIN   251

CHAPTER 15   SEA DOGS   265

INTRODUCTION

British businessman Malcolm Robertson had long cherished the ambition to sail around the world. He bought the 44ft cutter *Mr Bean* and when he retired, he and his wife Linda set off. They spent ten happy years at sea. Then on the night of 24 March 2009, they were moored off La-Ngu in southern Thailand, near the border with Burma. It was hot that night. Malcolm and Linda were sleeping in separate cabins.

'I was naked,' said Mrs Robertson. 'It was a very hot night.'

Just after midnight, three young Burmese migrants climbed on board, armed with hammers. They burst into the stern cabin where Linda was sleeping, grabbed her, tied her up and gagged her. Then they went forward. By this time her husband was awake. She heard him shouting: 'Get off my boat!'

She heard a scuffle, then a splash. Malcolm Robertson had been bludgeoned and thrown overboard. His body was found four days later. Linda was left trussed up naked like a chicken. Her feet and hands began to swell.

'It was all very degrading,' she said.

Meanwhile, the invaders ransacked the whole boat, opening every can and bottle, and eating everything they could find.

'It was like three boys having a picnic,' Mrs Robertson said. 'They were eating food, they were laughing and joking' – even though they had just killed her husband. 'The younger boy was playing on my mobile.'

But they were not unsympathetic. At one point they loosened her ropes and one of them massaged her swollen feet.

'He kept saying, "Sorry," all the time,' she said. 'And he stroked my feet which were in agony. I asked him if they were going to kill me and he said, "No." I asked when they would leave and he pointed nine o'clock on the cabin clock.'

Eventually, they took her up to the cockpit and asked her to show them how to work the controls of the yacht. There was blood on the deck.

'As I walked through the boat I realised I was walking through the blood of my husband,' she said. 'From that moment on I knew I was just fending for my life and might have to fight for it or take my chance in the ocean.'

At one point, she tried to throw herself overboard, but stumbled.

Instead of taking the yacht, the pirates decided to make off in the dinghy. They loaded it with the Robertsons' mobile phones, their laptop, cameras and other valuables. However, she knew that there was something wrong with the dinghy's outboard motor and when she heard them leave she quickly freed herself.

'They had only got 30 yards when the engine began to splutter, as I knew it would,' she said. 'They turned back to the boat, so I rushed to pull up the anchor. Then I put our boat into full throttle and headed out to sea, leaving them behind. I saw them head to shore and I knew my ordeal was over.'

Linda found some fishermen and raised the alarm. The police came in a patrol boat and shortly afterwards arrested the three pirates in the dinghy. They confessed to killing Mr Robertson but claimed that they were fleeing from a Thai fishing boat where they were being held as virtual slaves. They had not been paid for months and had only intended to steal a boat to make for shore. The murder of Mr Robertson, callous though it was, had been part of an escape attempt gone wrong.

Although this case made the front pages of the British newspapers, there is nothing unusual about it. Yachtsmen the world over face a growing number of attacks. Some are murdered. Piracy generally is on the increase. Luxury liners have been attacked. Supertankers and container ships have been hijacked and held to ransom. In some parts of the world, these attacks are carried out by bands of organised criminals. In the Far East, ships are stolen and their cargos offloaded. The vessel is then repainted, renamed and sold on. There are indications that the Triads may be involved.

However, most piracy takes place in areas where people are poor. Their livelihood has been taken from them by globalisation, civil unrest or war. There, men turn to piracy simply to survive and often go to great lengths to ensure that the crews of the vessels they seize are not hurt. Even *The Economist* and *The Times* have compared the modern-day buccaneers to Robin Hood. But that's not the whole story...

CHAPTER 1

THE SEIZING OF THE
SIRIUS STAR

The *Sirius Star* should have been safe. The supertanker was some 500 miles off the coast of east Africa, well outside the danger zone plied by the anti-piracy patrols of the world's navies. But with her tanks laden with two million barrels of heavy crude, she lay low in the water and was slow and hard to manoeuvre. In fact, she was a sitting duck. She was easily outrun by the powerful speedboats of the pirates who seemed to appear from nowhere.

The *Sirius Star* might have been 1,080 feet long with a deck the size of three football pitches and a displacement three times that of the largest aircraft carrier, but she had a crew of just 25. There was no way that such a small bunch of men could defend the gunwales against a determined bunch of Somali buccaneers armed with Kalashnikovs and rocket-propelled grenades (RPGs). Shoulder-launched anti-tank weapons that can rip a hole in the side of a ship, RPGs can be bought for as little as $10 in the world's trouble spots. So when a handful of well-armed pirates scaled the sides of the *Sirius Star* on 15 November 2008, the unarmed crew did not stand a chance.

The supertanker had filled up at Fujairah in the Persian Gulf with around a quarter of Saudi Arabia's daily output. She had headed out into the Arabian Sea via the Gulf of Oman, and was making for the United States around the Cape of Good Hope because she was far too big to go through the Suez Canal. Besides, heading that way would have taken her through the Gulf of Aden at the mouth of the Red Sea. That was the real danger zone. More than 50 ships had been hijacked there already that year.

All vessels sailing through that area are told to maintain strict 24-hour radar and anti-piracy watch using all available means. Crews are told to look out for small, suspicious boats converging on their vessel. Once alerted, the master can call on the naval patrols for assistance, but with vast areas of ocean to cover, the patrols are rarely in a position to respond in time. Crews are told not to resist, so the pirates are usually successful. Once a ship has been seized, it is sailed towards the Somali coast where it is held for ransom. When the *Sirius Star* was taken, there were 19 other hijacked ships moored off shore.

The *Sirius Star*'s route had taken her along the coast of Somalia, but she had heeded the warnings of the International Maritime Bureau (IMB) to keep as far as possible from the coast, ideally more than 250 nautical miles. The supertanker had stayed well outside that zone and had passed Somalia unmolested. In fact she had sailed on beyond Kenya and was off Tanzania when she was attacked. This was well outside the normal danger area: the IMB had only warned that pirates in that area were targeting ships in ports and anchorages – not those out to sea.

The *Sirius Star* was also at least 100 nautical miles further from the coast than any ship previously attacked. To make attacks further afield, Somali pirates had taken to carrying their high-speed attack craft on larger 'mother ships'. But it would have taken any mother ship three or four days to reach that position, which put the seemingly casual piracy off the coast in a different light. 'The distance from the shore would suggest a highly organised operation,' said Pottengal Mukundan, director of the IMB. 'This is not mere opportunism.'

The *Sirius Star*'s Polish captain Marek Nishky was not expecting an attack that sunny morning. There was no wind and the sea was like a millpond. 'It was flat calm – good pirate weather as we found out,' said Second Officer James Grady. 'When the first mate came and told me he thought we were being followed, the speedboats were just like little dots in our wake. You could barely see them. I thought, No – they're not following us. But they were gaining on us as we watched.'

Chief Engineer Peter French was in an officers' meeting when it was interrupted by a phone call from the third mate, alerting them that they were being followed. Two dinghies were visible in the distance, they were told, and closing fast.

The standard advice on how to get away from pirates is to speed up and zigzag. 'It's practically impossible to do both at the same time,' said Grady, and in a very large crude carrier (VLCC) it's impossible to do either effectively within the time available.

'It was obvious we were being menaced by pirates,' said French. 'I went down to the engine room to increase speed while Captain Nishky ordered the Filipino crew to man the fire hoses. Jets of water were our only defence.'

Few civilian vessels carry firearms as this can cause problems in the ports and territorial waters of some nations. Captains are also fearful of mutinies, and if you are carrying a flammable cargo – such as oil – the last thing you want is a shoot-out. Pirates are well aware of this and take advantage of the fact.

Twenty-seven-year-old Saudi sailor Hussein al-Hamza was napping after his night shift when the alarm went off. He rushed up on deck with the rest of the crew. 'I looked down and saw eight Somali pirates in two boats, each about 18 feet long,' he said. 'They looked scary.'

Very quickly a speedboat came alongside and the pirates, equipped with AK-47s and RPGs, flung a ladder with a hook over the rail. Realising they had no chance, Captain Nishky stood down the crew members with the fire hoses, and no one challenged the raiders as they scaled the few feet from ocean to deck. 'The ship was loaded with oil,' said al-Hamza. 'Imagine the catastrophe if weapons had been fired.'

'Our ship was low in the water so they didn't find it too hard to get on board,' said Grady. 'They had a 12ft ladder roughly tied together. They hooked it on to the side and climbed on. All we had to fight them was fire hoses but when we saw how heavily armed they were we thought it best not to even try. We didn't fancy our chances against Kalashnikovs.'

Pirate leader Abdullah Hassan later explained how the hijacking was done. The raiders operated from Russian-built trawlers. Once in sight of the target, they would launch a number of fast, high-powered motorboats. Within minutes, the ship would be surrounded by a dozen or so gang members firing AK-47s into the air and threatening to shoot RPGs at the unarmed merchantmen. After the flurry of gunshots had died away, the pirates would use grappling irons and ladders to clamber aboard and take control of the ship.

'The secret of a successful attack is the speed with which it is carried out,' said Hassan, who reckoned that his team of pirates could identify, catch, board and take control of a ship in less than 15 minutes. 'All without bloodshed,' he insisted. The Somali pirates, he said, take pride in carrying out 'clean' attacks where each man follows strict orders and the hostages remain safe.

Initially the *Sirius Star* was taken by just eight men (later the number on board rose to 30), so it proved to be a 'clean' attack. But to pull it off the crew had to be intimidated. 'I put my life in God's hands,' said al-Hamza. 'There were moments of fear, especially when a gun was put to my head.'

Chief Engineer French remained in the engine room during the attack. He gathered the crew together and locked the doors. Thanks to the ship's intercom, he was still in contact with Captain Nishky, who told him that there were armed men on deck. 'Everyone kept calm but we were obviously nervous,' said French. 'At sea, shit happens quite a lot and we deal with it – but never quite like this.'

One of the pirates made for the locked bridge and fired a single shot in the air, motioning to Nishky to open the door. He was then ordered to stop the ship. 'But Marek kept his cool and told them he couldn't stop the engines immediately for fear of damage,' said French. 'They would have to slow down gradually. He was slowing down the pirates with his own agenda. He was doing everything they asked but in his own time.'

The crew was then assembled so that everyone could be accounted for. This was French's first encounter with pirates and he was not impressed. 'They looked a motley crew, some wearing trousers and cheap shirts and sandals while others were barefoot in sarongs,' he said. 'This wasn't exactly *Pirates of the Caribbean*. Most of the time they were high from chewing drugs. This made them docile, which we liked. It was when they ran out that they got excitable.'

The first thing the pirates asked for was shoes – they were worried about damaging their feet on the deck. They then asked for cigarettes and crewmen handed over packs of Marlboros. The crew were then ordered to lift the pirates' two boats on to the deck using the ship's crane. Later they picked up the fuel barge that carried the pirates' petrol.

The pirates wanted money, phones and computers and they plundered the ship for valuables. Most of the pirates could speak only a few words of English, Grady said, but they made themselves understood. Then a few ground rules were laid down. As those who pay the ransom are concerned about the crew's well being, the captives were to be well fed and, to ensure their safety, they were confined to their own area on the ship. All contact with the pirates would be through a designated translator.

A pirate calling himself Daybad explained the situation on board the *Sirius Star* in an interview with the BBC World Service via satellite phone on 24 November. He assured the BBC that the ship's crew were being treated humanely.

'They are fine,' he said. 'We are treating them according to the charter of how you treat prisoners of war. They are allowed to contact their families. The crew are not prisoners – they can move from place to place, wherever they want to. They can even sleep on their usual beds and they have their own keys. The only thing they are missing is their freedom to leave the ship.'

Apart from the pirates' occasional petulant outbursts, nervously loosing off their Kalashnikovs, the crew's main complaint was the constant pilfering. It had begun when the captain was led at gunpoint to his office and ordered to open the safe. It contained $7,000 in cash. Later the pirates searched each cabin in turn, although they surprised the crew with their politeness. According to French, 'They said, "Good morning – can we look around?" and opened and closed drawers carefully, taking what they wanted. We had already stashed our valuables in the engine room in tool boxes but we left a bit of money and odd things. We decided to let them have something.'

This was going to be a problem throughout their captivity as new pirates came on board. 'We agreed to leave certain things on display for them in the hope it would stop them looking for other stuff,' said Grady. 'We knew they wouldn't believe we didn't have any money so we left cash in accessible areas. They kept asking for working shoes. They were wearing sandals but they were desperate for shoes.'

Grady noted that the pirates were eager to purloin anything shiny 'but all they got from me was the case for my reading glasses.' Everything else was hidden away safe and sound. 'I turned off the lift to the engine room to make it difficult for them to get in there, so I figured it was safe to hide my computer and my camera there. I took photos when I thought I was at a safe enough distance but I had to hold the camera at my waist, pointing out of my jacket and hope for the best.'

Daybad complained to the BBC that, after nine days, the owners had not yet made contact with the pirates. The only people they had had contact with were men claiming to be intermediaries. 'These are people who cannot be trusted,' he said. 'We don't want to make contact with anyone who we can't trust.'

This was very frustrating for the pirates, who saw hijacking ships as a business. 'We captured the ship for ransom, of course, but we don't have anybody reliable to talk to directly about it.'

Daybad said that once genuine negotiations began they would be seeking 'the usual asking price' but denied reports that they had been asking for a ransom of up to $25million as had been reported. 'That doesn't exist, there is nothing of the sort,' he said. 'We are warning radio stations and other people about broadcasting these unreliable stories.'

However, a ransom of $25million was not unreasonable. The oil on board alone was worth $100million. Indeed, the capture of the supertanker had sent a shudder through the world markets and the price of oil had climbed $1 a barrel. The brand new ship itself was worth another $150million. Built by the Daewoo Shipbuilding & Marine Company in Koje City, South Korea, she had been launched in March 2008. Sailing under the Liberian flag with Monrovia registered as her home port, she was owned by Vela International Marine Ltd, a wholly owned subsidiary of the Saudi Arabian state oil company, Saudi Aramco, based in the

United Arab Emirates. Vela own 24 tankers, 19 of which are VLCCs. The *Sirius Star* also had the distinction of being the first to be launched by a woman, Saudi Aramco's director of Human Resources, Policy and Planning, Huda M. Ghoson. For the pirates, the ship was something of a prize.

In his interview Daybad admitted the pirates knew that seizing the *Sirius Star* was illegal and wrong, and they were fully aware of the consequences of their actions. But the political situation in the country had left them no other choice. In 1991, the socialist government of President Siad Barre had fallen and Somalia had descended into anarchy. Warlords had taken over and begun dividing up the country. In 1992, a United Nations peace-keeping force, led by the Americans, went in. The result was a series of gun battles known as the Battle of Mogadishu and the Black Hawk Down incident, in which 19 American and one Malayan soldier were killed. Estimates of Somali deaths ranged from 200 to 1,500 and some 24 Pakistani peace-keepers were also killed in the fighting. UN casualties continued to rise and on 3 March 1995 the peacekeeping force pulled out. Order had yet to be restored.

As if Somalia had not suffered enough, its coastline was hit by the tsunami that devastated Sumatra, Thailand and Sri Lanka on 26 December 2004. Although Somalia was on the other side of the Indian Ocean, some three thousand miles from the epicentre of the tsunami, numerous coastal villages and towns were flooded. The confirmed death toll was 298 with more than 50,000 displaced. In all, some 1,180 homes and 2,400 boats were destroyed, and wells and reservoirs were rendered unusable. Debris dumped illegally in Somali waters was flung up on the shore. Worst hit was the semi-autonomous state of Puntland in northern Somalia, the area most pirates come from. Eyl, one of the centres of their operations, was flooded. Boats and fishing equipment were lost. Roads and bridges were washed out. Little food aid got through, and because of factional fighting in the area the relief agencies could do little to help.

'The world has to realise the problems we are facing here at home,' said Daybad. 'There has been no peace for 18 years. There is no life here. The last resource the Somalis have is the sea. Foreign fishing trawlers have come here to plunder our fish. How can they allow the Somali people to die? It is not possible. This is what drove us to piracy. We have to do anything we can to survive.'

Piracy had become a matter of life or death, he explained. 'Our fish were all eradicated, so we can't fish now, so we're going to fish whatever passes through our sea because we need to eat.'

The real problems, he said, lay deeper. 'The lack of government causes problems. If we solved the problem with the government, everything would be solved.'

Daybad quickly became the acceptable face of piracy and even allowed the ship's captain to speak to the BBC.

'We are generally OK,' said Nishky. 'All the crew and officers are in good shape and we reckon everything is going in the right direction.'

Were the pirates treating them well? Were they locked up?

'I would say there is not a reason for complaints,' he said. 'We were given already the opportunity to talk to our families and today I was negotiating with a gentlemen here about another such possibility. I am promised it will be soon, today or tomorrow, my crew will again be allowed to yet again talk to their families. As you can realise, these are the most important things for us now. Once we are grounded it is a good thing for us.'

He could not say how many pirates there were on board.

'I can't tell you exactly. I am not sure.'

Nor did he know whether negotiations over a ransom were taking place.

'I believe this is a secret that only the gentlemen on board know and someone on shore who is dealing with the matter. I am not the one knowing such things here, you know. And actually, to be honest, that is not my biggest concern now. The safety of my people and the vessel is what is taking the first place.'

The ship, he said, was stationary at the moment, but he begged not to be asked about where it was or where it was being taken.

'Please do not ask me such questions because I will not be allowed to talk to you any more.'

When asked what actually happened when the pirates took over the *Sirius Star*, he said, after a pause, 'Well, I am afraid we will have to finish our conversation now. Thanks very much for calling. Thanks for your concern.'

The 25-man crew under Nishky's care were a mixed bunch. They included 19 Filipinos, two Poles, one Croatian, one Saudi and two Britons. These were James Grady and Peter French, and they managed to speak to ITN on 25 November.

'The pirates are no problem whatsoever,' French told the interviewer. 'We have had no mistreatment or anything. Hopefully we are going to get some more phone calls to our families soon.'

It was plain that French was being supervised by his captors during the call, but even so he did not seem distressed by the situation. 'Our families don't have too much to worry about at the moment. All in all, we are not too badly off. The boys are quite happy. We are talking to them all the time, reassuring them. Apart from the inconvenience of being locked up, our life is not too bad.'

He confirmed that the crew were allowed a measure of freedom by the pirates. 'I don't mean we're locked up as in we're not locked up in cabins or anything, we go about our normal daily work,' said French. 'We're just continuing doing our normal day.'

In fact, he was more concerned about the football scores. He wanted to know how Newcastle United had done that weekend. When told his team had drawn 0–0 with Chelsea, he said, 'Excellent, that's a good score for us.'

On a more serious note, Grady said that the crew did not know how long it would take to resolve the situation. They had already been held for ten days and the pirates were becoming restive. 'They didn't trust us, especially the five Europeans.'

As the pirates became increasingly anxious, they chewed constantly on the narcotic weed khat to keep them calm. 'When they ran out of that they were a lot more twitchy,' said Grady. 'One of the pirates got shot. We don't know how it happened. There had been a burst of automatic fire and one of the pirates got shot in the arm. Another time they pushed a lifebelt into sea and fired at it.'

'We were frightened,' said French. 'They were twitchiest at night when they feared a rescue bid. "If they rescue you, we will shoot you," they said.'

On one occasion the pirates had panicked. 'They saw flashing lights in the distance and thought it was special forces coming to storm the ship,' French said. 'They were running around shouting and screaming and waving AK-47 rifles around. What they saw was from a lighthouse – but it took the captain ages to convince them.'

Al-Hamza complained that most of the days on board were 'boring'. However, he was allowed to make a couple of brief calls to his family in the Shiite city of Qatif in Saudi Arabia's Eastern Province. Meanwhile, the pirates amused themselves with internet porn and stealing things from the crew.

By the morning of 18 November the *Sirius Star* was anchored close to a headland called Raas Cubad, near the dusty coastal village of Hobyo, a pirates' lair 320 miles up the coast from Mogadishu. A fisherman named Abdinur Haji described the scene. 'As usual, I woke up at 3am and headed for the sea to fish, but I saw a very, very large ship anchored less than three miles off the shore,' he said. 'I have been fishing here for 30 years, but I have never seen a ship as big as this one.'

He also saw two small boats making their way out to the ship and 18 men he took to be pirates climbing aboard using a rope ladder.

Among the dozens of spectators who assembled on shore were a group of journalists, who had made the ten-hour drive up a potholed desert track through a no-man's land of sand and rocks, populated only by camels and small groups of armed men. They were taking their lives in their hands. On 26 November, two of their Western number – a Spaniard and a Briton – were kidnapped en route to the airport at the port city of Bosasso on Somalia's northern coast.

When journalist Manon Querouil reached Hobyo, he said he could see not just the hazy silhouette of the *Sirius Star*, but also Japanese, Greek and Ukrainian ships being held for ransom. The journalists then trekked up the desert beach for a rendezvous with the pirates. They were greeted by a truckload of armed men festooned with ammunition and each carrying a machine gun. Then a small white boat with seven men aboard approached across the calm blue water of the Indian Ocean. They checked in with those on shore via satellite phone to make sure it was safe to land, then ran ashore.

The man the reporters were to meet was Abdullah Hassan, the mastermind behind the hijacking. The 39-year-old – known as 'the one who never sleeps' by his men – had a fearsome reputation. For three years he had headed a gang of 350 former fishermen and disenchanted militiamen who called themselves 'The Coast Guard'. The ex-fishermen had the nautical knowledge required to stage the attacks and were regarded as the brains behind the enterprise. The brawn was provided by former militiamen, who had learned how to use weapons in Somalia's civil war. The pirates also employed a number of young electronic wizards who knew how to operate the GPS systems and communications equipment used to track their targets and coordinate the attacks. Then there were the lawyers and accountants who carried out the ransom negotiations and handled the money.

Under Hassan's command, the Coast Guard had taken more than 30 ships in 2008, including, in collaboration with another group of pirates, the Ukrainian MV *Faina*, carrying Russian tanks and other heavy weapons.

Hassan alighted from the speedboat carrying a rusty RPG launcher on his bony shoulder and a sweatshirt wrapped around his head like a turban. He too blamed the surge in piracy on the collapse of the rule of law and the invasion of trawlers from all over the world, who had plundered the rich fishing grounds off the coast of Somalia. 'Before, I was an honest fisherman,' he said, crouching on the scalding sand. 'But since the commercial fishing boats emptied our seas, we have had to find a way to survive.'

Despite his ragged appearance, Abdullah admitted he was doing pretty well. He had taken around £7million in 2008 – and that was before the hijacking of the *Sirius Star* or the ransoming of the *Faina*. He could now afford to take care of his family and pay his men handsomely. The rest of the money was reinvested, buying better weapons and faster boats from Kenya or Dubai. 'Money is no longer a problem,' he told the journalists.

But there was a problem with Islamic militants in Somalia, who were angry that the pirates had targeted a Muslim-owned ship. One faction of Islamists was threatening to take over the *Sirius Star*. 'We have organised our fighters,' said Islamist spokesman Abdirahim Isse Adow. 'The first step is to cut off pirates inland from those on the Saudi ship by restricting their supplies and cutting their communications.'

The Islamists had promised to stamp out piracy if they regained control in Somalia. The Union of Islamic Courts had managed to put a halt to it when they took over the country in June 2006, but they had been kicked out of

Mogadishu when the Ethiopians invaded that December. But the Islamists had not disappeared. By 2008, factional fighting had put Somalia's Transitional Federal Government on the back foot again, but the Islamic militants were making slow progress in their advance on Mogadishu and were now split. One group had turned up in Harardhere about 180 miles north of Mogadishu, residents said.

'A group of Islamists met some of the pirates here and asked for a share of the ransom,' a local man called Farah told the journalists. The pirates promised them something after the ransom was paid. But there is no deal so far.

In the midst of negotiations, the pirates moved the supertanker further offshore. Not surprisingly, the Islamists were put out by this move. We are against this act, said Abdirahim Isse Adow, and we shall hunt the ship wherever it sails, and free it.

The *Sirius Star* was then moored along with three other hijacked ships, the 33,000-tonne Philippine-flagged chemical tanker *Stolt Strength* (seized in the Gulf of Aden on 10 November), the 60,000-tonne Panamanian bulk carrier *African Sanderling* (taken on 15 October) and the 83,000-tonne Turkish bulk carrier *Yasa Neslihan* (hijacked on 29 October). Together these ships carried a total of 64 seafarers, two-thirds of them from the Philippines. At the time some three hundred seamen were being held hostage along the Somali coast.

Dr Fehmi Ulgener, a lawyer for the shipping company that owned the *Yasa Neslihan*, said the ship's crew of 20 were in good spirits. 'They have no health problems, but they are bored – although that is to be expected,' he said. 'The company's personnel department is dealing with the crew's families and we are giving them information. At the moment, they are completely calm and are waiting for the good news.'

Dr Ulgener said the pirates who attacked the ship, which was laden with 77,000 tonnes of iron ore, had 'popped up out of the blue' at midday on 29 October. He had no idea how long the hijacking would go on. 'Our only source is the other examples, and so it could last for between 60 and 70 days,' he said.

The Panamanian company that that owned the *African Sanderling* had taken delivery just five months before, while Martin Baxendale, a spokesman for Stolt-Nielsen, the Norwegian-Luxembourgeois company that had chartered the *Stolt Strength*, said he believed the ship's 23-strong Filipino crew were well after being held for 17 days. 'If there's any silver lining, it's that these pirates don't seem to be out to harm the crew,' he said. 'It's purely a financial thing, but it's extremely distressing for the families of the crew. And although they're not setting out to hurt the crew, accidents do happen.'

The company was all too familiar with Somalia's hijacking problem. Another of its ships, the *Stolt Valor*, had been the subject of a hijacking that lasted more than two months and its crew had had only been released 12 days earlier. 'In humanitarian terms, it's very unpleasant,' Baxendale added. 'The sooner we get them out the better.'

The four ships were being held five miles off the coast at Hen Daier, 20 miles south of Hobyo and a hundred miles from Haradheere. The pirates had moved the centre of their operations south in September 2008, after President

Sarkozy had ordered French Navy commandos to free the luxury yacht *Carré d'As*. Retired French couple Jean-Yves and Bernadette Delanne had been delivering the 53ft vessel from Australia to France for its owner when it was boarded 90 miles off Somalia by a dozen gunmen from two fast boats. The raiders, Jean-Yves said, had fired a burst with their Kalashnikov rifles. 'They were quite threatening. One of them took command and became more reassuring, and told us they were not going to hurt us.'

In their case, too, the pirates were only interested in money. 'The next day they demanded $4million, then $2million the following day,' said Jean-Yves. 'I tried to talk to them a lot, saying it was impossible to find such a sum and that it wasn't our boat and that I was a workman like they were.'

Again the Delannes were not maltreated by their captors. However, the pirates remained single-minded. 'They stayed firm,' said Jean-Yves. 'They had no political demands.'

However, it was reported that they were also demanding the return of six Somali prisoners taken after the French Navy had released the French luxury yacht *Le Ponant* in April 2008 who were then facing trial in Paris.

'They just wanted money,' insisted Jean-Yves, 'but it was possible to talk with them. They were afraid that we would communicate by internet. After a while, they let us wander about on the boat.'

The pirates did let the couple communicate with the French authorities by text message on a satellite telephone and the *Carré d'As* was taken to an anchorage just off the village of Abot. Then, after a dispute between the pirates, it was moved along the Puntland coast to Bargaal. Meanwhile the French Navy kept it under observation and reported to the Élysée Palace. 'We were not really frightened,' Jean-Yves said, though he noted that some of the gunmen seemed unfamiliar with the use of their weapons. In the end the ransom demand came down to £800,000.

'When we were freed, I found out they were going to take us to Eyl, which is frightening because they would have put us on land. This would have been hard to escape from,' he said. 'We would still be there if the commandos had not intervened at sea.'

When it became clear the yacht was heading to Eyl, President Sarkozy had ordered the commando assault. Soon afterwards 30 French combat swimmers from the Commando Hubert unit, modelled on Britain's Special Boat Service, were parachuted into the sea nearby at night. Wearing night-vision goggles and undetectable breathing systems, they swam to the *Carré d'As*, clambered silently aboard and shot one pirate dead. Within ten minutes, the yacht was retaken and the couple rescued after their two-week ordeal. Six pirates were taken alive and sent for trial in France. 'This operation is a warning to all those engaged in this criminal activity,' said President Sarkozy. 'France will not accept that crime pays.'

Although Hassan's group had moved south, further from the French base at Djibouti, he claimed he was unimpressed by the rescue. 'The French scare no one,' he said. Nonetheless, his men now stayed out at sea keeping watch with their captives.

Meanwhile the Delannes had sailed through the Suez Canal to the Côtes d'Azure, and they had some advice for the crew of the *Sirius Star*. They should avoid confronting the gunmen holding their supertanker and engage them in conversation while waiting for outside help. 'You are powerless when faced with their firearms,' Jean-Yves said. 'It is best to stay calm. They should play for time and not give in to the temptation to rush things while the experts analyse the situation.'

According to the Saudi Foreign Minister Prince Prince Saud al-Faisal, negotiations with the pirates over the *Sirius Star* had begun by 19 November, but the owners Vela International Marine refused to comment. Meanwhile the British Foreign Secretary said that the Royal Navy was coordinating a European response to the incident.

Speaking for the pirates, Farah Abd Jameh told the television network Al-Jazeera that they were arranging for a ransom to be delivered to the tanker. 'Negotiators are located on board the ship and on land,' he said. 'Once they have agreed on the ransom, it will be taken in cash to the oil tanker. We assure the safety of the ship that carries the ransom. We will mechanically count the money and we have machines that can detect fake money.'

On 20 November, another pirate calling himself Mohamed Said told France's AFP news agency that Vela International had been given ten days to hand over a ransom of $25 million. 'We do not want long-term discussions to resolve the matter,' he said. 'The Saudis have ten days to comply, otherwise we will take action that could be disastrous.'

By 24 November, the ransom demand was dropped to $15 million. The ransom actually delivered seven weeks later was $3 million. On 9 January 2009, a small plane flew over the tanker and dropped a canister containing the ransom by parachute. Second Officer Grady complained that the pirates continued robbing the crew even after the ransom was delivered, but bit his lip. 'We didn't want to upset them – for obvious reasons,' he said. 'They thought they'd stolen everything there was to steal on the ship but I had a hiding place in the engine room that they never discovered.'

The ship's owners stayed tight-lipped but on the evening of 9 January, Mohamed Said said, 'All our people have now left the *Sirius Star*. The ship is free, the crew is free.'

The Kenya-based East African Seafarers' Assistance Programme announced that the gunmen had disembarked from the tanker and that it was 'steaming out to safe waters'. Soon afterwards, one of the pirates' negotiators confirmed that the pirates were heading back to their homes in central Somalia, and the vessel's crew was safe.

However, five of the pirates were far from safe: they drowned when their small boat capsized as they were speeding away from the *Sirius Star*. The skiff had overturned and some of the ransom money was lost. James Grady admitted that the crew were far from upset when they heard of their fate. 'A news programme said five of the pirates drowned,' he said. 'I told the others and I can't claim they were very sympathetic. Some pirates were worse than others and we hoped it was them. One of the crew drew a picture of them drowning with the names of the guys we hoped it had been.'

Grady heard the news because he had hidden a portable radio behind a ceiling tile in the toilet and tuned into the BBC World Service. 'It was like a film,' he said. 'When I was hiding things away, hoping the pirates wouldn't find them, I did think of those old war movies you see, with people hiding things from the Germans... I unscrewed a ceiling panel to hide the radio and I listened to it every night when they thought I was asleep.'

Three of the pirates made it to the shore from the capsized boat after swimming for several hours, but lost their share of the ransom. The body of one drowned pirate was found with $153,000 in a plastic bag in his pocket when it was washed shore. Abukar Haji, an uncle of one of the dead pirates, attributed the accident that killed his nephew to the naval surveillance organised by the British and Americans. 'The boat the pirates were travelling in capsized because it was running at high speed because the pirates were afraid of an attack from the warships patrolling around,' he said.

After its release, the *Sirius Star* headed back to the port of Fujairah, where the crew were given a medical check-up. 'We had eaten all that Somali food,' said joked al-Hamza. 'They wanted to make sure we were OK.'

The ship's owners turned out to welcome the crew back safely. The crew was replaced and the *Sirius Star* set out to sea again four days later. The bulk of the crew were flown home to the Philippines. Al-Hamza flew to the Eastern Province city of Dammam where he was met with applause and ululation from relatives at the airport. A fish dinner – his favourite food – awaited him at his home, which was filled with relatives and well-wishers.

CHAPTER 2
THE HOSTAGES' TALE

Safe and sound back home, Saudi sailor Hussein al-Hamza wondered if he'd had some premonition of the hijacking. 'Before leaving, while chatting with my friends, I would tell them, "There are pirates,"' he said. 'And they would say dismissively, "Yes, in the 19th century." It looks like I have a sixth sense... God has granted me a new life.'

When the two Britons rescued from the *Sirius Star* were interviewed by consular officials, they were said to be in high spirits. They went through a thorough debriefing and saw an occupational therapist to check their health. 'We had the chance to speak to a psychiatrist,' said Second Officer James Grady, 'but we all went off and got drunk instead.'

Afterwards they headed to Dubai, where Chief Engineer Peter French's wife Hazel was waiting. Grady's wife Margaret and his two grown-up sons, Paul and Phil, were also there. After a reunion in the Crowne Plaza Hotel on 20 January, the family flew back to the UK. The Gradys had a brief holiday before returning to Scotland. Although everyone was happy to have him back, there were no welcome-home parties. Instead, he preferred to have quiet time, walking his two dogs on the beach at Largs and getting back to normal.

'I'm not worried about going back to sea but I think I have been affected by this,' he said. 'After our release we were sailing to port. We were getting closer to shore and two little fishing boats were heading straight towards us. It was totally innocent but the three of us on the bridge at the time were immediately on edge, thinking, Oh no, not again. So there must be something in my subconscious, even if I'm not aware of it all the time.'

Grady also said he felt a bit of a fraud when people refer to him as a hostage. 'I'm not in the same league as people like Terry Waite, people who've been held on their own for a long time,' he said. 'What happened was just a shift for me. I might have been held hostage for 57 days but I still did my four-month stint as usual.'

And Grady was determined to ship out again. Now 52, he had been going to sea since he was 21. 'I'm a seafarer,' he said. 'I'll be going back to sea... What else would I do? There's no work around here. This isn't going to put me off. I am used to it. I'll probably go back on the *Sirius Star*.'

Grady brought home with him the computer and camera he had hidden in the engine room. On his laptop he had kept a daily log. He recorded that on 15 November, he was working in a sunken part of the deck when he saw crew setting up the fire hoses. He thought they were just testing them but a member of the crew came over and explained that they were being followed by two small speedboats.

Grady dismissed the thought that the speedboats belonged to pirates. They were too far out to sea, so he went back to work. The next time he looked, the speedboats there was no point trying as the pirates had AK-47s and rocket-propelled grenades. Within seven minutes the eight pirates had taken over the bridge and ordered the ship to stop.

At three o'clock that afternoon, the ship stopped again to pick up a third boat. Ten more armed men clambered on boat. There was no chance of putting out a distress call as the pirates kept the satellite phone in constant use. As they were a long way outside the area where pirates usually attack, there was no one they could call for help anyway. Soon they had turned for Somalia and the crew began to worry about what might happen to them when they arrived there.

The next day, the stealing started. First the captain's cabin was ransacked, then they went through Grady's cabin twice. Each cabin was rifled for money and mobile phones. Fortunately Grady had already hidden his computer and camera.

On day three, they arrived off the coast of Somalia and anchored at what the crew called Pirate Cove. It was then that the pirates visited Grady in the engine control room. They took a company laptop among other things, but did not find his personal computer. It was then that he turned off the elevator, hoping that it would keep them away. It didn't. The following day he got another visit, this time from a Somali who could speak good English. He asked Grady how he was keeping.

'OK – for a hostage,' he replied.

The Somali then asked for money. Grady explained that all his money had been taken by the previous visitor. This did not discourage the pirates. The next day they went around all the cabins again to see if they could find anything else to steal. Grady estimated that by this time there were between 20 and 25 pirates on board, but as the crew were not allowed to go outside it was difficult to tell. 'The saving grace is they know nothing about computers,' Grady recorded in his diary.

They were a week into their captivity when one of the crew was accidentally shot with a Kalashnikov. He needed medical attention and was taken ashore. The crew did not see him again.

On 24 November they moved 15 miles along the coast, as the pirates wanted the *Sirius Star* closer to shore. They did not seem to understand that such a big ship could not go any closer safely. Two days later, Grady was interviewed by ITV News via the satellite phone. He recorded in his electronic diary that he had given the pirates a good write-up. They had been standing close to him, listening to the interview, so he had no choice. Besides, they had promised to allow the crew to call home the next day and he did not want to risk putting that in jeopardy.

On day 13, the pirates and the crew fell out. The crew, Grady commented, had brought it on themselves. They had been watching internet porn on the computer, so the pirates wanted porn too and began bullying the crew.

A helicopter had been circling the *Sirius Star* once or twice a day for several days. A warship appeared in the distance which the crew identified as Spanish. Although it was five miles away there was a possibility that it was supposed to convey some subtle message to the pirates. Grady wondered whether the helicopter had come from the Spanish ship, but of more pressing concern was that his work shoes had been stolen.

By 2 December, the pirates were getting jumpy, especially when the crew tested the alarms. Guns were brandished. More pirates arrived. At nine o'clock that evening, the crew were ordered to report to the bridge. The pirates thought they were under attack when they mistook a distant lighthouse for an attack craft. Even when the situation was explained to the pirates, they forced the crew to sleep under armed guard in the officers' recreation room. It was cold and uncomfortable, Grady recorded. The captain's snoring didn't help. The following morning the cabins were ransacked again – for the fifth time.

The helicopter continued to circle. Grady found this a comfort. At least the crew knew that someone was keeping an eye out for them. They also knew that the European Union was taking over the responsibility for policing the waters off Somalia from the United Nations. The problem was that neither body knew what to do if they caught a pirate, Grady commented. The crew, of course, knew exactly what to do with them.

By 10 December, the helicopter was circling more frequently. There were checks on the crew that night and they were told they were going to be released the next day. Grady recorded a one-word comment: 'Bullshit'. A week later, the crew were awoken at 1.15am by the pirates firing at a lifejacket they had thrown overboard as a target. At 6.30am they fired a heavy machine gun at a fishing boat that approached the aft.

As their captivity dragged on, the helicopter visits grew rarer. There were no more phone calls home and the crew's lockers got broken into. However, on Christmas Day the crew were allowed to go fishing with the pirates, as supplies were running low. They were then informed that a good English speaker was coming on board, so they might be allowed a phone call home.

At one point the pirates threatened to dump the *Sirius Star*'s $100million cargo of oil unless they were paid, even though this would have polluted the Somali coastline. 'We know the risk of spilling the oil shipment,' said Shamun Indhabur, a pirate aboard another vessel, the MV *Faina*. 'But when evil is the only solution, you do evil. That is why we are doing piracy. I know it is evil, but it is a solution.'

On 4 January the crew were told that negotiations had been completed. Now they would have to wait maybe three days for the money to arrive. However, when Captain Nishky was allowed to call Vela International, they told him that it would take a week to ten days to get the money to the pirates. Four days later, on 8 January, the crew were mustered on deck at 6.30am, so that observers in a small plane flying over the ship could count them. Vela International wanted to check that they were all still alive before they paid the ransom. It was not until 8.05am that the plane flew over. It flew back and dropped half the ransom. Two pirate boats went out to collect it.

The plane was to return six hours later with the rest of the ransom. Captain Nishky was to count the money with the pirates, then the pirates would go. Grady recorded that the plane returned at 2.10pm. The rest of the ransom had been retrieved by 2.20pm, but at four o'clock the pirates were still on board stealing anything else they could find. They had been paid, Grady wrote, but they seemed in no hurry to go. At 4.30pm, 17 of them departed, but the others remained. At 7pm the crew were told that one of the boats had sunk and four pirates were missing, so the rest of the pirates were staying the night.

The following morning, the 57th day of their captivity, the crew were up early. At 5.34am, Grady recorded, the last pirate left the ship. Two minutes later the crew were making ready to sail and by 6.42am they were off. They did not know where they were going, however, as the company had not yet decided. An American helicopter flew by and gave them a wave; Grady waved back. Then he heard news of their release on the BBC, followed by the report of that five of the pirates had died, which the crew applauded.

The one close family member who did not join the reunion in Dubai was Peter French's 18-year-old daughter Amy. She was at home in Willington, County Durham because she was doing her A-levels. The night before the hijacking Amy had sent her father a text that said jokingly, 'Watch out for pirates, Dad.' He had replied saying that they were sailing in safe waters, though he later realised that by then the pirates were already watching the ship.

French described the pirates as 'motley crew of paranoid druggies' who were often high. 'Some would sleep on the deck while others roamed around,' he said. 'We kept our distance from the pirates who would patrol the boat posturing with their guns. Sometimes they would hold handguns to the heads of some of the crew.'

After the ship had been ordered to turn back to Somalia,

French said the crew settled into a relatively normal, if tense, routine. He admitted that at times he feared for his life, and the pirates said they would blow up the ship if there was a rescue attempt. But that did not mean French was not above a little deception: as they steamed back towards Somalia, he tampered with the controls. 'I changed the maximum speed on the ship's telegraph so it looked like we were going full speed ahead,' he said. 'But really we were going much slower. We wanted to arrive in Somalia in daylight.'

Back home, his wife Hazel was contacted by the company. They told her that the *Sirius Star* had been hijacked and that he had been taken hostage. 'I was dumbstruck,' she recalled. 'It was a heck of a shock and I burst into tears.'

Eight hours later, Peter was allowed to ring her briefly from the ship's phone. This was a comfort. 'I knew it was the ship-to-shore because of the familiar delay,' she said. 'I burst into tears and heard Peter saying, "I'm OK, I'm OK. I love you." I told him, "Don't do anything daft. Make sure the boys are OK, and take care."'

Over the next eight weeks they would speak twice more before he was released. They had to use the ship-to-shore phone as, even six miles off the coast of Somalia, their mobile phones would not work. Pretty soon these had been stolen by the pirates anyway.

Once the *Sirius Star* had anchored and negotiations with the company had begun in earnest, French recalled, tensions eased marginally. The crew settled into a daily routine, carrying on as near to normal as possible. Although French did not keep a diary, he had a detailed recollection of what had happened.

While initially the crew had plenty of food and water, he said, the pirates preferred their own fare. Live goats were brought from the shore two at a time. The pirates would slaughter them on deck, then sling them over their shoulders and take them down to the cook, who would make a goat curry. However, there were always one or two goats roaming free around the deck.

'Ironically, for pirates they weren't particularly hard,' French said. 'They were always pestering the chief officer, who controlled the medicines, for tablets for headaches, stomach pains and colds.'

It was clear, however, that the pirates had scant regard for human life. French recalled that when one of the pirates accidentally shot himself in the arm they gave him no help. 'We bandaged him up and said he needed to get ashore, but they wouldn't let him.'

He also noted that they picked on the Filipinos and were more aggressive when searching them. However, when one of the crew members pointed out that the Filipinos were as poor as the Somalis, they gave some of the cash back.

'One pirate complained to the captain that a coat he stole was too big and that he wanted another one,' said French. On another occasion they ordered the third officer to hand over his expensive watch. In return, they gave him a cheap one they had stolen from someone else. 'They came back the next day and made him adjust the good watch to Somali time as they couldn't work it.'

But the worst night was when the pirates were spooked by a lighthouse. Some new gunmen had come aboard so there were now about 25 of them. 'It was 9.30pm and I was in my cabin,' said French. 'But I could hear the noise of men running around and shouting. We were rounded up at one end of the bridge and told to sit down.'

The pirates were convinced that they were under attack and looked desperate. Things did not look good and the crew were convinced someone was going to be injured or killed. Captain Nishky tried to calm the pirates, pointing out that what they thought was a ship was, in fact, a lighthouse. Eventually the captain persuaded a fat Somali who spoke English that there was nothing on the radar. 'They weren't very professional,' French could only conclude. After that, the situation calmed down but relations between the crew and pirates continued to deteriorate.

By Christmas there was still no sign of a deal. 'The day itself was pretty awful,' French recalled. 'We were thinking constantly of our homes and families. Their Christmas dinner provided little comfort. 'We shared a box of biscuits and later turkey, but it was sombre. The only treat came when we were allowed on deck to go fishing. We caught snapper and grouper.'

They asked to ring home but the pirates would not let them make any calls. 'It was disappointing,' said French. 'But we weren't going to beg them. Not for that or anything. They would play on that weakness.'

Negotiations between the pirates and the shipping company continued. Contact was made daily but the situation was often tense. However, the crew sensed a breakthrough had been made on 27 December. 'Their attitude changed,' French recalled. 'They seemed more relaxed and happy and we were allowed to phone home.'

The deal was struck on 3 January. A few days later, French recalled, the entire crew were herded out onto deck so the pilot of a light aircraft could make a headcount before he dropped the cash. 'It was 8am,' French recalled. 'We were all at one end of the deck and the pirates were hiding under the pipes. The pilot did a once-round fly-past then gained speed and the parachute dropped. It was a pink capsule which landed out at sea. The pirates picked it up in their boat.'

The captain was taken to the main pirate's cabin to help count it. The rest of the cash was dropped six hours later. One by one the pirates went to the cabin to get their share. By that evening most of them had gone. Only the senior men stayed behind.

'We were getting excited about the prospect of leaving,' said French, 'but then one boat-load of pirates capsized, drowning five or six, and we feared reprisals.' He was seriously worried when he went to bed that night but at 4am he got a phone call from the bridge. It was Captain Nishky. 'Peter, can you get your engine ready?'

'Marek, that engine has bloody well been ready for 57 days,' French replied.

When the engine fired up, French recalled that its low thrumming noise was the sweetest sound he had ever heard. Etched on his memory was the fact that the last eight pirates had left at 5.34am and the captain ordered the ship to sail at 6.42am. 'I can't remember there being a cheer,' he said, 'but there were smiles. We thought, There is a God after all.' French then rang his wife Hazel to tell her he was free. 'I was only on for a minute as others were clamouring for the phone.'

Later, as the ship headed back to Fujairah in the United Arab Emirates, French – like James Grady – admitted to some nervous moments when they came across some small fishing boats and dhows. However, this brush with pirates was not going to stop him going to sea again either. He is a seaman, not the type who can stay at home. 'I'm back until my leave comes to an end, then I'm away again,' he said.

He believes that it is up to the world's navies to stop piracy, not arming merchant ships and their crews. 'Once you arm crew, the whole game changes,' he says. 'Pirates will step up their own weapons and come aboard all guns blazing. Armed protection of convoys are one way to tackle it.'

CHAPTER 3
SOMALI STANDOFF

The hijacking of the giant oil tanker *Sirius Star* brought the Somali pirates to the front page of newspapers around the world. However, the seizing of the MV *Faina* seven weeks earlier was of far greater strategic concern. This was because it was carrying a highly sensitive cargo of 33 Russian-built T-72 tanks, together with a large consignment of rocket-propelled grenades, anti-aircraft guns and 812 tonnes of ammunition. These were intended for Kenya, an ally of the West. They now risked falling into the hands of the Islamists who were now on the rise again in Somalia.

The *Faina* is a 14,000-tonne roll-on-roll-off cargo ship built in Sweden in 1978. Initially she sailed under the Swedish flag and was called the *Vallmo*. Later she became the *Matina*, the *Loveral*, the *Marabou* and, in 2007, the *Faina*. She also changed flags, first to Luxembourg in 1991, Panama in 1996 and latterly Belize. Owned by Waterlux AG, based in Panama City, she was operated by Tomex Team of Odessa, the Black Sea port in the Ukraine.

In September 2008, the *Faina* was heading from the Baltic, where she had picked up her dangerous cargo, and was heading to Mombasa in Kenya via the Suez Canal. On 25 September, she was around two hundred miles off Mogadishu when she was boarded by a bunch of Somali pirates who called themselves the Central Regional Coast Guard. But the weapons the *Faina* was carrying were not the motivation for the hijacking. 'We just saw a big ship, so we stopped it,' said one of the pirates. According to pirate leader Shamun Indhabur, the hijackers were from the same group that later seized the *Sirius Star*.

'It is an astonishing ship to take,' said maritime expert James Wilkes about the 17-knot *Faina*. 'It defeats a number of the previously held conceptions that they'd go for slow-moving ships. This ship is built like a castle; how they managed to make it stop, I don't know. I can imagine that they possibly laid quite a bit of weapon fire on the ship.'

According to Januna Ali Jama, a spokesman for the pirates in the breakaway province of Puntland, he and his men hid out on a rock near the narrow mouth of the Red Sea and waited for the big grey ships with the guns to pass before pouncing on slow-moving tankers. They were not worried by the foreign navies that were being sent to the area. Even when his men were arrested their only punishment was a free ride back to shore as no one seemed to have the jurisdiction to prosecute them. 'We know international law,' he said.

Justifying the attack, Jama said: 'I do not think we are in the wrong. Our country is destroyed by foreigners who dump toxic waste at our shores.'

According to Jama, the *Faina*'s crew tried to fight off the pirate assault. Eventually, the attackers, estimated to have been about a hundred strong, succeeded in using 'tactical manoeuvres' to overpower the crew. The leader of the boarding party, Shamun Indhabur, said fighting between the pirates and the crew went on for over an hour, and the captain only decided to surrender after the pirates fired some rockets as a warning. 'We were close to destroying the ship if they didn't surrender,' he said. 'The captain tried to escape, but he didn't succeed. He had a pistol and he refused to surrender until we were close to killing him.'

When the pirates saw that the *Faina* was carrying a shipment of arms, they feared that these were going to the Ethiopian Army that was supporting the Transitional Federal Government in Somalia. However, the captain told them that the arms were bound for South Africa. 'Later, after we forced the captain to show us the manifests, we saw that the shipment was actually destined for Southern Sudan,' said Indhabur. The Kenyan government denied this.

At the time of capture, the *Faina*'s crew comprised one Latvian, three Russians and 17 Ukrainians, including a 14-year-old boy. The pirates turned the ship around and headed for Eyl, but the USS *Howard*, an American guided-missile destroyer, was in the vicinity. It caught up with the *Faina*, forcing it to stop at the coastal village of Hinbarwaqo, north of Hobyo, another haven for pirates that lay some two hundred miles south of Eyl. However, the *Howard* made no attempt to approach the hijacked vessel.

Three days after the hijacking, the *Faina*'s first mate Viktor Nikolsky reported that the ship's Russian captain, Vladimir Kolobkov, had died, it was thought, from a hypertension-related or sun-induced stroke. However, there have been allegations that the cerebral haemorrhage that killed him was brought on by the psychological warfare waged by the encircling warships, overflying helicopters and planes, loudspeakers and the jamming of communications.

According to some reports, these tactics also caused a rift between three members of the Majerteen clan from Puntland – the hard-core Habr Gedir – and more moderate members of the pirate gang. There were around 50 men on board at the time, supported by at least another hundred heavily armed militia warriors on shore.

'There was a misunderstanding between the moderates and the radicals on board who do not want to listen to anyone,' said Andrew Mwangura, president of the East African Seafarers' Assistance Programme, who was monitoring the situation from Mombasa. 'The moderates wanted to back-pedal. The Americans were close, so everyone was tense. There was a shoot-out and three of the pirates were shot dead.'

The dead men were said to have been the three Majerteen. Fortunately, the crew had escaped injury. However, Mwangura's claims were immediately refuted by the pirates' spokesman Sugule Ali. He said that there had been neither a disagreement nor a shoot-out. What had happened, he claimed, was that the pirates had fired several rounds to celebrate the Muslim festival of Eid, 'despite being surrounded by American warships and helicopters'.

Viktor Nikolsky, who had assumed nominal command of the *Faina* after the death of the captain, said that he could see three warships nearby. One was carrying an American flag. At that time the USS *Howard* was just five miles away. One of the other ships were reportedly Russian. '*Howard* is on-station,' said her captain Commander Curtis Good-night. 'My crew is actively monitoring the situation, keeping constant watch on the vessel and the waters in the immediate vicinity.'

The USS *Howard* was part of the Ronald Reagan Carrier Strike Group based in San Diego, which had been deployed to the US Navy's Fifth Fleet area of operations to conduct Maritime Security Operations – in other words, to keep the sea lanes open. Lieutenant Nathan Christensen of the US Fifth Fleet, based in Bahrain, confirmed the *Howard* was in visual range of the *Faina*, which was 'anchored off the Somali coast, near the town of Hobyo, along with a couple of other pirated vessels'. Two other hijacked vessels, the MV *Captain Stefanos* and MV *Centauri*, were known to be at anchor in the area. US Navy officials said they had allowed the pirates to re-supply the *Faina* with food and water, but they would not permit it to unload any of its military cargo.

The USS *Howard* had been in contact with MV *Faina* using VHF radio, but the pirates claimed that they were not intimidated by the presence of the US Navy. 'They can't catch us like goats,' said one. 'We will fight, and everyone here will die with us.'

Sugule Ali maintained that the pirates did not know that the *Faina* was carrying weapons until they were on board. 'As soon as we get on a ship, we normally do what is called a control,' he told the *New York Times* via satellites phone on 30 September, five days after the cargo carrier had been taken. 'We search everything. That's how we found the weapons. Tanks, anti-aircraft, artillery. That's all we will say right now.'

Asked whether he was surprised, he replied, 'No, we weren't surprised. We know everything goes through the sea. We see people who dump waste in our waters. We see people who illegally fish in our waters. We see people doing all sorts of things in our waters.'

The pirate then calmed the West's fears that the weapons would be sold on to insurgents in Somalia. 'We don't want these weapons to go to anyone in Somalia,' said Ali. 'Somalia has suffered from many years of destruction because of all these weapons. We don't want that suffering and chaos to continue. We are not going to offload the weapons. We just want the money.'

So how much were they asking for?

'$20million, in cash,' said Ali. 'We don't use any other system than cash.'

But they were happy to negotiate. 'That's deal making,' he said. 'Common sense says human beings can make deals.'

The pirates knew that the coalition navy had them hemmed in. American helicopters and other planes constantly flew over the *Faina*. But they were not scared. 'We are not afraid because we know you only die once,' said Ali. 'If we are attacked, we will defend ourselves until the last one of us dies.'

Somali officials urged the Americans to resolve the standoff by storming the ship. But American military officials said that, while they were keeping a close watch on the ship, there were no plans to raid it. There was a large naval contingent on hand at the time, as from the third week in August the Combined Maritime Forces had set up a secure shipping lane through the Gulf of Aden. Both US and French warships were in the area, and the Royal Canadian

Navy frigate *Ville de Québec*, which was to have been withdrawn after protecting UN-chartered merchant vessels carrying South African grain between Mombasa and Mogadishu, remained on station. The Russian Navy was also sending a frigate, the *Neustrashimy* (*Fearless*), from the Baltic. The commander of the Baltic Fleet, Viktor Mardusin, said the frigate would stay off Somalia for more than two months to guarantee the safety of Russian shipping. But the heavy presence of warships and aircraft from Western navies did not seem to have deterred the pirates. 'Anything that happens is their responsibility,' said Jama.

The standoff was particularly nerve-racking for the crew of the USS *Howard*. They remembered the suicide attack on the USS *Cole* off Yemen. On 12 October 2000, the American warship had been refuelling in Aden harbour when two suicide bombers sailed alongside and detonated their explosives-packed boat, killing 17 American sailors and wounding 39 more. The US government got a $150million repair bill and had to pay out a further $8million to compensate the families. On 14 March 2007, a federal judge ruled that the Sudanese government in Khartoum was liable for the bombing, and there were already indications that Sudan might be involved in the hijacking of the *Faina*.

Sudan's possible motive for the hijacking was provided by Andrew Mwangura, president of the East African Seafarers' Assistance Programme. He maintained that this was not the first cargo of arms that had been shipped through Kenya. 'One of the cargos arrived at the port of Mombasa in October last year, two in February this year,' he said. 'The military equipment was destined for southern Sudan.'

The largely Christian south of Sudan had been fighting the Muslim north for decades in Africa's longest-running civil war. This was supposed to have ended in 2005 with an agreement that would give southern Sudan full independence in 2011. However, in May 2008 there were renewed clashes in the oil-rich flashpoint of Abyei that ignited fears of a renewed civil war.

'The pirates are saying that if they are not going to be paid the ransom, they will spill the beans,' said Mwangura. 'Maybe they are going to say what is happening in this region because we understand South Sudan is under a United Nations arms embargo and why Kenya allows the military equipment to pass through Kenyan waters is not known.'

Sudan denied having anything to do with the hijacking. 'Sudan should not be dragged into this issue,' an envoy said, 'because it does not concern us.'

The US Fifth Fleet continued to monitor the situation actively. 'We will maintain a vigilant watch over the ship and remain on station while negotiations take place,' said Rear Admiral Kendall Card, the task force commander who was leading the efforts to prevent the weapons aboard MV *Faina* from being unloaded. 'Our goal is to ensure the safety of the crew, to not allow off-loading of dangerous cargo and to make certain the *Faina* can return to legitimate shipping.'

As the standoff dragged on, at least nine foreign navy vessels gathered off the coast. On the shore more militiamen arrived. Large numbers – there were thought to be as many as a thousand – were members of the Habr Gedir clan from Mogadishu. (It had been an abortive attempt to capture the Habr Gedir warlord, Mohamed Farrah Aidid, that led to the Black Hawk Down incident in 1993.) Indeed, there were so many different clans and militia groups in the village of Hinbarwaqo that the negotiations got bogged down in discussions and rivalries. But the one thing they all agreed on was that the talks had dragged on too long.

Fearing that there was going to be military intervention or that the ship might explode, around 750 people – mainly women, children and old men – from Hinbarwaqo left their homes and moved inland with their livestock, camping out in makeshift shelters. Elders from Hobyo and the nearby village of Ceel Xur also debated if their inhabitants should also be evacuated. At night, military aircraft buzzed the area or hovered above without any lights. There had been several missile attacks on the civilian population of Somalia in the recent past, it was hardly surprising that innocent locals were so terrified.

In an attempt to defuse the situation, the pirates said they had no plans to kill the crew of the *Faina*. They were not interested in politics nor the arms on the *Faina*. All they were interested in was money. The reason they wanted cash, Ali said, to 'protect ourselves from hunger'. Ali agreed the $20million they were asking for was a lot just to protect them from hunger, but they had to divide it among a lot of men. Nor were they prepared to leave the ship without the money, even if they were promised immunity. 'We're not afraid of arrest or death or any of these things,' he said. 'For us, hunger is our enemy.'

Ali also maintained that the pirates and their captives were getting on well, and that the hostages were given regular meals prepared by their own chef. 'We interact with each other in an honourable manner,' said Ali. 'We are all human beings. We talk to one another, and because we are in the same place, we eat together.'

According to Ali, the Somali hijackers did not consider themselves pirates or sea bandits. 'We consider sea bandits those who illegally fish in our seas and dump waste in our seas and carry weapons in our seas,' he said. 'We are simply patrolling our seas. Think of us like a coastguard.'

Nor did Ali's group consider holding the crew at gunpoint a crime. 'If you hold hostage innocent people, that's a crime,' he said. 'If you hold hostage people who are doing illegal activities, like waste-dumping or fishing, that is not a crime.'

What crime had the crew of *Faina* had committed? he was asked. They had sailed into Somali waters carrying weapons without permission, was his reply. 'We are sticking to the demand for $20million,' said Ali. 'This is not ransom, but a fine for unlawfully transporting weapons on Somali waters.'

Ali would not say if his group had hijacked before.

On 1 October, Somali president Abdullahi Yusuf Ahmed spoke up on the need to combat piracy in the lawless nation's waters, where more than 60 ships had been seized in 2008 alone. 'The pirates are imposing an embargo on the Somali people and the international community because they are blocking movement between the Mediterranean and the Indian Ocean, which affects not only Somalia but the whole world,' he told reporters in Mogadishu. 'I call on the Somali people to fight against the pirates. I also call on the international community to act quickly on what is happening in Somali waters as well as on shore.'

But few Somalis heeded the call. The pirates of Puntland lay beyond his jurisdiction. The United Nations did take the situation seriously though. On 7 October, the Security Council passed a resolution drafted by the French that urged member states to deploy naval vessels and military aircraft against the pirates. It specifically sanctioned the use of force. Somalia gave its permission for the international community to take on the pirates. Even the regional government in Puntland advocated a commando raid on the *Faina*.

The al-Shabaab militia – the youth wing of Somalia's Islamist movement – also attempted to intervene by urging the pirates 'to either burn down the ship and its arms or sink it' if they did not get the money they asked for. 'It is a crime to take commercial ships but hijacking vessels that carry arms for the enemy of Allah is a different matter,' said their spokesman Sheikh Mukhtar Robow. 'We believe that the military shipment belonged to Ethiopia and was headed to Mogadishu seaport, where it would have been unloaded with the intention of destroying Somalia, but that never happened.'

On 10 October, Ali gave the ship owners four days to pay up or lose the ship with all those on board. 'We held a consultative meeting for more than three hours today and decided to blow up the ship and its cargo – us included – if the ship owners did not meet our ransom demand,' said Ali. 'After three days, starting from tomorrow, the news of the ship will be closed. Either we achieve our goal and get the ransom or perish along with the ship, its crew and cargo.'

Meanwhile observers feared that the vessel might soon run out of fuel for the generators. Without electricity, they would lose light and communication, along with air-conditioning, fresh water, toilet systems, pumps and the ability to start the main engine. Essential units of the kitchen would be shut down, along with the cool room where the body of the ship's captain was being kept. Communication with the ship confirmed that fuel was getting low and a tonne of diesel oil was delivered to the ship – enough to keep them going for a few days. However, they refused fresh food and drinking water for the crew. This was unnecessary given the circumstances.

'Either we receive our money by tomorrow, or never,' said Ali.

The company still had not come up with the ransom, which seemed to have dropped from an initial $35million to below $10million. The relatives of the crew then tried to put pressure on the Ukrainian government. When Ukrainian president Viktor Yushchenko refused to meet them, they occupied the his office and vowed not to leave. The Ukrainian opposition party then started fund-raising. Meanwhile Kenya, the supposed owner of the cargo of weapons, also refused to pay any of the ransom, after the Somali ambassador Mohamed Ali Nur – nicknamed 'Ali America' – had dismissed the pirates' threat to blow up the ship.

Indeed, the threat did prove an empty one as the *Faina* was still afloat on 14 October, when the Islamic Courts Union of Somalia complicated the situation further by declaring war on all Western warships in Somali waters. ICU spokesperson Abdirahim Isse Adow said the Western warships, including those of NATO, were helping the deployment of what he called 'Christian soldiers into Somalia and their aim is to re-colonise Somalia'. There was speculation that jihadis might blow up the *Faina* or that the coalition might anticipate the outcome with a torpedo or a special forces' demolition squad and blame it on the pirates.

Somali Foreign minister Ali Ahmed Jama now urged caution. 'The pirates are holding hostages,' he said. 'Human lives are at stake. Ultimately, force could result in casualties.'

Muslim leaders in Kenya said it would be a sin for either side to blow up the *Faina* and the pirates saw sense. On 15 October, Sugule Ali announced that they had withdrawn their threat. Speaking by satellite phone, he complained that an excessive number of mediators had been hampering the negotiations and insisted again that the pirates did not plan to harm the crew. Meanwhile people on shore said that the pirates had recently hauled aboard enough spaghetti, rice and goat meat to last them several months.

Complex negotiations were now going on with money being offered for some of the light armaments and ammunition. 'There's not much they can do with the tanks – they can't get them off,' said an analyst with a network of Somali informers. 'But the rest of the weapons they are trying to move ashore.'

Indeed the Islamists sent pick-ups from Mogadishu to collect the small arms. 'The Ukrainian ship is loaded with military hardware that is very important for our holy war against the enemy of Allah,' said al-Shabaab's Sheikh Mukhtar Robow.

Fresh arms were certainly helping their cause. Somali insurgents were making impressive gains around the time the *Faina* was being held. They had taken control of the port of Kismaayo, 250 miles to the south of Mogadishu, and were equipping their own pirates as part of a campaign to control the sea. It seemed that some piracy had acquired an ideological dimension. According to Bruno Schiemsky, a Somali analyst based in Kenya, al-Shabaab militia had joined forces with the pirates and were offering weapons training in return for lessons in plundering at sea. 'This has now gone beyond money,' he said. 'The Shabaab are now at sea looking for Israelis, Americans and other Westerners. This is getting very nasty now.'

The navy ships surrounding the *Faina* were using loudspeakers warning the pirates not to unload the cargo. One local clan elder said that they were also inviting the pirates aboard the navy ships for talks.

Then on 17 October the ruling coalition in the Ukraine collapsed and President Viktor Yushchenko called an election to be held on 7 December. Meanwhile the country descended into financial turmoil and the International Monetary Fund had to step in with a loan. After a meeting, Yushchenko's officials said that they were working 'every hour' to liberate the Ukrainian sailors on board the *Faina*. The ship had now run out of fuel and supplies of fresh water and diesel oil were being turned away. For electricity the crew were now relying on the ship's three wind-turbines.

On 19 October, the crew were allowed to line up on an upper deck so that the US sailors on the *Howard* could see them and photograph them. According to Lieutenant Christensen, they looked healthy. The pirates who lined up along with their captives, it was noted, looked very young.

By then the *Neustrashimy*, which had been steaming

through the Suez Canal, had arrived in Somali waters on 28 October after stopping at Aden to be reprovisioned. This again raised fears that the hijacking might be broken by the use of force – with potentially disastrous consequences. The Russians had a reputation for bungling hostage rescues after their use of special forces to free an audience held by Chechen terrorists in a Moscow theatre in 2002 and again in a school in North Ossetia two years later. However, Russia's central command ruled out a direct military engagement with a weapon-laden ship pinned down by several US and EU navy ships. But, submarines had been spotted in the area, a little to the south near Mogadishu harbour.

Newspapers reported that Nina Karpechava, a Ukrainian member of parliament and human rights mediator, was in Kenya and in regular contact with the pirate negotiators as well as with diplomats on the scene. The ship's owners then revealed that the crew had run out of food and water the previous week and that the pirates had been feeding the sailors with supplies brought from the mainland.

A Russian news agency reported that the pirates had threatened to kill the crew the next day, quoting a pirate as saying, 'Tell everybody that the crew will die. Possibly, tomorrow.' However, it was widely held that the pirates were merely expressing their fears that the crew would begin to face starvation and dehydration due to the critical shortage of food and water. More fuel had been provided, but only enough for the ship's generators to run for another 30 hours, it was reported.

On 23 October, the operators of the *Faina* said that they

could not raise the multi-million dollar ransom. So far they had only managed to raise $1million. However, a spokesman said the crew had received food and water, and were in satisfactory condition. The Ukrainian Foreign Ministry renewed its guarantee that its priority was to save the lives of the hostages and was in talks with pirates but the Ukrainian government issued a statement distancing itself from direct involvement in events.

'We would like to note that Ukraine as a state cannot be a party in the negotiating process with the pirates,' it said. 'According to the international practice, if pirates hijack ships, government structures don't participate in talks directly with assailants. The mechanism of holding the negotiations foresees talks between a ship-owner or a managing company and pirates, directly or through mediators. According to this practice, the *Faina* ship-owner has empowered a professional legal company to hold the talks with the pirates.'

Meanwhile Sugule Ali restated the pirates' position. 'Either we get the money or hold on to the ship,' he said. 'And if attacked, we will fight back to the bitter end. The important thing, though, is if we die they – the crew – will die too.'

By 11 November the Ukrainian Foreign Ministry was reporting that the health condition of the crew members was satisfactory. 'The Ukrainian Foreign Ministry has daily contacts with the Ukrainian sailors' family members and informs them of the situation.' Food and water was still being delivered as negotiations between the company and the pirates went on. The ransom had dropped to $5million, but the nature of the *Faina*'s cargo was still creating tension between the pirates and the Islamic Courts' militia, who wanted the weapons to retake Mogadishu.

'We simply want the money so our families can live,' said pirate leader Abdullah Hassan, 'but they want to recover the weapons to fight the government troops.' He bristled at the accusation that the pirates were in league with the Islamist militia and were helping to train them. 'If anyone has lessons of war to learn, it is certainly not us,' he said.

As Sugule Ali continued to negotiate, seeking to prevent the unloading of its deadly cargo into a country already shattered by civil war, the authorities in Puntland urged the use of force. 'A military operation has to be taken,' said Ahmed Said Aw-nur, minister of fisheries. 'If the Islamists get the arms, they will cause problems for all of Somalia.'

The US Navy was also worried about that possibility. 'We're deeply concerned about what's aboard, as well as the safety of the crew," said Lieutenant Nathan Christensen of the US Navy's Fifth Fleet. 'We're hoping the arms don't make it to shore.'

From neighbouring Galmudug province, president Mohammad Warsame suggested a simple solution – bomb the *Faina* and blow up its cargo of Russian armour. Killing the crew on board would be merely 'collateral damage' in the war against piracy and the loss of the ship will help show the pirates the error of their ways. Kenya's Foreign Minister Moses Wetangula also said force should be used to rescue the weapons from the pirates. The United Nations had sanctioned it and, in the face of the seeming impotence of the US and NATO, he appealed to the Chinese and Indian navies to put a stop to the acts of piracy around the Horn of Africa.

Their views carried little weight, however. Pentagon spokesman Geoff Morrell said, 'At this point, what we are most concerned about is seeing a peaceful solution to this problem.' America's main concern, he continued, was 'that this cargo does not end up in the hands of anyone who would use it in a way that would be destabilising to the region'.

Ali Sugule made the pirates' position clear. 'Somalia has suffered from many years of destruction because of all these weapons,' he said. 'We don't want that suffering and chaos to continue. We are not going to offload the weapons. We just want the money.'

There was little danger of the pirates being able to unload the tanks, as the small ports of Puntland lacked the specialist heavy-lifting gear required. But that did not discourage the pirates. They wanted booty in the form of cash on board and ransom money, which ship-owners now seemed increasingly willing to pay, given the huge values of ships and their cargoes and the daily costs of maintaining them at sea. On the same day as the *Faina* was captured, another Puntland pirate syndicate released a Japanese bulk carrier, the *Stella Maris*, and its crew of 21 after a £1million ransom had been paid – and it had only been carrying zinc and lead ingots, not very expensive weapons. And even as the *Stella Maris* was being freed, Somali pirates were hijacking a Greek chemical tanker with 19 crew as it sailed through the Gulf of Aden.

On 9 December, the pirates announced they had put down a hostage revolt. 'Some crew members on the Ukrainian ship are misbehaving,' said a pirate. 'They tried to harm two of our gunmen late Monday.' The pirates had been taken by surprise. 'Maybe some of the crew are frustrated and we are feeling the same but our boys never opted for violence. This was a provocation. This is unacceptable – they risk serious punitive measures.'

Other sources said that those involved would be 'seriously punished'. 'Somalis know how to live and how to die at the same time,' said the pirate, 'but the Ukrainians' attempt to take violent action is misguided.'

A Russian news agency claimed that the story was fabricated. Quoting a maritime expert who had spoken to the owners of the *Faina*, it said what really happened was that two pirates who were heading for the shore by boat were seized and detained by the Americans. The pirates on board the *Faina* had then called intermediaries and the ship-owner to ask them to speak to the Americans and request the release of their accomplices, but had been told this was impossible. The pirates had then made up the story of the hostage revolt and possibility of the punishment as a veiled threat.

Eventually a ransom was agreed, but then there was another hold up. 'The middlemen tried to steal some of the money we agreed on,' said pirate leader Shamun Indhabur. 'And now we can't trust them. They're trying to take the money, and we are the criminals. We can't accept that.'

On 4 February a ransom – thought to be $3.2million – was paid. The pirates spent the night counting the haul, which they did not consider unusual. 'No huge amount has been paid,' said Sugli Ali, 'but something to cover our expenses.'

Early the next morning the pirates began leaving the ship. 'We have released MV *Faina*,' Ali told journalists.

'There were only three boys remaining and they delayed the release for one hour, but now the ship is free.'

The *Faina* then set sail for Mombasa, where the crew were re-united with their families. The body of the captain was sent to the hospital morgue, before being airlifted to Russia. The controversial cargo was then unloaded. The Kenyan government insisted that it was the end user of the weapons consignment, even though Kenya had not been to war since the 1960s. A fresh crew was ready to join the ship, but first the algae that had built up on its bottom during its four months at anchor had to be scraped off by a team of 12 divers. As on the *Sirius Star,* the pirates had looted the ship of valuables, and the inside had to be cleaned and made good as a great deal of damage had been done.

'They vandalised the cabins and defecated in the accommodation blocks,' said Mombasa Port International Transport Federation inspector Juma Khamis. 'The vessel will have undergo a major facelift before it becomes habitable.'

CHAPTER 4

THE PRISONERS OF
LE PONANT

The three-masted *Le Ponant* is a 850-tonne luxury yacht, sailing under the French flag. She is 88 metres long with accommodation for 64 passengers in 32 air-conditioned state rooms. There are two restaurants, a grand saloon with a terrace, a show area, nightclub, library, video salon and four hundred square metres of sundeck. And for those who have to work, she has a telex, fax and satellite phone. For any pirate, she is quite a prize.

On 4 April 2008, she was sailing through the Gulf of Aden en route from the Seychelles to the Mediterranean. She was carrying no passengers at the time, just 30 crew members – one Cameroonian, one Ukrainian, six Filipinos and 22 French, including six women. The pirates had to be fast to catch her – under sail she can reach 14 knots and she has a 2,200 horsepower engine. Nevertheless, the pirates caught her late that morning in their high-power Zodiac rigid inflatables, and 12 Somalis, armed with Kalashnikovs and rocket-launchers arrived alongside in two dinghies and boarded without a shot being fired. However, the captain, Patrick Marchesseau, had time to alert the French authorities and the frigate *Commander-Bouan* of the Coalition's Task Force 150 – the naval wing of Operation Enduring Freedom in Afghanistan – set off in hot pursuit.

François Fillon, the French Prime Minister, immediately condemned the hijacking. 'This is a blatant act of piracy,' he told reporters. 'The defence and foreign ministries are mobilised to act.'

The *Commander-Bouan*, under Commander Hervé Couble, was just two kilometres behind *Le Ponant* when she reached the coast of Puntland. By then, she had 18 marine commandos on board. They had parachuted from a Transall military transport aircraft onto the Yemeni island of Socotra off the tip of the Horn of Africa, where they were picked up. A Canadian helicopter from HMCS *Charlottetown* was also keeping an eye on the captured ship, as were Atlantic 2 long-range reconnaissance aircraft from the French base at Djibouti.

The first contact between *Le Ponant* and the *Commander-Bouan* took place on the morning of 6 April. Captain Marchesseau reported by radio that his men were well and being well treated. The pirate leader spoke English and insisted that the conversation was carried out in English, but Captain Marchesseau frequently lapsed into French, which made his captor nervous. The pirates refused to give their names, only referring to themselves as the 'Somali people' or the 'Somali Marines', who had a reputation for being courteous to their captives, provided the ransom is paid. According to Andrew Mwangura, president of the East African Seafarers' Assistance

Programme, of the four rival groups of pirate operating off the Somali coast, 'They are the best organised. They have an almost military structure and training, plenty of weapons and boats, and excellent communications.'

A French journalist, Gwen Le Gouil, had been held for eight days by the Somali Marines in December 2007. He said they were 'former fishermen, who have converted to illicit operations of various kinds, including hostage-taking and trafficking in people, money and archaeological remains... They have no particular political allegiance. Only money counts as far as they are concerned.'

Mwangura was already familiar with the way the group pursued its goal. 'The size of the ransom depends on the value of the ship, its proprietor and the nationality of the crew. In this case, they will ask for a fortune, millions of dollars, and then lower their demands and everything will go well.'

Despite their reputation for being civil, the pirates were taking no chances. At night, the crew were kept together in the reception room. During the day, they were confined to the upper deck. After some protest by the captain, they were moved to another deck where they could make themselves more comfortable.

The pirates made the most of their stay on *Le Ponant*. The first night they raided the bar. It seems at least these pirates lived up to the 18th-century image of buccaneers. But there was considerable concern about what they might do under the influence of alcohol, to which, as Muslims from a Muslim country, they were unaccustomed. Indeed, one night one of the pirates disappeared. Captain Marchesseau thought he had fallen in the water while dead drunk, and there was little hope he had been able to swim to shore.

Le Ponant anchored off the village of Garacad, 530 miles north of Mogadishu and a short way up the coast from Eyl. Villagers brought fish and water to the yacht and the pirates made frequent trips ashore to sell what they had looted. Their mother ship was thought to be in the vicinity, but the French Navy could not locate it. 'The boats of the pirates and fishermen are all alike,' said Vice-Admiral Gerard Valin, commanding the area from his flag ship the FS *Var*.

Indeed, the pirates sometimes used old fishing boats as their mother ships and lookouts, using satellite phones to direct the speeding pirates to their targets. But with money from successful raids, the pirates have subsequently upgraded their mother ships. More recently, the International Maritime Bureau (IMB) has told shipping to be on the lookout for long, white Russian-made stern trawlers with the names *Burum Ocean* and *Arena* or *Athena*. The latest attack craft are skiffs painted blue or white, as these colours are difficult to distinguish when the sun is reflecting off water. They are low in the water and made of wood, so it is difficult to spot them by radar.

On the evening of 6 April, the owners of *Le Ponant* – CMA-Compagnie Generale Maritime – got in touch with the pirates. Rodolphe Saadé, son of the owner and general manager, spoke to them several times a day from the company's headquarters in Marseilles. Again the conversation was in English. During the negotiations, he was advised by the GIGN, France's anti-terrorist squad, and agents of the Directorate-General for External

Security. Soon, the pirates became concerned not so much about the ransom but their safety. They were hemmed in to seaward by the French Navy, while on land rival clans were assembling with an eye to the loot.

While negotiations were under way, Rodolphe Saadé's wife Véronique, head of cruises in the family business, made contact with the families of the crew. Rodolphe's father, Jacques Saadé, was a friend of President Nicolas Sarkozy with whom he had regular meetings in Paris. Saadé agreed to pay the ransom, though Sarkozy was against it.

As the days passed, the French forces built up around *Le Ponant*. The *Commander-Bouan* was joined by the *Var*, the frigate *Jean Bart* and the training ship *Jeanne d'Arc*, which had been diverted from a world tour. An oil tender also turned up to keep them supplied. The *Jeanne d'Arc* had brought with her six helicopters, and a squad of airborne marine commandos from the French base at Djibouti were also on hand. The tactical operation was put in the hands of Rear Admiral Marin Gillier, commander of the marine commandos who had parachuted into the sea near the *Var* that Sunday. He was followed the next day by Colonel Denis Fravier of the GIGN, whose men had also been deployed.

The two men discussed taking advantage of the pirates' habit of getting drunk at night to stage a commando raid on the ship. However, the combat swimmers pointed out that they would not be able to make an armed assault as the current along that part of the coast was too strong. Besides, such an attack broke their prime directive, which was that any intervention must not endanger the lives of the hostages. Nevertheless, the 50 marine commandos and ten GIGN men readied themselves for action.

By 9 April, negotiations were near completion. The owners and the pirates had reached an agreement and the crew were to be released the next day. But then the pirates changed their minds. Nicolas Sarkozy, who had promised the crew members' families that their loved ones would be released, then stepped in. He was determined to take action and got permission from the Somali government. The Saadés continued talking to the pirates – indeed the negotiations seemed to be accelerating – but the pirates were becoming increasingly nervous. There were 18 of them, though only seven were on board. Captain Marchesseau, keeping a look out with his binoculars, prayed that the navy would not approach any closer as the crew of *Le Ponant* were surrounded by armed guards. Any attempt to rescue *Le Ponant* would result in a bloodbath.

On 11 April, the military put Operation Thalathine into action – *thalathine* is Somali for 30, the number of hostages. It began with the delivery of the ransom on the water. Three pirates met two GIGN men and a marine commando, who handed over a sum thought to be in the region of $2.5million. The hostages were then released and they clambered into one of the Zodiacs, which they would use to take them over to the navy ships. Last off the ship was Captain Marchesseau, who was encouraged to jump into the water to speed up the operation.

With the hostages safe, the second phase of the operation began. Surveillance aircraft patrolling ten kilometres off shore monitored the movements of the pirates and could identify some of them in the village of

Garacad. 'We could not intervene immediately to avoid causing injuries to civilians,' said Rear Admiral Gillier. Then they saw a large 4x4 leaving the village. 'That's when we launched the ambush.'

As the 4x4 headed out into the desert, four helicopters – one Aérospatiale Gazelle, one Eurocopter Panther and two Aérospatiale Alouettes – took off from the *Jeanne d'Arc* and *Jean Bart* with marine commandos and GIGN men on board. A French Navy sniper in the Gazelle put a 12.7mm ball from his MacMillan Tac-50 sniper rifle into the engine of the 4x4, bringing the vehicle to a halt. 'The pirates did not understand what was happening,' said Gillier. 'They did not see the helicopter.'

The GIGN and French marine commandos on other helicopters then closed in. The six occupants of 4x4 were reluctant to surrender, even though they were outnumbered. Warning shots were fired and three GIGN men landed, loosing off one or two bursts of automatic fire into the air. This was enough to intimidate the pirates, who realised they were not going to be able to escape and surrendered. The French quickly had them down on the ground, where their hands were tied behind their backs. Then they were bundled into the helicopters and flown back to the *Jean Bart*.

'No one was killed during the operation,' said Gillier. However, one of the men in the front of the 4x4 was slightly injured in the calf. It seems he was hit by a ricochet from the engine.

'It was an intervention, not a pulverisation,' French Army chief of staff General Jean-Louis Georgelin. 'We made shots and intimidated them, forcing them to abandon their vehicle. There was no direct fire on the pirates.'

However, local officials claimed that three people were killed in the raid and a further eight wounded. The district commissioner of the Garacad region, Abdiaziz Olu-Yusuf Mohamed, said that three French helicopters landed and tried to intercept the pirates after they came ashore. 'Local residents came out to see the helicopters on the ground,' he said. 'The helicopters took off and fired rockets on the vehicles and the residents there, killing five local people.'

Witness Mohamed Ibrahim said: 'I could see clouds of smoke as six helicopters were bombing the pirates. The pirates were also firing anti-aircraft machine guns in reaction. I cannot tell the exact casualties.'

Naval captain Christophe Prazuck, the spokesman for the French military chiefs of staff, countered this by reiterating the French version of the incident. 'There were four helicopters involved,' he said. 'A sniper shot out the motor of the pirates' four-wheel drive vehicle. A second helicopter then landed nearby, allowing the six pirates to be arrested under covering fire from two other helicopters. We are absolutely sure that there were no collateral victims.' President Sarkozy also denied anyone had been killed.

Troops also recovered some of the ransom money paid by the owners of the yacht. The six captured pirates, all aged between 25 and 40, were then flown to Paris to face trial. 'It is the first time that an act of piracy in this area has been resolved so quickly... and it is also the first time that some of the pirates have been apprehended,' Admiral Edouard Guillard told a press conference.

The Transitional Federal Government in Mogadishu called for other nations to join the battle against pirates off Somalia. 'If each government conducts operations like the

French, I think we will see no more pirates in Somali waters,' said a spokesman, Abdi Gobdon Haj.

The freed hostages turned out to be full of praise for their captors. The pirates said they had had a good-conduct manual on how to seize a foreign vessel. They were not supposed to shout at hostages and were to give them food and drink regularly. Hostages were allowed to use the lavatory and sleep when they wanted, and pirates were not to sexually molest any female captive. The freed crew said the pirates had made them feel 'relaxed and cheerful' during their captivity. The gunmen had even brought goats on board and invited the captives to join 20 friends from their village for a barbecue. None of the crew claimed to have been abused by the pirates and there seems to have been only one act of violence. The man that Captain Marchesseau thought had got drunk and fallen overboard had, in fact, been shot by another pirate in a row about drugs.

'We really didn't have a bad time at all,' one crewman told the newspaper *France-Soir*. 'At first it was frightening when men with guns boarded but we soon realised they were pretty nice guys. They were calm and polite and hardly even raised their voices. Luckily they got what they wanted and left, because they didn't look like they really wanted to kill us.'

CHAPTER 5
THE *SEABOURN SPIRIT*

The German-built five-star cruise ship MV *Seabourn Spirit* was launched in 1989. She is one of a number of luxury liners owned by Seabourn Cruise Line, based in Miami, and takes holidaymakers from North America and Europe around Africa.

In late October 2005, she set off on a 16-day cruise from Alexandria in Egypt to Mombasa in Kenya, carrying 151 passengers – mostly Americans, but also Australians, Canadians, Britons and a number of other Europeans each paying £500 a night for the trip. Also on board were 150 crew. By 5 November, the 440ft ship had already passed through the Suez Canal and down the Red Sea. As the cruise-line's brochure said: 'Along the Red Sea shores, majestic granite mountains and sweeping dunes enfold Bedouin tents and lost Egyptian temples. These are the exotic dreams of a lifetime, waiting to be made real.' Any romantic dream of rollicking adventures with pirates on the high seas was about to become all too real – and with a very modern twist.

At 5.35am, the *Seabourn Spirit* was cruising some 70 miles off the coast of Somalia when she was attacked by pirates aboard two small, high-speed inflatables. They were carrying automatic weapons and rocket-propelled grenades (RPGs).

On the bridge, Captain Sven Erik Pedersen saw them coming alongside. The masters of merchantmen and liners are told not to resist when attacked, but Captain Pedersen was determined not to give up without a fight. He did not hit the alarm button to alert the passengers to the emergency as he feared they would run up on deck where they risked being shot. Instead, he calmly announced the looming danger over the ship's Tannoy and told the passengers to stay in their cabins.

Passenger Mike Rogers of Vancouver, Canada said, 'It was about 5.30 in the morning and we were awakened by the sound of what we figured out was bullets ricocheting off the side of the boat.'

Then he heard the voice of Captain Pedersen over the Tannoy saying, 'Stay inside, stay inside, we are under attack... This is not a drill. We have a boat alongside that appears to be armed. Please get low to the floor and stay away from the windows.'

But Rogers did not stay down. Looking out of the porthole, he saw the pirates shooting and firing RPGs at the *Seabourn Spirit*. 'The captain tried to run one of the boats over,' he said, 'but they were small boats, about 25 feet long. Each one had four or five people on it, and the captain said he was going to do anything to keep them from getting on board.'

The boats were now approaching from the port as well

as the starboard side and passengers were advised to lock themselves in their cabins.

Harry Hufford of Oakmont, California, said, 'The captain swerved the ship sharply to the left trying unsuccessfully to ram the oncoming boat and then took off at full speed.'

'My daughter saw the pirates out our window,' said passenger Edith Laird from Seattle. 'At least three RPGs hit the ship, one in a stateroom four doors down from our cabin. Our captain, Sven Erik Pedersen, and the rest of his crew did a wonderful and amazing job getting us out of the area as fast as possible. We had no idea that this ship could move as fast as it did! And he did his best to run down the pirates.'

It was later revealed that the captain had been trained in these protective and evasive tactics.

Another passenger, Norman Fisher from Hampstead Garden Suburb in north-west London, also saw the attackers. 'I was awake doing some work when I heard what sounded like a crack from outside,' he said. 'I looked out of the window and saw a small boat with about five people in it, about 20 yards away. One of them clearly had a rifle. Later I realised that two of them had rifles and one had some kind of rocket launcher.

'At first I didn't know what was going on, but when I saw the rocket launcher I started getting a bit scared. They were firing the rifle and then fired the rocket launcher twice. One of the rockets certainly hit the ship – it went through the side of the liner into a passenger's suite. The couple were in there at the time so it was a bit of an unpleasant experience. Fortunately they weren't hurt but you can just imagine what it would have been like if they had been standing up because obviously the cabin was very badly damaged.'

It was some 15 minutes later when Captain Pedersen made his announcement. 'He told us to go the restaurant in the middle of the ship and wait,' said Fisher. Many of the passengers were dressed in nightclothes. 'The atmosphere in the restaurant was a little tense. People were pretty good and they weren't panicking, but one or two were certainly looking nervous.'

Then Captain Pedersen came into the restaurant and said he was confident he had outrun the attackers. 'Of course he got a massive round of applause,' said Fisher. 'It was all a very surreal experience – not the kind of thing you expect on a cruise.'

But it wasn't just a matter of outrunning the pirates. On deck, two brave crewmen had taken them on directly. As soon as the ship's security officer Michael Groves, an ex-policeman who had also served in the Royal Navy, heard that two speedboats were approaching, he headed up to the deck. 'As soon as I went on deck I came under automatic fire,' he recalled. 'Then a rocket grenade blew me off my feet. The next thing I remember is rolling around, trying to check for shrapnel.' He was uninjured, but instead of ducking for cover, he then braved the bullets to unwind a high-pressure hose and aim the jet at the attackers, forcing them to withdraw.

The pirates soon returned, however. This time the liner's master of arms Som Bahadur Gurung, an ex-Gurkha, went to activate a sonic weapon known as a Long Range Acoustic Device. An LRAD looks like a loudhailer but it emits a concentrated beam of sound of more than 150 decibels – above the threshold of human pain – and is capable of causing permanent damage to hearing at a distance of more than a thousand feet.

But no sooner had Gurung got the LRAD out than Groves saw him fall. He had been hit in the upper body by a bullet. 'I saw a spray of blood and he just went straight down. I thought he was a goner but he opened one eye. He looked like half his head had been blown off.'

Groves dragged Gurung to safety, then turned the sonic canon on the attackers. Meanwhile, Captain Pedersen was trying to ram the raiders. He hit one of the boats, sinking it. After 30 minutes the pirates were forced to retreat and the captain directed the liner to safer waters, though the pirates continued circling the liner until it sped out of range.

The ship did not escape undamaged. 'There were bullet holes at several locations and two of the floor-to-ceiling windows in the lounge at the rear of the ship were shattered by bullets,' said Harry Huffords. An RPG shell had also wedged itself in the wall of a cabin, but after the raid, the USS *Gonzalez*, an American destroyer patrolling the waters, sent a Navy ordnance disposal team to deal with unexploded munitions. Its leader, Lieutenant John Stewart, inspected the cabin where the RPG had struck and his team removed the remains of the grenades. 'We made sure that the remnants of the RPG were no longer hazardous to the ship or the passengers,' he said.

There was other minor damage – 'There was no water, for instance, in some places,' said Mark Rogers – but the *Seabourn Spirit* remained seaworthy, and at least the passengers were uninjured. Gayle Meagher from Sydney Australia, who had wanted to take an exciting cruise, said, 'It was a little bit more exciting than we planned for.'

'It was terrifying,' added Groves. 'There was a lot of screaming on the lower decks.'

The *Seabourn Spirit* then rerouted to the Seychelles to keep away from the Somali coast, and Seabourn Cruise Lines began to consider route changes for their cruises.

Som Gurung recovered from his gunshot wound, but Michael Groves' hearing had been damaged by the LRAD and he now suffered from tinnitus. He made a claim for damages against the shipping company, seeking compensation of more than £300,000. He told the High Court in London that his impaired hearing, coupled with post-traumatic stress disorder, had meant he was unable to carry on working as a ship's security officer. He claimed the company were guilty of negligence by ignoring warnings that pirates were active in the area, and by taking the ship within 63 miles of the coast of Somalia, instead of staying at least 150 miles off shore as advised by the International Maritime Bureau (IMB). He also alleged that he was told wrongly that the ship was 140 miles off the coast. Further, he said, the ship was travelling too slowly, making it more vulnerable to attack.

On 16 May 2007, Michael Groves and Som Gurung, who had settled in Southend, were summoned to Buckingham Place. Groves was awarded the Queen's Gallantry Medal, while Gurung got the Queen's Commendation for Bravery.

The *Seabourn Spirit* was the first liner to be attacked in those waters, but other ships had fallen victim to other activity. Just a few days before, pirates had thwarted efforts to deliver relief supplies to northern Somalia. According to the IMB, nearly 30 hijackings had been recorded off Somalia's 1,880-mile coastline in the previous eight months compared to just two attacks the previous year. They warned ships to stay at least 150 miles away from Somalia's waters; further out to sea, international waters were patrolled by NATO warships.

On 27 June 2005, a UN-chartered ship, the MV *Semlow*, was on a humanitarian mission to tsunami victims in Somalia when 15 gunmen boarded and took over the ship in 15 minutes. Its crew of ten were held for over three months while pirates tried to get the United Nations to pay a ransom.

'We heard some gunshots,' said the *Semlow*'s commander Captain Sellathurai Mahalingam. 'These pirates, they came in three boats fully armed, and within seconds they boarded the vessel. The head of the gang then came to the bridge and ordered the vessel to be stopped. They asked me about money, and they put the gun on my face.'

The gunmen stole $8,500 from the ship's safe and ransacked the crew's cabins, taking anything of value. Then came the most frightening part, an interrogation of sorts by the nervous pirates on the bullet-scarred bridge. 'The question that scared me the most was when they wanted to know the religion of the people on the ship,' said Kenyan crewman Patrick Ogudu, a Christian. 'I decided to name myself Abubakar, to be in a safe position.'

The gunmen were freelance militia men, members of one of Somalia's many criminal gangs who depend on hijacking and kidnapping for money. They demanded $20,000 for the ship's release, but the UN refused to pay up. As the days passed, the pirates and crew reached an uneasy understanding. Though they said they were Muslims, Ogudu said he never saw the pirates pray. The only time they appeared to care about Islam was when he moved a Qur?an without washing his hands first.

On 14 September, the crew thought a deal had been secured for the ship's release, but the pirates apparently decided at the last minute to demand another ransom. Then on 23 September they used the *Semlow* to seize the MS *Ibnu Batuta*, an Egyptian ship carrying cement. As negotiations dragged on, the *Semlow* ran out of fuel, so the hijackers got the *Ibnu Batuta* to tow it to the port of El Maan. Along the way, the gunmen left the ship by speedboat and the ships were freed, though the pirates had vandalised the ships' communications equipment. Most of the *Semlow*'s 937 tons of rice – donated by Germany and Japan – was still on board, but the pirates had looted some of it. The rest was unloaded in El Maan, but never reached its intended recipients.

On 12 October, eight days after the *Semlow* was released, her sister ship, the MV *Miltzow* was seized in the harbour at Merka, 45 miles south of Mogadishu, while unloading humanitarian aid for the 78,000 starving people of the Jilib district. At 3.30pm six gunmen stormed the ship and forced it to leave the port with an estimated 450 tons of maize beans and vegetable oil (out of a total cargo of 850 tons) still on board. One hundred days later, the *Miltzow* was released and returned to Merka to finish unloading.

Again on 12 October, Somali pirates seized the MV *Torgelow*, also carrying relief supplies. After 53 days she was released and returned to her home port of Mombasa. 'I am surprised these people are doing this and especially in the holy month of Ramadan,' said one of the ship's owners.

Typically freighters carry only a handful of crew members but it was feared that the pirates, emboldened by these hijackings, might now try hijacking cruise ships full of rich Westerners. This did not materialise and the attack on the *Seabourn Spirit* was the last known attempt to board a passenger ship, though the menace did not go away. Indeed, on 24 November, the *Seabourn Spirit* – which was still plying the same waters – radioed for help when she spotted small boats closing on her off the coast of Oman. The distress call was picked up by HMS *Campbell* 120 miles away. Her captain, Commander Gordon Abernethy, dispatched a Lynx helicopter armed with missiles and as it approached the cruise liner at 180mph, the pirates dispersed, leaving the *Seabourn Spirit* unmolested. 'It is extremely rewarding to be of assistance,' said Commander Abernethy.

Apparently undeterred, the Seabourn company was still offering a 17-day luxury cruise on its sister ship *Seabourn Pride* from Alexandria to Dubai – a route that would take it through the Gulf of Aden – as late as April 2009.

CHAPTER 6
THE SOMALI SEA

According to the secretary general of the Shipping Federation, hijacking off Somalia was just a blip on the radar screen when modern-day piracy reached its peak in 2000. Since then it has became a big problem, costing international shipping an estimated $150million in 2008. The first attack that brought the Somali pirates to world attention was the taking of the liquefied petroleum gas tanker MV *Feisty Gas* on 10 April 2005. It was released when the owners paid $315,000 to a representative of the pirates in the port of Mombasa, the second-largest city in neighbouring Kenya.

One major cause of piracy in Somali waters is the failure of central government. After years of civil war, a Transitional National Government was set up in 2000 after a peace conference in Djibouti. However, it was opposed by the Somali Reconciliation and Restoration Council, which was formed the following year. In October 2004 another attempt was made to make peace between the warring factions with the creation of a Transitional Federal Government.

At first, its parliament had to meet in Kenya; then it had to move to Baidoa in southern Somalia, as the capital Mogadishu had fallen into the hands of powerful warlords. In June 2006, the Union of Islamic Courts defeated the warlords and was soon threatening the Transitional Federal Government in Baidoa, but fearing a militant Islamist regime on its borders, Ethiopia intervened and defeated the Islamic Courts. However, the Transitional Federal Government continues to be weak and unable to establish its authority over the whole country. It also faces violent resistance from extremist elements, such as the al-Shabaab militia previously affiliated with the Union of Islamic Courts. Nevertheless, it is still recognised as the legitimate government of Somalia.

In 2005, following the hijacking of three UN relief ships, the Somali government appealed for help. 'Until we establish our own marine force, we want neighbouring countries to deploy their navies to protect Somalia's coastline against the pirates,' said Mohamed Ali Americo, a senior official in the prime minister's office. 'We need help from all the nations along the Indian Ocean and the Red Sea. The pirates use ransom to buy weapons. Their operations are also intended to destabilise and discredit the transitional government now that it has relocated to Somalia.'

Small vessels off the coast of Somalia had been under threat for some time. On 28 April 1999, the 33ft sloop *Violetta* was seized. It belonged to Pertti and Pirkko Pulkkinen from Finland who had been sailing enthusiasts for 20 years. Pertti had built the *Violetta* so they could sail around the world when he retired and on 30 June 1994, they set off. It was not until they reached the waters off Somalia, by which time they'd completed two-thirds of their journey, that they even heard of a pirate attack.

They kept 60 miles off the coast, thinking they would be safe. But at 2am on 28 April, Pertti heard the noise of a motor in the distance. Alarmed, Pirkko joined him in the cockpit. Another boat was gaining on them fast. The men on board fired shots in the air and then three of them boarded the *Violetta*. Pirkko asked if they were from the coastguard. It was clear that they were not.

The Pulkkinens were manhandled onto the pirate boat, but Pertti was then allowed to climb back onto the *Violetta* to take the sails down. The pirates then tried to take the *Violetta* in tow, but the autopilot was on and kept steering the yacht towards Djibouti. Three gunmen got back on the yacht with the couple and ordered Pertti to switch on the engine and follow their boat, which was heading for the port of Bosasso. Despite their rough handling at the outset, the Pulkkinens found the pirates quite congenial. They offered to share their water with the couple and had even brought their own food. However, the pirates subsequently asked for paper so they could smoke hashish, which made them more menacing in the Pulkkinens' eyes. Nevertheless, they did not mistreat their prisoners, and pirates and captives dozed together in the heat of the day.

The *Violetta* dropped anchor in Bosasso, but the Pulkkinens were taken ashore eight or nine miles away and held in a small village of seven or eight mud huts with straw roofs. The couple were give a hut of their own and slept on straw mats on the floor. They were fed twice a day and given the choice of meat or fish. Twice they were taken to the pirates' headquarters in Bosasso where they met local clan chieftains. After a week the United Nations Development Programme learnt of the couples location and put pressure on the chieftains to have them released. Although a ransom still had to be negotiated, the Pulkkinens were allowed to go to the nearest UN base so they could phone home to tell family and friends they were alive. The pirates also allowed them to send out faxes, which said the pirates were demanding a ransom of $50,000. A UN official managed to secure the Pulkkinens' release without a ransom being paid, but the pirates hung on to their yacht which contained just about everything they owned. Fortunately, Pirkko had had the foresight to hide her Visa card in her bikini bottoms, so they could get home.

A couple of months after the Pulkkinens returned to Finland, they received a fax from the pirate chief in Bosasso asking for $50,000 for the return of their boat. In the ensuing months, the insurance company managed to get the *Violetta* released in Aden. No ransom was paid, though money for 'docking fees' did change hands.

In June 1999, the charter yacht *Nono* was being delivered from the Seychelles to Turkey, via the Suez Canal. On board were the captain, Boris Kulpe, and a crew of four German sailing enthusiasts. Leaving Victoria Harbour on Mahé Island in the Seychelles on 12 June, they made good time across the Indian Ocean and were off the coast of Somalia six days later when a gale hit. The skipper decided to take the westerly route around Socotra Island, believing that pirates would not venture out in a storm, but just as they entered the channel the wind dropped. The

Nono had lowered her sails and switched on her engine when the skipper spotted a low-slung motorboat heading for them. He gunned the engines and put out a distress call to the freighter on a parallel course about a mile-and-a-half to starboard. There was no reply, so he fired off a flare, but by then the pirates were alongside. One fired a pistol in the air and others clambered aboard carrying assault rifles.

The *Nono* was taken to the small fishing village of Allula, where a translator joined them. He asked how much money they had. The crew had about $400 in cash between them, which they handed over. The pirates laughed at this paltry sum and demanded a ransom of $200,000. After a day, they dropped their demand to $100,000, but that too was beyond the crew's means. Boris Kulpe tried to explain to the pirates that the yacht did not belong to them and that they were merely a delivery crew. If the pirates let them go, they would go back to Germany and get the owner to pay a ransom to get his yacht back. The suggestion was met with some interest, but nothing happened.

The *Nono* was then taken up the coast towards Bosasso. The pirates tried to contact their chieftain there, but could not get through. It was fiercely hot, hitting 105ºF under the awning on the yacht. The crew were allowed to cool off in the water, though Barbara Cojocura – the only female crew member – had to wear a blouse and skirt over her swimming costume. Despite these strictures, the pirates were friendly. The only time they became aggressive was when other pirates sailed by. It was clear that they had no intention of giving up their prize without a fight.

As their captivity dragged on, Kulpe managed to radio a distress message, but received no reply. The idea of attempting to overpower their captors was quickly dismissed. One of the crew members started drinking. Another wanted to videotape the pirates secretly. The pirates were certainly not fearful that their captives would turn on them. When they ran short of water, one member of the crew and one of the pirates were sent to get some from a nearby well. On the way back, they took turns – one carrying the water, the other the Kalashnikov.

Eventually, a UN representative turned up. He arranged for the crew to be taken in a UNICEF jeep to Bosasso, where they were put up in a hotel surrounded by barbed wire and armed men. They could see the *Violetta* in the harbour below. It was then that they learned that the local coast-guard commandant was also commander-in-chief of the pirates. The lighthouse on the tip of the Horn of Africa was used as a pirates' lookout and all the fishing boats along that part of the coast were ordered to report when a foreign boat was in their waters. That was how the *Nono* had been picked up so easily.

The UN representative then arranged for them to be flown to Dubai, from where they were returned to Germany. Eventually, the *Nono* was released, but the insurers banned Kulpe from sailing the boat on to Turkey. They claimed he had been negligent in taking the vessel so close to the coast of Somalia and threatened to sue, but later withdrew their threat.

In December 2005, the International Maritime Organisation grew so concerned over the growth in piracy off Somalia that they approached the United Nations to do something about it. In March 2006 the Security Council urged member states to use their navy vessels and military aircraft to fight piracy off the coast of Somalia. In November 2007, the General Assembly adopted a resolution on piracy in Somali waters that, among other things, asked the Transitional Federal Government for its consent for the ships of other nations' navies to enter their territorial waters and for military aircraft to enter their air space in pursuit of pirates. This had little effect, so the UN had to adopt a new resolution in November 2008 following the hijacking of the *Sirius Star*.

While piracy in Somali waters still went on, the world's navies rode to the rescue, not without some success. On 16 January 2006, pirates seized the India-registered MV *Safina al-Birsarat* along with its 16-man Indian crew. The US Navy were alerted to the attack by the Piracy Reporting Centre, which had been set up by the International Maritime Bureau in Kuala Lumpur in 1992 at a time when the Straits of Malacca were the most active area for pirates. The guided-missile destroyer USS *Winston S. Churchill* set off in pursuit. It located the captured ship some 55 miles off the coast of Somalia on the evening of 20 January. The *Churchill* then shadowed the vessel through the night and into the morning of the following day.

At 8.03am, the *Churchill* tried contacting the *Safina al-Birsarat* over ship-to-ship radio. The *Churchill* requested that the crew leave the vessel and board the two small boats the ship had in tow. Repeated attempts were made to establish communications, but there was no reply. The *Churchill* then began aggressive manoeuvring in an attempt to stop the vessel, but the *Safina al-Birsarat* continued its course and speed.

At 11.31am, the *Churchill* fired warning shots across the

Safina al-Birsarat's bows. The vessel cut its speed and went dead in the water, but still the *Churchill* could not raise anyone on the radio. At 1.02pm, it broadcast a warning that it would take further action and use force if the crew did not to respond to questioning and depart the vessel. Nothing happened. At 2.21pm, the *Churchill* fired more warning shots. The pirates on the *Safina al-Birsarat* then got on the radio and said they would begin sending men over to *Churchill*. They started going across at 2.54pm, after which marines boarded the *Safina al-Birsarat* and found a cache of small arms. They freed the rest of the crew and arrested ten suspected Somali pirates, who were handed over to the Kenyan authorities in Mombasa.

In court, the Somalis said they had been abducted from their fishing boat and claimed they were the criminals' victims. However, the Indian sailors countered that they had been tortured by the Somalis. They also said that the pirates had also demanded a ransom of $50,000 for their release. All ten pirates were convicted and the prosecution urged the court to hand down life sentences. When the sentence was read, the packed courtroom fell silent and the accused bowed their heads to pray. When they heard they had been given just seven years, their faces brightened and they clapped their hands. Even so, the defence lawyer appealed against their sentences, arguing that some of the defendants were minors.

On 18 March 2006, the USS *Cape St. George* and the USS *Gonzalez* were involved in a firefight with suspected pirates. The destroyer *Gonzalez* had intercepted a suspicious vessel towing two skiffs some 30 miles off the coast of Somalia. She contacted the cruiser *Cape St. George*, asking for assistance and the cruiser duly arrived before dawn. At sunrise the *Gonzalez* sent two rigid-hulled inflatable boats (RIBs) carrying a nine-man boarding party to investigate, but their attempts to board were repulsed by the pirates.

'When the *Gonzalez* RIB crews approached, the suspected pirates started brandishing rocket-propelled grenade launchers and opened up on the RIB crews,' said Captain James Russell Yohe, commander of the *Cape St. George*. 'The RIB crews returned their fire and manoeuvred. At the same time, gunners on our ship laid down covering fire to keep the pirates' heads down so the *Gonzalez* RIBs could get out of the way.'

The two American ships continued laying down covering fire long enough to allow the boarding parties to escape, whereupon the pirates opened fire on the capital ships with RPGs and other small arms, instigating the US Navy's first surface action of 21st century.

'From there, it evolved into a surface action, where the suspected pirates started shooting back at us, raking down our side,' said Captain Yohe.

Yohe ordered his ship to full speed to get ahead of the three pirate vessels. From there he could attack them without risking hitting *Gonzalez* or its two small boats. The *Cape St. George* engaged the two smaller, high-speed vessels with its machine-gun fire, disabling them. Meanwhile the *Gonzalez* raked the larger pirate vessel, a 40ft diesel. A tracer round hit a 55-gallon drum of diesel, setting the boat on fire. It burned to the waterline.

'I was simply amazed they were firing at us, to be so bold as to actually continue the engagement,' said Captain Yohe, who added that his men responded with what he considered appropriate force. 'Once the suspected pirates started waving their arms and we could tell they were giving up, they ceased firing and everyone stopped firing,' he said.

Immediately, the *Cape St. George* launched its small boats to recover the injured and arrest the other suspects. One pirate suspect was dead and five were wounded, two seriously. Chief Petty Officer Patrick Modglin, the senior corpsman on the *Cape St. George*, set up a triage area on the ship's fantail while eight stretcher-bearers carried the wounded to the ship's sick bay. Modglin complained that he got just 30 minutes sleep during the 30 hours he spent treating the wounded. They were then treated further on the amphibious assault ship USS *Nassau*, which had a full medical staff, before being transferred to the Dutch fast combat support ship, the HNLMS *Amsterdam*.

In all, 12 pirates were captured. In what remained of their boats, a number of grenades, grenade-launchers and automatic weapons were found, and these were impounded to be used in evidence.

No Navy personnel were injured but the *Cape St. George* suffered minor superficial damage, although it was not until the action was over that Yohe learned some rounds had hit his ship. 'One of the crews said, "Hey, there are bullet holes on the hull,"' Yohe reported. 'You could see the paint chipped off and little dimples in the steel.'

Later, there was some dispute over the incident. Saleban Aadan Barqad, a spokesman for the Somalis involved in the incident, said the US Navy had opened fire first. He also claimed that the men involved were not pirates at all. Rather they were militiamen 'in an operation to protect the country's sea resources from illicit exploitation by foreign vessels'. Geraad Mohamud, of the same militia group, said that in future the militiamen would kill any hostage they captured and attack any ship unlawfully plying Somalian waters unless their men were released.

Captain Yohe denied that the US ships had fired first. 'I can tell you, we have some footage that I think will resolve that,' he told the *Virginian Pilot* newspaper. 'It will clearly show the suspected pirates firing at the *Gonzalez* RIB crew first.'

In the meantime the US ships continued their search-and-rescue missions with Task Force 150, under the command of Royal Netherlands Navy Commodore Hank Ort.

The MV *Rozen*, a freighter registered in St Vincent and the Grenadines, had several scrapes with pirates. On 13 March 2006 she was attacked by armed raiders in broad daylight off the Somali coast. About five pirates with machine guns and RPGs chased the vessel and fired shots that hit the bridge and superstructure. The chase continued for almost an hour with the pirates firing from both port and starboard, and signalling the ship to stop. When the pirate boat came alongside and attempted to board, the captain quickly changed course and rammed it, leaving her dead in the water.

The following year the *Rozen* was not so lucky. On 25 February 2007, she was returning to Mombasa after delivering 1,800 metric tons of food aid to the ports of Bossaso and Berbera in northern Somalia when six gunmen boarded her and took control. The raiders then took the freighter and her crew of 12 – six Sri Lankans, including the captain, and six Kenyans – to Garacad, where she was moored.

On 27 February four of the pirates went ashore to buy supplies and were arrested by the Puntland authorities in the coastal town of Bargaal. That evening there was a firefight between the coastguards and the remaining pirates that took out all the glass in the *Rozen*'s bridge. One of Sri Lankan crew was slightly injured in the shoulder, and two coastguards were thought to have been killed. Negotiations opened on 6 March, and the ship and its crew were released a month later.

The same day the Indian-flagged MV *Nimatullah*, which was carrying more than 725 metric tons of cargo, including cooking oil, second-hand clothing and rice, was also released. A representative of the East African Seafarers Assistance Programme said a ransom had been paid for the ships' release but would not give the amount.

On 15 May 2007 two South Korean fishing vessels – the *Mavuno I* and the *Mavuno II* – were hijacked 250 miles off Mogadishu on their way to Yemen. Between them they had 25 crewmen – ten Chinese, four Koreans, four Indians, four Indonesians and three Vietnamese. Within two days the ship-owner's representatives in Mombasa learnt that the men were safe. They were being held with a hijacked Taiwanese fishing vessel, the *Ching Fong Hwa 168*, in the port of Ras Assuad, north of Mogadishu. After six months, they were released. Once they set sail, they rendezvoused with the US Navy who provided humanitarian assistance and escorted them out of Somali waters. However, the captain of the *Ching Fong Hwa 168*, Lin Sheng-hsin, had a harrowing tale to tell.

On a sunny afternoon in April, his ship had been stormed by some 15 pirates armed with automatic rifles, machine guns and RPGs. One of the unarmed crew had been shot in the back, though he survived. However, when negotiations with the ship's Taiwanese owners were going badly, the pirates grabbed a young Chinese sailor, 32-year-old Chen Tao who had served with the ship for two years, and took him over to the other side of the boat. Then six shots rang out. Tao had been executed.

'He was very unlucky because they just took him at random,' said Captain Lin. 'We were in shock. Just for money they took a life – they are not human.'

'After they shot that guy, I was really afraid,' said Lin Shang-yu, the captain's 22-year-old son who was also on board.

Four crew members were ordered to drag Tao's bloody body into the ship's freezers, where the captain insisted it was stowed so that it could be buried on land. The pirates had wanted to throw it to the sharks.

As the kidnapping dragged on, the ship's supply of vegetables ran out and the crew came down with scurvy. They also endured frequent mock executions and beatings from guards when the crew – Chinese, Taiwanese and Filipino – failed to understand orders given to them in Somali and broken English.

To increase the pressure on the ship's owners, the crew were forced to call home and beg for their lives. Captain Lin listened as his wife wept over the fate of her husband and her son. Then when negotiations broke down, the pirates said they were going to execute Captain Lin's son. The only response Captain Lin could think of was to threaten to throw himself into the shark-infested sea. Four pirates had to rush forward to keep him from jumping overboard. 'It was a test,' he said. 'I wanted to see how much the pirates valued me... They know if the captain dies, they will get less ransom.'

After five months, the ship's owners paid up – the pirates had originally demanded $1.5million. When the pirates got the ransom, the crew thought they were going home, but the pirates held out for more money. Then the US Navy intervened. They got the pirates on the radio and pressed them to leave the ship. On 5 November, the pirates took to their skiffs and headed for shore. It is not entirely clear why they left. However, a few days earlier the US had made a show of force. An American vessel had fired on pirate skiffs tied to a Japanese-owned ship and, earlier, a warship had shelled suspected al-Qaeda terrorists ashore. Over the previous months, the US Navy had freed five hijacked ships.

The *Ching Fong Hwa 168* was then escorted out of Somali waters, and its crew were given food and medical assistance. After reaching Mombasa, they celebrated with chicken and lobster in a Chinese restaurant and toasted their regained freedom in saké.

But in June 2007 a US Navy warship failed to rescue the crew of the MV *Danica White*, a Danish bulk carrier seized on the morning of 1 June. She was carrying drilling equipment from Dubai to Mombasa, and had almost passed the coast of Somalia in international waters. The captain had not received notification that he should remain at least two hundred miles offshore, though they were in fact 205 miles from the coast. Due to wind and current, the ship had slowed to five knots. The master was alone on the bridge, where he was preparing some paperwork for the new captain who was taking over in Mombasa.

Sometime shortly before 10am, the captain heard screams coming from outside. At first he thought that it was the ordinary seamen joking around. Then he heard a few crashes and realised that somebody was pulling at the door to the wheelhouse. The pirates had boarded the ship from three fibreglass boats – one large boat with an inboard motor and two smaller boats with outboard motors. Getting on board had been easy as the ship was heavily laden and low in the water.

The first mate had been off duty at the time. At around 9.45am he had looked out of the porthole in his cabin to see the stern of a fibreglass boat. He rushed to the bridge with the cook, who had been alerted by the sound of crashes, to tell the captain he thought they were under attack. He found the captain was working at his computer and had not seen anything. Suddenly, there were ten to 15 men with weapons in the wheelhouse.

The captain immediately hit the Ship Security Alerting System (SSAS) and the button lit up, confirming transmission. The alarm signal would be picked up by a satellite and relayed to warships nearby. Then he put his hands up in the air and told the pirates that they could take whatever they wanted, and that the crew would do as they said. Then he set off the ship's general alarm to summon the rest of the crew to the bridge. The cook had a machine-gun pointed to his head and was sent to get them.

The two ordinary seamen had been taking a break when they heard the crashes. One of them was in his cabin and had looked out of the porthole to see the pirates on their way up the ladder to the bridge. The other ordinary seaman had spotted the pirates on the deck. The two of them ran to the engine room and locked themselves in. After a while, they thought better of it. Fearing that the other crewmen might be punished if the pirates thought that some of the men were hiding, they unlocked the door and made their way to the bridge. When they assembled, the pirates did not believe there were only five men on board.

At around 1pm the following day, the shipping company's office in Copenhagen got a call from the USS *Carter Hall*, telling them they had just spotted the *Danica White* heading towards Mogadishu with three boats in tow. The owner then tried contacting the vessel, but received no reply. Meanwhile the office checked whether the ship's destination had been changed by the charterers and called the warship back to tell them it was not supposed to be heading for Mogadishu. The *Carter Hall* reported that they had noticed a large number of people on the bridge and there had been some sort of disturbance.

It was plain that the pirates were in control on the bridge and had taken the crew hostage. The *Carter Hall* now fired machine-gun bursts – at first warning shots, then more serious rounds. Disabling shots were aimed at the pirates' three skiffs in tow behind the *Danica White*, pretty much destroying them. But the pirates were still able to sail the ship into Somali waters where, at that time, the US warship had no permission to follow them. The ship and its five-man crew were held for 83 days. It was not clear if any of the ransom had been paid, but the pirates had demanded $1.5million.

In the first week of June 2007, the US Office of Naval Intelligence (ONI) reported that at least four vessels had been fired upon as far as 230 miles from the Somali coast, all within a 60-mile radius of 01:37 North 049:36 East. The gunmen had attacked in small white speedboats and been armed with machine guns and RPGs.

'Given the distance from shore these recent attacks have occurred and poor weather conditions typical for this time of year, ONI assesses pirates are likely utilising a larger merchant vessel as a mother ship to support their small-boat attacks,' the report said. 'If so, this would extend their attack range beyond two hundred nautical miles, and increase the number of attack groups (typical three-vessel configuration of one nine-metre centre-console support skiff and two six-metre outboard-motor attack/boarding skiffs with ten to 15 pirates per group) as well as increase their time on station.'

Until then, the International Maritime Bureau (IMB) had recommended that ships should stay at least 86 miles from shore. That recommendation was duly increased to 230 miles. The Office of Naval Intelligence also advised ships to stay at least 75 nautical miles from the position 01:37 North 049:36 East until the mother ship threat could be evaluated. 'Vessels transiting the east coast of Somalia, regardless of distance from shore, should increase anti-piracy precautions and maintain a heightened state of vigilance,' it said.

The ONI also pointed out, 'Vessels that have successfully prevented pirates from boarding are those that have taken evasive manoeuvres that maximise the amount of wake turbulence with the minimum amount of momentum loss. Vessels with high freeboard and wide gunwale railings fare better than vessels with low freeboard and readily available hook-points for the makeshift six-metre hook-ladders used by Somali pirates.'

Meanwhile, NATO was setting up seaborne rapid reaction forces and discussing security with maritime nations.

On 20 September 2007, the Greek fishing vessel FV

Greko 2 was seized by pirates about 130 miles west of Berbera and anchored near the village of Raas Shula. All 16 crew, plus four Somali security personnel, were taken off the vessel. The pirates also destroyed equipment and stole everything they could remove. This included diesel fuel, although they left the engines intact. The crewmen were intimidated, but not harmed. The boat was released on 23 February and sailed for Aden. The owners said no ransom had been paid.

On 28 October 2007 the Japanese chemical tanker MV *Golden Nori,* carrying highly explosive benzene, was seized by pirates only nine miles off the coast near the Socotra archipelago. The 12,000-tonne tanker's distress call was picked up by the destroyer USS *Porter*, which had permission from the government to enter Somali waters. The *Porter* opened fire, sinking the pirates' skiffs tied to the stern, but broke off because of the danger of igniting the benzene. The USS *Arleigh Burke* then took over shadowing the *Golden Nori*. Meanwhile the tanker's captain phoned home, telling his family that the 21-man crew was safe. US and German naval vessels blockaded the port of Bosasso to prevent the *Golden Nori* entering the harbour there. Eventually, after demanding a ransom, the pirates freed the ship and its crew on 12 December.

On the night of 29 October 2007, eight pirates seized North Korean cargo vessel the *Dai Hong Dan,* about 70 miles off Mogadishu. However, while the hijackers took control of the bridge, the 22-man crew managed to hold onto the engine room and steering compartment. Their distress signal reached the IMB in Kuala Lumpur, who immediately called the Combined Maritime Forces

Headquarters in Bahrain. They in turn contacted the USS *James E. Williams*. The destroyer was some 60 miles from the *Dai Hong Dan* but sent a helicopter to investigate.

When the *Williams* caught up with the hijacked freighter at midday on the 30th, she contacted the pirates by radio and ordered them to give up their weapons. At this point, the crew stormed the bridge and, after a struggle, took back control of the ship. A team from the *Williams* then came aboard. They found two pirates dead and five more captured. Three Koreans had been wounded and were transferred to the *Williams* for medical attention. The *Dai Hong Dan* finally docked safely in Aden on 6 November.

The Koreans were in a good position to defend themselves. Most North Korean sailors have been through at least ten years of military service before they go to sea. They also receive martial arts training to be ready for such an eventuality. Normally, security agents are on board vessels headed overseas to keep an eye on the crews' activities and they would have ordered the men to fight. North Korean merchant ships also carry small arms.

'If the crew members were captured and the incident forced the North Korean authorities to step in, that would have ruined their career,' a defector told a Hong Kong newspaper. 'The crew members upon their return to North Korea would have faced severe ideological verification and lost their job. I imagine that the crewmen of the *Dai Hong Dan* must have fought very hard against the pirates, risking their life.'

As it happened, the *Dai Hong Dan* was already famous in Korea after defying the South Korean Navy in the Jeju Strait in June 2001. Park Yong Hwan, her captain of 27 years, received the title of 'Hardworking Hero', North Korea's top award for workers.

According to the IMB, piracy rose by ten per cent in 2007, the year that *Dai Hong Dan* was seized, thanks to the Somali pirates who, despite the world's navies patrolling off their coast, were becoming increasingly audacious.

On 1 February the Danish-owned, Russian 114ft tug boat MV *Svitar Korsakov* was seized. This was unusual as she was carrying no cargo or anything of any value to the pirates. In fact, she was on her maiden voyage. Having been built at the shipyards in St Petersburg, she was on her way to her first job at Sakhalin Island, between Japan and Russia, travelling via Singapore. This took her through the Suez Canal and the Gulf of Aden, a journey expected to take 17 days. When she was seized, she was 70 miles off the coast and following the approved route well north of the island of Socotra.

'We heard or saw shouts or shots or something,' said her British captain Colin Darch. 'I saw a boat coming towards us and I raced up to the bridge. I put the propulsion into hand and increased the revs and the pitch, by which time the boat was close to the starboard quarter. I sort of threw the stern at him and he sheered away, and I did that two or three times.'

There were five armed men in the large speedboat but as the pirates circled, Captain Darch managed to fend them off with the tug's powerful engines. Then the pirates started firing so the crew – four Russians and Irish engineer Fred Parle – ducked. 'When they started firing at the wheelhouse we decided enough was enough,' said Darch.

Then a second boat appeared. 'At first there was just one

boat and I was able to fend him off with the thrusters so every time he tried to get close he risked being sunk,' said the captain. 'But then he went off for reinforcements and it wasn't possible to keep two boats at bay.'

Soon after the second boat turned up someone shouted, 'They're aboard!'

Darch closed the engines down to idle as the pirates came rushing up to the bridge, firing their guns. There was no way they crew could resist 20 armed men. One of the first two pirates on the bridge was a short, fat man who called himself Andrew and spoke English. He introduced the other man. 'This is Omar, our captain,' he said. 'You only take orders from us two.'

For the first few hours, Darch and his crew felt very threatened by the pirates. 'We didn't know how wild and desperate they were,' he said. However, they soon made it clear that all they were interested in was money and that the crew would be quite safe provided they cooperated. 'We were told if we behaved no one would get hurt. If we did something wrong, we would be shot... They wanted money and said the tug had been hijacked for ransom. We could see they were not religious or political, and they told us they had to rob to survive.'

Meanwhile the pirates looted the crew's cabins, stealing their phones, cameras, laptops and clothes. 'They didn't bother so much with mine because they were too old-fashioned,' said the 70-year-old captain, 'but they told us we were all Muslim brothers and must share.'

The tug was taken to Eyl and anchored off shore. An American warship turned up, but did not attack in case the crew got hurt. The pirates were reinforced by others and a standoff began. Gradually, the young gunmen began to become impatient. They feared they would never be paid, believing that the protracted negotiations were just a big trick and they would be eventually attacked and killed. Darch tried to calm the situation by remaining neutral in the negotiations, merely playing the role of telephonist and messenger.

However, by the twelfth day of their captivity, the captain had devised a plan to escape with the help of the warship. The idea was to black out the ship that night, while the crew took refuge in the engine room, where they could barricade themselves behind the steel watertight doors in the stern. He hoped the Americans would see the blacking-out of the ship as a signal and knowing the crew were safe, send a boarding party. After they had killed the pirates, or frightened them off, they could hand back the ship to the crew. Darch spelled out the plan in 'an almost plain language message to that effect' he sent to the American warship.

At one o'clock they put the plan into action and barricaded themselves in the ballast tank that was partly full of water. But the pirates quickly worked out what was going on. 'Then we heard, all day, them bashing and smashing at the steel doors, trying to get through to us,' said Darch. 'But we didn't hear any American attack.'

At five o'clock the following afternoon Darch and his crew decided to give themselves up. But they were in for a surprise. The door would not open. The pirates had bolted them in. It was now the crew's turn to bang on the bulkhead. This went on for a couple of hours and eventually at around seven o'clock the pirates released them.

'We didn't know then what they were going to do to us,' said Captain Darch. 'They had spent all day smashing away, trying to get at us. But apart from shouting and firing their guns and generally doing a bit of a war dance, they didn't actually touch us. The young guns were shouting abuse at us and shooting their guns. Then Omar, their leader, appeared. He grinned and held out his hand. It was like we'd just had a good game of squash and I'd lost.'

However, the crew did lose all their privileges. From then on they had to sleep in the wheelhouse rather than their cabins, and they could only go to the toilets and mess room under armed guard. They got only Somali tea for breakfast and dinner, but lunch was provided by the pirates who had brought goats on board.

As the hijacking dragged on and negotiations stalled, there was talk of taking the crew ashore. Captain Darch began to get concerned about their safety and got permission to send an uncensored email to the tug's owners in Copenhagen. He told them that for over 30 days, their lives had been balanced against the expectation of money. If no money was forthcoming, the crew's lives would be worth nothing to the pirates. Eventually the owners agreed to pay the ransom. But the real problem lay with the pirates and the practical difficulties of working out how to pay a ransom.

'It was like a syndicate of workers who had won the lottery but couldn't find the ticket,' said Captain Darch. 'They were unsophisticated hoodlums. They couldn't drive the ship away because they didn't have the skill to control it.'

In the end, the pirates settled for a much reduced figure – $678,000. The money was delivered secretly by sea and after

47 days, the *Svitar Korsakov* and her crew were released. After she had sailed away from Eyl, she rendezvoused with the American warship, which sent two officers aboard to debrief the crew. Darch asked them why they had not attacked when they had seen his signal. One of the officers said they had not got the message he had sent. Another said that even if they had got the message, to put American lives at risk to save four Russians, an Irishman and an Englishman whose lives were not immediately in danger would have needed permission from very high up which they probably would not have been granted.

After the US Navy had escorted them to a safe port, the tug continued on its journey with a new crew, while Darch talked to the world's media about the hijacking. 'It was all about money, but our captors told us there were much worse pirate gangs around the Somali capital Mogadishu. They hinted that these gangs were linked to terrorists. One dreads to think what would happen if a cruise ship fell into their hands.'

The British seaman's union Nautilus said that one notorious gang, calling themselves the Somalia Coast Guard, had links to al-Qaeda and that unless something was done about the pirates, the world was giving 'a green light for a terrorist outrage'.

The incident has not put Darch off globetrotting. 'It keeps me young,' he said. 'I can't resist the call of the open sea... I will continue – but not in pirate areas.'

CHAPTER 7
THE GULF OF ADEN

Every year about 22,000 ships pass through the Suez
Canal and the Gulf of Aden, where regional instability
and 'no questions asked' ransom payments have led to a
dramatic rise in attacks on vessels by heavily armed Somali
raiders. But it is not just certain Somalis who are cashing
in on the business of piracy. The northern shore of the Gulf
of Aden belongs to Yemen, another poor country with a
history of political instability. Yemeni pirates have also
been putting to sea to take advantage of the rich pickings
within close range of their shores.

In March 1999, the American Zoltan Gyurko and his
girlfriend Jennifer Hile were following the Yemeni
coastline from Salalah in Oman to Aden in his yacht *The
Way*. Zoltan had set out single-handed from California in
1994 as a novice sailor; Jennifer had come aboard at
Singapore. Sailing on around the world, the two of them
were making their living from freelance journalism and
documentaries about their adventures.

On the night of the attack, Jennifer was sleeping, while Zoltan was on watch. At about 3am they were seven miles off the coast of Yemen when Zoltan heard an outboard motor in the distance. Unable to see it in the darkness, he decided it could have been a fishing boat. But as it drew near, he saw four masked men aboard. They were carrying guns. He awoke Jennifer and told her to hide under the bedding.

Zoltan had a flare gun and a sheath knife, but they would be no match for an AK-47. The pirates switched on a spotlight, blinding him, and then rammed *The Way*, knocking him off his feet. When he got up, he put his hands in the air. 'What do you want?' he shouted. 'I have money. Dollars.'

Two pirates slung their Kalashnikovs over the shoulders and tried to board. But the sea was rough and at that moment the boats were hit by a huge swell. Zoltan was knocked from his feet again while the pirates were still on their boat, now about ten feet away. 'Dollars! Dollars!' shouted Zoltan, gesturing that he could deliver the money without anyone coming aboard. He doubted that the pirates could understand much English, but some words are universal.

'Moonhee! Moonhee!' shouted the pirate leader.

Zoltan scooped into the cabin to get his wallet, but there was only one $50 bill in it. The rest of his money was in travellers' cheques. Then he had an inspired idea. He grabbed a carton of Marlboros and a bottle of Sri Lankan whiskey. This might do the trick as alcohol was banned in the Yemen. He had to lean over the rail to hand over the goods, and the pirate leader had to drop his gun take them. Another wave pushed the two boats apart again so pirate boat started another approach, but the pirate leader was closely studying the whiskey bottle. Satisfied, he ordered his helmsman to break off and *The Way* continued its way to the Red Sea and the Suez Canal.

In June that year, the 36ft catamaran *Gone Troppo* sailed out of Darwin harbour in Northern Australia. On board were Stephen Phillips and Gail Dawson, two Aussies who had 'gone troppo' – become crazed by the heat and humidity of the tropics – years before. After a number of adventures in the Pacific, they were headed for the Indian Ocean, then Aden. On the morning of 27 January 2000, they were in the Gulf of Aden 70 miles off the coast of the Yemen, 115 miles from Somalia, and still some 250 miles from Aden. The steering was in the hands of the autopilot and the GPS. It was hot and all they had to do was relax and scan the horizon.

Then a small grey aeroplane flew over. Gail later suspected that it might have been a spotter plane for the pirates. At the time, they did not have the foresight to change course. Soon afterwards they spotted a small black dot on the horizon. Fearing an attack, they now changed course. Stephen fired up the engine to give them more speed, but it was little help. Within a quarter of an hour, the pirates were upon them.

The *Gone Troppo*'s maydays had gone unanswered and the pirates pulled alongside. They were well turned out, clean-shaven and wearing Western clothes. Stephen recognised them as Yemenis. They started firing at the rigging, then at the catamaran's hulls. One of the bullets passed through the side of the boat and hit Gail in the leg. Stephen, who had been below hiding valuables, came up with his hands held high and the shooting stopped. The pirates gestured for Stephen to take in the sails.

Four men boarded and forced Stephen and Gail into the netting that was strung between the two hulls of the catamaran. A young man in his twenties kept his AK-47 levelled at them as if he was looking for an excuse to shoot. Stephen was convinced they were going to be killed, but the leader of the pirate gang, a man in his fifties, came and shoved the gun aside. The pirates began stripping the equipment out of the *Gone Troppo*. Then they asked Stephen and Gail for money, which they went below to retrieve. The looting complete, the pirates got back on their boat and made off.

Stephen and Gail reckoned they had lost around $10,000, but that was the least of their worries. The port hull was filling with water. At first, they thought it had been holed below the waterline, but it turned out a bullet had severed the line from the freshwater tank. They ran up the sails again and headed west, putting out more mayday calls on a transmitter the pirates had overlooked. Eventually in the late afternoon, they got a reply from a large merchant ship that passed on their piracy report to the authorities.

The following evening they were still 90 miles from Aden when they spotted a small blip on the radar screen. They could not see the vessel as it was running without lights, but then *Gone Troppo* was also running without lights so it would not risk being spotted by the pirates. Again they altered course and switched on the engines to increase speed. The other boat increased its speed too and would not answer over the radio.

They spotted the lights of a large ship and managed to make contact on the radio. Stephen explained that they had been attacked by pirates. His girlfriend had been wounded and they were now being followed by an unlit vessel. If it came any closer, he said, he would fire off some red flares. The officer on watch said he would keep his eyes peeled.

It seems that overhearing this conversation was enough to discourage the pirates. The vessel that had been following *Gone Troppo* suddenly turned away and headed off. The large ship kept in contact and informed other ships that there were pirates in the area. The following morning, Stephen and Gail arrived in Aden, where they went straight to the police. The officers refused to believe the attackers looked like Yemenis. They must have been Somali, the Yemeni police insisted.

On 23 February 2001, the British cruising yachts *Mi Marra*, *Ocean Spray* and *Shady Lady* were attacked by Yemeni pirates in the Gulf of Aden. The pirates were waiting for them because they had revealed their plans when picking up diesel. *Mi Marra* escaped, but the catamaran *Ocean Spray* was towing *Shady Lady* and they were taken.

The story was broadcast on CNN, so the skippers of 11 bluewater cruisers that had stopped at Salalah in Oman before making their way through the Gulf of Aden met to have a cold beer and make plans to avoid the same fate. They decided to form a convoy, staying within a quarter of a mile of the leader. They would stay 35 miles from the coast and enter the same way points on the GPS. They would motor their way through without sails or lights, and one VHF channel would be reserved for distress calls between them.

Everything went well until they were a day out of Aden. Then three speedboats loomed on the horizon behind them. One of them sped up to the last vessel in the column and asked for food and drink. The skipper switched to the emergency channel. The entire convoy then turned, surrounded the pirates and took photographs of them. This rattled the Yemenis as piracy is punishable by death in the Yemen, and they made off.

Federico and Fulvia Pettenella had been sailing the high seas since 1984. Even the birth of their children had not stopped them: the youngsters' education was simply conducted by correspondence course. In October 2000, the family set sail from Viareggio in northern Tuscany in their yacht, the *Daisy Duck*, and headed for the warmth of the Red Sea. They spent four months in the Sudan and Eritrea, from where they headed for Sri Lanka and Thailand. However, when they reached the Gulf of Aden, the wind dropped and they had to continue under power. They had travelled around seven hundred miles when they saw a huge container ship coming up astern. Federico got on the radio to its captain and explained that they were getting low on diesel. The captain of the container ship said that he could not stop if he was to keep to schedule.

It was then that Federico spotted a small skiff off his port side. The captain of the container ship saw it too when his ship passed between the *Daisy Duck* and the skiff. As soon as the ship had passed, the skiff speeded up. There were four men aboard and when they had come within 15 yards, they gestured for the Pettenellas to stop. The children were sent below and Fulvia handed Federico the shotgun they carried. Federico then opened the throttle. One of the men on the skiff pulled out an AK-47 loosed off a round, but when Federico returned fire with the shotgun, the pirates veered away and made off.

The Pettenellas then sent out a series of maydays. The container ship that had just passed them was still only half-a-mile away but it did not reply. Nor did three other large merchant vessels they could see from their radar were in the vicinity. It seemed that the traditional laws of the sea counted for nothing.

On 8 March 2005, two sailing yachts, the *Mahdi* and *Gandalf*, were travelling from the port of Salalah in Oman to Aden. At around 9am they were travelling southwest around 30 miles off the coast of Yemen when two outboard-powered boats, about 25 feet long, passed across their stern moving south at about 25 knots. There were three men in each boat. An hour or two later they returned. One came in quite close and appeared to be inspecting the yachts carefully. The second boat passed their bows but at quite a distance.

'These boats were obviously not engaged in a normal activity such as fishing,' said retired US Navy officer Rodney J. Nowlin on board the *Mahdi* who reported the incident to the Yemeni coastguards, as well as to the US Coalition Fifth Fleet and the US Embassy. 'At that time we were south of Al Mukalla, Yemen. The area around Al Mukalla is well documented as being a piracy problem area and we started watching carefully for anything out of the ordinary. At about 16.00 we observed two different boats approaching us head on from the southwest. These boats were 25-30 feet long, had higher freeboard [a greater distance between the waterline and the deck] and were diesel powered. They were coming very fast directly at us. There were four men in each boat. The boats separated at about two hundred yards, one boat ahead of the other, coming down *Mahdi*'s port side and firing into the cockpit. The other boat was firing an automatic weapon at both *Gandalf* and *Mahdi* from ahead, more at *Gandalf*. These guys were shooting directly at the cockpits and obviously intended to kill us. The first boat swung around behind *Mahdi*'s stern to come up and board us.'

At this point, Nowlin took out a twelve-gauge shotgun loaded with 00 buckshot and started shooting at the boat behind. 'I forced them to keep their heads down so that they could not shoot at us,' he said. 'I am not sure I hit anyone at that point, although I could see the driver of the boat crouched down behind a steering console.'

After firing three shots at them, their engine started to smoke, so Nowlin swung around to shoot at the boat ahead. 'At that point, I saw Jay Barry on *Gandalf* ram that boat amidships, almost cutting it in two and turning it almost completely over. I turned back around to shoot again at the boat behind *Mahdi* and that was when they turned away from *Mahdi* and were heading toward the stern of *Gandalf*.'

Gandalf was beside the *Mahdi*, about a hundred feet away. The bow of the pirate's boat came right up against *Gandalf*'s stern and two men stood up on the bow to board. 'That was a serious and probably fatal error on their part,' said Nowlin. 'I shot both of them. That boat then veered away and I shot the driver, although I am not sure of the outcome because they were farther away and I did not knock him down like the other two.'

The *Mahdi* and *Gandalf* both kept going at full speed to put as much distance between them and the pirates as possible. As soon as they were out of rifle range, Nowlin looked back and saw that both boats appeared to be disabled and drifting.

'If Jay on *Gandalf* had not had the presence of mind to veer over into one boat and ram it,' said Nowlin, 'the outcome of this attack would have been totally different. All they needed to do was stand off a ways and shoot us to pieces with automatic weapons. We were extremely lucky.'

Mayday calls had been broadcast on all VHF and HF radio frequencies, including two HF emergency frequencies given to them by the US coastguard a few days before. The Coalition Forces in the area were supposed to be monitoring these frequencies, but there was no response except from a commercial ship that approached and observed the disabled pirates for a bit. It then sailed alongside the yachts for the next few hours until darkness fell to make sure they were safe.

In his report, retired naval officer Nowlin said, 'The pirates were well organised and well armed. There were at least four boats involved. They had set up a picket line out from the Yemen coast probably at least for 50–75 miles, so if you transited the area during the day they wouldn't miss you. The two boats that attacked us appeared to have come from the south. There has been speculation in the past that this ongoing piracy problem off the Yemen coast was being carried out by Somali pirates. Given the number, type of boats involved and the direction the spotter boats came from, this does not appear to be correct in this case. This problem is getting worse and the pirate attacks are getting deadly. One could only expect that the Yemen Government will take more direct action. At the very least, allow yachts to group in Salalah, Oman and at some point on the northwest Yemen coast to request an escort along the Yemen coast.'

Two years later another five yachts were attacked in the Gulf of Aden. Two other yachts had been attacked by pirates the previous week only 20 miles away, so the *Narena*, *Penyllan*, *Imani*, *Gypsy Days* and *Sea Dove* were sailing in convoy. Those on board had already met to plan what to do. They had decided to sail in a close formation not more than half a mile apart, maintaining a minimum speed of four knots under sail and five knots under power. They had heard that the pirates had VHF radios, so they decided to keep radio silence on Channel 16, and they would not give out their position on any radio frequencies. However, they would make regular reports on HF 2 MHz every three hours.

At 8am on the morning of 9 March 2007, Bruce Matthews on the *Narena* was scanning the horizon and saw three small craft coming in his direction. He radioed the other yachts and warned them. As the boats drew closer, Bruce could see plastic tarpaulins covering their hulls and the heads of a lot of people. He immediately realised that these were people-smugglers. However, they were also possibly the same boats that had attacked the two yachts the previous week; they too had had plastic sheeting wrapped around their hulls. The boats now approaching were about 65 feet long, wooden and loaded with terrified people, believed to be Somali refugees being trafficked into Yemen.

'We were later told that the refugees are often thrown

into the sea off the coast of Yemen, regardless of whether or not they can swim and left to their own devices,' said Cheryl Matthews. 'The people-smugglers are ruthless.'

The yachts closed ranks, switched on their engines and put on as much speed as they could, while sticking together in a tight group. The Matthews on *Narena* were at the rear of the formation on the port side and particularly vulnerable to attack. Inside them, was the *Imani*. The Matthews were happy about that because the *Imani* had children on board.

When the pirates were about two hundred yards from the *Nareni*, they started shooting. Bruce ducked down to the floor of the cockpit, and all the yachts began putting out distress calls. The Matthews got no reply. Then Cheryl heard Mark, a Frenchman on the *Imani*, talking in his mother tongue to the French base in Djibouti. They would send an Orion plane but it would take about an hour to reach the threatened yachts. The yachtsmen were not sure they could hold out that long.

The *Sea Dove* managed to raise the *Maersk Antwerp*, a merchant ship that was also about an hour away. It said it would relay the distress call to the Piracy Centre in Kuala Lumpur but again that offered no immediate help. Mark then raised an American aircraft carrier that they had passed the day before and watched as it practised landing its Harrier jump jets. It could reach their position in three hours.

'That is not good enough,' said Mark. 'We need help now.'

The aircraft carrier promised to send assistance immediately, but the yachtsmen did not believe it would arrive in time.

Cheryl had still not managed to raise any response to her maydays on the HF international distress frequency 2.182 MHz. But the *Sea Dove* then got a response from the Panamanian merchant ship *Royal Pascaderas*, who said she was altering course to come to their assistance. She was only about five minutes from visual contact: all the yachts had to do was keep the pirates at bay for a little while longer.

Bruce Matthews was still lying in his companionway to avoid bullets. He was steering the yacht by reaching up and pressing the autopilot panel. He told Cheryl to stay below in the cabin. Much of it was below was the waterline, so the sea would provide some protection against being shot. Despite the danger, Cheryl looked out of the cabin window. She could see one of the boats that were pursuing them. It was crammed with human cargo, packed in like sardines. On the bow, she could see a man with a rifle. Further away she could also see another two boats circling the behind the yachts. 'I wasn't sure if they had given up the chase or were they going around behind to flank us,' she said.

However, the main boat that was chasing the yachts was gaining slowly, and Cheryl realised the pirates intend to board the *Narena* as she was the closest. 'We were surprisingly very calm. Bruce put his arms around me and said, "We'll get through this, Cherie. Just give them anything they want and they won't hurt us. They only want to rob us, so just let them have what they want."'

After going up into the cockpit to check they were not going to run into the yacht in front, Bruce jumped quickly back below and grabbed the radio. He told everyone on the yachts to look back. The pirates were slowing down and dropping back. Perhaps they had given up the chase. It was then that they saw the *Royal Pascaderas* coming over the horizon. As she was headed for the convoy, the three pirate boats made their way quickly towards Yemen and one was blowing a lot of smoke.

About half-an-hour later, the Coalition Orion flew overhead and circled them a few times. By then the yachtsmen were on the deck waving and shouting like children. The Orion then headed off to patrol the area, but the *Royal Pascaderas* sailed slowly beside them. Around an hour later the Orion patrol plane returned from the opposite direction. The pilot radioed to say he had seen numerous small local craft, but none were coming in their direction or appeared to be a threat to them. Knowing the yachts were safe, the *Royal Pascaderas* bid them farewell and returned to her original course.

Half-an-hour after she had left, a large US helicopter flew overhead and spoke to the convoy by radio. Soon afterwards Coalition Taskforce 200 called and asked if they still needed assistance: they were on their way and would arrive in a few hours. The yachtsmen told them the Orion had said they were no longer in danger. Nevertheless, that evening the Coalition Warship 992 contacted them by radio. She would stay close by that night and the next day. By then they were out of the danger zone, and so went their separate ways. It was only later that Bruce and Cheryl Matthews realised the Coalition ships were not there just to protect them. They were on station ready for the invasion of Iraq.

CHAPTER 8

THE NAVY STRIKES BACK

After the hijacking of *Le Ponant* on 4 April 2008, piracy in Somali waters picked up pace. The pirates did not seem to be put off by the display of French military might. On 20 April a Japanese oil tanker was hit by a rocket. The same day, the Spanish-registered Basque tuna-fishing boat *Playa de Bakio* was hijacked about 250 miles off the coast. Four pirates seized the vessel, taking hostage its crew of 13 Spaniards and 13 Africans of various nationalities. The boat was slightly damaged in the attack but it remained seaworthy.

The Spanish government sent the frigate SPS *Méndez Núñez* to locate the hijacked ship. A team of combat divers were put on alert, though the Spanish government claimed to be seeking a diplomatic solution. The vessel was moored off southeast Puntland, but it was moved along the coast when security forces were sent to chase away the pirates. On 26 April the *Playa de Bakio* and her crew were freed and the frigate escorted the ship to safety in the Seychelles.

It was reported that a $1.2million ransom had been paid. The Spanish government denied this and it was thought that the ship's owners might have paid up.

Later it emerged that a deal had been secured through negotiations in London between the Spanish government, the ship's owners and the hijackers. London has traditionally been a hub of the maritime industry. With its brokers and specialist lawyers, it has now also become the centre of the Somali ransom industry, with most deals being brokered there. London firms also provide specialists to deliver the cash – usually men who have retired from the Special Forces.

News of the *Playa de Bakio* ransom deal caused outrage in Spain. Owners of other hijacked trawlers who had previously negotiated through Britain began to question whether the Somalis or the lawyers in London were the bigger pirates. Gustavo d'Aristogee, the foreign affairs spokesman for Spain's main opposition party, unequivocally condemned the UK's role in the Somali ransom business.

'If we know of a Spanish law firm helping, mediating, facilitating in any way the relationship between pirates or other kinds of criminals with the company of families of the victims of hostage-taking, you can be absolutely certain that we would denounce it in parliament and we would take legal measures against them,' he said. 'It is completely immoral and, in some countries, would be a crime. And we really have to be extremely harsh with this. I believe that some people are making a very handsome living out of it. To what extent are they just being intermediaries and to what extent are they actually encouraging this criminal industry? This is what needs to be sorted out.'

The one good thing that came out of the hijacking of the *Playa de Bakio* was that the Puntland security forces had been involved. They had shown they were serious when a cargo ship from the United Arab Emirates, the MV *Al-Khaleej*, and its crew of 16 Pakistanis were seized off the Somali coast near Bosasso on 21 April 2008. The following day, Puntland security forces stormed the ship, freeing the hostages, killing one of the pirates and capturing seven. Less than a week later, the survivors stood trial. They were convicted of piracy and sentenced to life imprisonment, along with four collaborators.

On 23 April the 150,000-ton Japanese tanker *Takayama* was attacked by pirates 274 miles east of Aden. The German warship FGS *Emden* picked up its distress call, 'Tanker is being threatened by boat with weapons and being fired upon.' A helicopter took off from the *Emden* and headed for the tanker. When it arrived, the pirate boat retreated, but bullet holes were visible in the *Takayama*'s hull and fuel was leaking into the ocean. However, no one on board was injured.

On 17 May, another ship carrying aid was seized by pirates who had chased her in three speedboats. The MV *Victoria*, a Jordanian vessel carrying four thousand tonnes of sugar donated by Denmark, was hijacked 35 miles off the Somali coast. The ship and her 12-man crew from Bangladesh, India, Pakistan, and Tanzania had been en route from Mumbai to Mogadishu, but diverted to Garacad. The Indian Navy was put on high alert as several of the crew were Indian, and the destroyer INS *Delhi* put on standby.

The pirates released the ship on 23 May and it continued

its journey to Mogadishu with Somali soldiers on board to ensure safe passage. According to local clan elders, Islamists had threatened to attack the pirates if they did not release the ship. Once on shore, there was shoot-out between the pirates and Islamists. Two Islamists were killed, along with four pirates. An Islamist commander named Kheyre Mohamed Mohamud confirmed the death toll, but pointed out that the Islamists had captured six of the pirates alive.

The following day, the MV *Amiya Scan*, a Dutch vessel with a crew of five Filipinos and four Russians, was seized in the Gulf of Aden. She was carrying a damaged oil platform from Mombasa to Constanta in Romania. Released after 31 days, the *Amiya Scan* sent out a mayday as she was low on food, water and fuel. Again the *Emden* went to her aid.

On 28 May the German MV *Lehmann Timber* was on her maiden voyage when she was seized in the Gulf of Aden. Concern for the 15 people on board the cargo vessel – its Russian captain, four sailors from the Ukraine, one from Estonia and nine from Burma – mounted after she ran out of food after two weeks. She was released after 41 days. The German Foreign Ministry would not say how the release had been achieved, but Ali Farah Warfa, the acting district commissioner of Eyl, said a ransom of $750,000 had been delivered by ship to 18 pirates in the town. The Ukrainian Foreign Ministry announced that that captain had declared the condition of the crew to be satisfactory. The USS *Momsen* provided the liberated crew with food and water, but the ship's main engine broke down as a storm approached. The *Momsen* stayed on station until a tug arrived to tow her to Oman.

At the beginning of July, the Canadian frigate HMCS *Calgary* claimed to have chased two skiffs from the sea lanes with her Sea King helicopter. But throughout July and August 2008, the hijacks continued apace. On 20 July, pirates seized the Japanese bulk carrier MV *Stella Maris* and her crew of 21. They were released on 26 September after a $2million ransom had been paid.

On 8 August the USS *Peleliu* heard a distress call from the Singaporean cargo ship *Gem of Kilakarai* in the Gulf of Aden. She reported being under attack from pirates armed with small arms and rifle-launched grenades aboard two skiffs. The *Peleliu* was only ten miles away and sent three helicopters, which drove the pirates away. That same day a group of gunmen freed two German tourists held captive for two months in northern Somalia after their yacht had been attacked in the Gulf of Aden. An accomplice said the ransom paid was $1million.

Later that month the MV *Thor Star* and her crew of 28, seized a hundred miles off the coast of the Yemen, were released after 64 days following payment of a ransom. A Nigerian tug boat, the MT *Yenegoa Ocean*, was also seized around the same time.

On 19 August, pirates seized a Malaysian tanker, the *Bunga Melati Dua*, with 39 crew on board. One Filipino crew member was killed. The ship was carrying 32,000 tonnes of crude palm oil, worth $2.5million, from Indonesia to Rotterdam. The pirates wanted $4.7million to release the *Bunga Melati Dua* and her sister ship the *Bunga Melati 5* seized on the 29th. She was carrying 30,000 tonnes of petrochemicals from Saudi Arabia to Singapore and had 36 Malaysian and five Filipino crew on board.

On 21 August, pirates seized the German cargo ship MV *BBC Trinidad* with nine crew on board. She was taken to the port of Eyl. The owners paid ransom of $1.1million.

A week after the seizure of *BBC Trinidad*, another Basque fishing boat was attacked by three speedboats some 325 miles off the coast of Somalia, but managed to escape by fleeing out into the open sea. However, the pirates did manage to hijack a Japanese-operated tanker, the MV *Irene*, and an Iranian bulk carrier, the MV *Iran Deyanat*. Both were taken to Eyl. The *Irene* was released the same day as the *BBC Trinidad* after a ransom of $1.5million was paid.

The *Iran Deyanat* had been 94 miles off the coast of Yemen when the crew were alerted by gunfire. 'Many of us ran out on the deck,' said 28-year-old crewman Jeevan Kiran D'Souza. 'We saw a group of men in two tiny speedboats close to the ship. The ship's radar had failed to pick them up. The men were firing in the air... There were 16 of them. They threw a ladder fitted with grappling hooks over the side of the ship and clambered aboard. They stormed all cabins and herded the entire crew into one small room, and told the captain to cut the engine.'

Fellow crewman Anthony Clive Timudo had a slightly different recollection. 'It was early on 21 August, when two armed men came on a speedboat and at gun point ordered our ship's captain to stop. Minutes later, another 18 pirates came in another speedboat and wrested control of our ship.' Others said there were as many as 40 pirates.

'Most of us had had a chance to speak with our families over the satellite phone,' said Jeevan. 'We knew what was happening: the ship had been hijacked. Soon afterward, the pirates sealed the communications room and, for the

Above left: Thai police officers help Linda Robertson after her husband, Malcolm, was murdered on board their yacht off the coast of Southern Thailand during an attempted robbery.

Above right: The oil-tanker *MV Sirius Star*, which was hijacked by Somali pirates in November 2008.

Below: *MV Faina* was seized by pirates in September 2008 and forced to anchor off the Somali Coast. This picture shows the crew of the vessel following a US Navy request to check on them.

Above: New Zealand yachtsman, Sir Peter Blake, who was murdered when armed pirates stormed his boat, the *Seamaster*, while it was docked in the Brazilian port of Macapa.

Below: Malaysian Special Forces climb aboard a vessel during an anti-piracy demonstration in the Straits of Malacca.

Above: French soldiers arrest presumed Somali pirates in the eastern part of the Gulf of Aden. They were apprehended while trying to hijack a cargo vessel.

Below: Recovered pirates' weapons.

Above: *Le Ponant*, the French luxury yacht which was boarded by pirates off the coast of Somalia.

Below: The pirates who seized the yacht are dramatically arrested by the French military.

rest of their time on board, manned the entrance round the clock.'

The pirates locked the 29 crew members in one room. Initially, they asked for just $10,000, which the captain handed over. Then the pirates ransacked the crew's quarters, taking away all mobile phones and the crew's clothes.

'We thought that we would be released after they had taken our possessions,' said Anthony Timudo. In fact, the crew's ordeal had only just begun.

The pirates said their boats were out of fuel, and asked for them to be towed to a nearby port. The ship travelled to Reassban on the Somali coast, where she was detained for a day. Then the pirates took her to another port, Reassaaf. 'We spent two days at Reassaaf,' said Jeevan. 'Then the pirates said we must move again, to escape other gangs in surrounding waters. They said they were taking us to the Eyl coast where their boss, Abdul Hakeem, would meet us.'

But this was not how things unfolded. For the next two weeks, the *Iran Deyanat* shuttled between the Gulf of Aden and Reassaaf. The pirates did not seem to have any clear destination in mind, and their indecision only succeeding in making their hostages feel insecure and exhausted. 'They frequently threatened to sell our ship to the most dreaded hijackers in the region,' said Jeevan.

After two weeks, provisions were running out. The pirates emptied the ship's store, leaving the crew with only sliced bread. Their daily ration soon came down to two cups of water and four slices of bread. The hijackers themselves ate well, slaughtering sheep on the deck and feasting on chunks of mutton while sitting around a large plate. They also constantly chewed on khat.

'They navigated our ship to four different places,' said Anthony Timudo, 'and finally dropped anchor at a place surrounded by deep forests.' The *Iran Deyanat* was anchored some six miles off Eyl, where several ships were being held. She was secured by a larger contingent, with 50 pirates on board and the same number on shore. Abdul Hakeem came on out to them on a speedboat, accompanied by a retinue of bodyguards, all carrying modern weapons. He asked for $5million in ransom, and negotiations lasted for a month.

In appearance and behaviour, the pirates were a paradox, Jeevan said. They seemed like crude, illiterate men who wore nothing but filthy, torn lengths of cloth tied around their waists. However, they were skilled at handling sophisticated weapons and GPS navigation equipment. Jeevan also noted that they operated within a highly disciplined organisation with hierarchical ranks of officers, and on shore they had a well-equipped central control room where they constantly monitored the movement of every ship in the area.

'Our ship seemed to be getting a somewhat sympathetic treatment because it belonged to a Muslim nation. They asked us every day if there were any non-Muslims on board,' said Jeevan, a Hindu. 'I was asked my name several times. I made up a name to save my skin, as did another Indian from Goa, the only two non-Muslims on board.'

In Eyl, the question arose of what the *Iran Deyanat* was carrying and where she was bound. The ship belonged to the Islamic Republic of Iran Shipping Lines, a state-owned company run by the Iranian military that saw sanctions applied to it by the US Department of the Treasury on 10 September. According to the US Government, the company regularly falsifies shipping documents to hide the identity of end users and uses generic terms to describe shipments to get round UN sanctions. 'IRISL's actions are part of a broader pattern of deception and fabrication that Iran uses to advance its nuclear and missile programmes,' said Stuart Levey, US Undersecretary of the Treasury for Terrorism and Financial Intelligence.

According to her manifest, the *Iran Deyanat* had set sail from Nanjing in China at the end of July and was heading to Rotterdam with 42,500 tons of iron ore and 'industrial products' for a German client. She arrived in the Gulf of Aden long before schedule, but then expected to take seven days to reach the Suez Canal – a journey that should have taken four or five days at most.

Within days of the ship's arrival in Eyl, the pirates who had ransacked the ship began to lose their hair and exhibit burns on their skin. Some 16 of them died. Experts have said that the accounts of the illness sound more like radiation than chemical poisoning. 'It's baffling,' said Jonathan Tucker of the James Martin Center for Nonproliferation Studies in Monterey, California. 'I'm not aware of any chemical agent that produces loss of hair within a few days. That's more suggestive of high levels of radioactive waste.'

News about the illness and the possibility that the cargo was toxic quickly reached Garowe, Puntland's capital. The Minister of Minerals and Oil, Hassan Allore Osman, was sent to investigate, but the pirates, who were demanding $9million for the release of ten ships, refused to allow him to inspect the ship – even threatening to blow it up if the authorities tried to inspect it by force.

During talks, the pirates told Osman that they had got sick after they had tried to inspect the cargo. The Iranian ship was carrying seven locked containers and they did not have the access codes to open them. However, the pirates had blasted open one of the units to find an unidentified powdery substance. Within days, they had fallen ill.

Osman was allowed to speak to the ship's captain and engineer by cell phone. They told him first that the cargo was crude oil, later saying the cargo was minerals. The owners flatly denied that the ship was carrying a dangerous cargo.

The pirates set the ransom at $2million. It was then said that the Iranian government had given a local broker $200,000 to 'facilitate the exchange' Iran denied this. Then, when the sanctions were applied to IRISL on 10 September, the company told the pirates that all deals were off. They said that they could not come and deliver the ransom, or take back the ship, because of the presence of the US Navy.

The Iranian press then claimed that the US had offered $7million for permission to search the vessel, saying that the *Iran Deyanat* was carrying 'uranium and chemical weapons'. The US government refused to comment. Without inspecting the cargo, it was impossible to tell what the *Iran Deyanat* was carrying. However, Puntland officials believed that the ship was carrying weapons to Eritrea for Islamist insurgents. Iran had previously broken US sanctions by shipping shoulder-fired surface-to-air missiles and Sagger anti-tank missiles to the Union of Islamic Courts during the Somali civil war.

Andrew Mwangura of the East African Seafarers'

Assistance Programme said that after the initial payment the ship was supposed to be released 'but now they are saying the $200,000 was for facilitation only. They want more money for the ransom.' According to *Lloyd's List* (the leading daily newspaper for the maritime industry) the IRISL ultimately paid $2.5million to free the ship.

'In the last ten days of captivity, fungus grew on the bread,' said Jeevan. 'As the ransom negotiations dragged on, the pirates sometimes got restive, threatening to shoot us. Sometimes, they shot at bubbles in the water, thinking the ship was being stormed, when it was probably only some ocean creature like; perhaps, a whale.'

'I had lost all hope of escaping and reaching home safely,' said Anthony Timudo. 'But God was kind to me and made this reunion with my family possible... The toughest part was surviving without water for days on end.'

In early October, the crew were told that an Iranian vessel had reached Somali waters with the ransom money. The pirates sent the ship's chief officer to fetch it. He was warned that the captain would be held on the ship with a gun to his head until he returned with the money. 'When the money came into their hands, the pirates scanned them with fake-currency detectors,' said Jeevan. 'Ten people then left, and once the money was safely on land, the rest left too and the ship was released. That was on 10 October.'

They had been held for 51 days.

Iranian naval ships then escorted the *Iran Deyanat* to Oman, where the crew disembarked and Jeevan and the two other Indian crewmen flew home. The ship eventually arrived in Rotterdam on 11 November 2008. It was searched but no hazardous substances were found. The paperwork also seemed to be in order. The German ship's charterer then said there had never been any evidence that pirates had suffered illness during the hijack, but pointed out that anyone entering the holds mid-voyage risked immediate suffocation because of oxygen degeneration. However, this claim contradicts what the authorities in Puntland said to Reuters and other news agencies.

While the authorities were puzzling over the mysterious cargo of the *Iran Deyanat*, the pirates had been far from inactive. On 23 August, they opened fire on a Japanese general cargo ship in the Gulf of Aden, but it managed to survive the hijacking attempt. The yacht *Carré d'As* was seized on 2 September, but was retaken by French commandos two weeks later. The following day the MV *Al Mansourah* was attacked by 12 pirates armed with automatic guns and RPGs. They boarded the ship, hijacked her and stole cash and the crew's personal belongings. She was released on 27 September after a ransom of $1.2million was paid.

The following week the MV *Bright Ruby* was taken and ransomed a week later. Next it was the turn of the *Stolt Valor*. Its captain, Prabhat Kumar Goyal, believed he had taken every precaution to prevent pirates taking his ship. He had crossed the Gulf of Aden twice in the previous two months. Both times he had witnessed hijackings, so he sailed down the 'designated safety corridor' though the Gulf of Aden, patrolled by the world's navies, keeping to the northern edge and as far as possible from the Somali coast.

Once the ship entered pirate-infested waters, all entrances to the accommodation area were locked and additional lookouts were placed on the bridge to keep track of all passing or approaching boats. Pirates usually approach from the stern with two or more skiffs. However, they also attack from the port quarter as those on the watch tend to concentrate on the starboard side, keeping an eye out for crossing traffic. The skiffs can easily outrun any merchant ship as they can make 20 – 25 knots, while more most cargo vessels can only make 13 – 14 knots. Captain Goyal knew that if pirates attacked, he could only send distress calls. Once they were aboard, the game was over.

By that time, most ships travelling through the Gulf of Aden had installed security systems and developed contingency plans. But few merchant ships carry weapons and there is little an unarmed crew can do against armed pirates. Vessels under attack make evasive manoeuvres, creating a large wake in the hope of swamping approaching speedboats, or use high-pressure jets of water – ineffective in the case of the *Stolt Valor*. Once the pirates are aboard the vessel, there is no option but to surrender.

Rahul Singh, a young Indian marine engineer on board the *Stolt Valor*, complained that the protection from the navies patrolling these waters was not adequate. On one occasion, they saw a chemical tanker just 24 miles behind their ship being hijacked. 'It was desperately calling for assistance but no warship responded,' he said.

Captain Prabhat Kumar Goyal described their two months in the hands of the pirates as a nightmare. The ship was taken to Eyl and the crew were confined to the wheelhouse. 'The pirates were very rude and kept all the 22 crew members in very unhygienic conditions,' said engineer Seema Kumari. 'They used to threaten us constantly. However, they never assaulted us.'

The ship and crew were released after a ransom of $2.5million was paid. Seema Kumari insisted that he would go back to sea after a six-month break. 'Did people of Delhi or Mumbai leave the city after bomb blasts? Then why should I change my job?'

On 17 September the Greek cargo MV *Centauri*, carrying a cargo of salt from Port Nassau in Ethiopia to Kenya with a crew of 25 Filipino seamen, was seized two hundred miles off the Somali coast by five pirates in three speedboats. She was taken to Eyl where several vessels were being held for ransom. The seamen were released 71 days later.

The same day that the *Centauri* was taken, another Greek vessel, the Liberian-flagged *Peter S* with a crew of 22, was attacked by gunmen off the coast of Somalia. However, the crew managed to hold off the pirates with high-intensity jets from the ship's fire hoses. They were lucky in this case. Captain Giorgos Tsouris explained how difficult it is to repel attacks by armed gunmen.

'When confronted with pirate attacks there is very little the captain and the crew can do,' he said. 'We can use hoses to shoot water at them as they approach the ship, but this is dangerous as pirates are heavily armed with machine guns and grenade launchers. The safety of the crew must come first. I remember in 1991 a ship I captained was hijacked at a port in Brazil, when three gunmen sneaked in and held us at gunpoint. Even though we had rifles in the ship it never crossed my mind to use them against the pirates. You have to remember these people are ruthless and they will kill anyone who resists them without thinking twice. I gave them everything they asked for and just pleaded with them not to harm my crew. There is nothing else you can do.'

Four days after this incident four Somali pirates boarded another Greek-owned freighter, the MV *Captain Stephanos* and took its 19 crew members hostage. They were released after 11 weeks. Then, just four days later, the MV *Faina* was seized with its consignment of tanks. On 25 September the chemical tanker MV *Genius* was seized. It was released on 20 November after a ransom was paid.

On 9 October, the MV *Wail*, with a crew of two Somalis and nine Syrians, was transporting cement from Oman to Bosasso when she was a seized. On this occasion, the Somali security forces engaged in a shootout with the pirates on the 12 October, resulting in the death of one Somali soldier and one pirate. The security forces also captured two pirate speedboats, preventing them from escaping. Two days later, Somali forces arrested ten hijackers and freed the ship. The *Wail* was slightly damaged in the gun battle, but was still seaworthy and continued its journey to Bosasso.

There were more casualties when the chemical tanker MV *Action* was hijacked on 10 October. The ship was released two days later but by then three of the crew were dead. The MT *African Sanderling* was seized on 15 October and released on 13 January 2009. On 29 October 2008 the MV *Yasa Neslihan* was hijacked near the Gulf of Aden and released on 4 November. The Danish-owned MV *CEC Future* was seized on 7 November and released on 15

January. Then came the MV *Stolt Strength,* which was seized on 10 November.

However, the following day, the Indian Navy rescued two ships. The frigate INS *Tabar* was cruising in the Gulf of Aden when, at 10am, she received a frantic distress call from the Saudi Arabian oil and chemical tanker NCC *Tihama.* Two to three high-speed boats, carrying several armed men, were trying to hijack the ship as it headed westwards. The *Tabar* immediately launched a Chetak helicopter – an Indian-built variant of the Aérospatiale Alouette – carrying a team of four marine commandos. When the helicopter reached the *Tihama,* the pirates had surrounded her and were attempting to board. The marine commandos opened fire with their automatic weapons and the pirates turned tail and fled back into Somali waters.

At around 10.30am, while the Chetak was still in the air, the *Tabar* received another SOS – an SMS from the MV *Jag Arnav.* Owned by the Mumbai-based Great Eastern Company, the 38,265-tonne bulk was carrying a consignment of barley from Odessa to Jubail in Saudi Arabia. She had passed through the Suez Canal a few days earlier, but around 70 miles east of Aden, she had been ambushed by another band of pirates in two small boats. The *Jag Arnav* was less than 30 miles from the *Tabar.* While the *Tihama* was instructed to follow the frigate for safety, the Chetak was diverted towards the *Jag Arnav*'s position. This time there was no need to fire warning shots. Seeing the helicopter approach, the pirates promptly abandoned their hijack and sped off. The *Tabar* then escorted the *Tihama* and the *Jag Arnav* to safety.

That same day, the Royal Navy rescued MV *Powerful,* a

Danish cargo ship that had been attacked by pirates aboard a dhow 60 miles south of the Yemeni coast in the Gulf of Aden. The pirates had made two attempts to seize the vessel, opening fire on her with a machine-gun, but before they could board, the frigate HMS *Cumberland* turned up. She sent a Lynx helicopter and the pirates made a run for it.

The *Cumberland* then launched two rigid-raider craft carrying Royal Marines to stop the dhow. As they approached, several of the pirates – a mixed crew of Somalis and Yemenis – opened fire on the Marines with their assault rifles. In the ensuing firefight, two Somali pirates were killed. A third, thought to be a Yemeni, suffered gunshot wounds and died later. By the time the Marines boarded the dhow, the terrified pirates were ready to surrender. The commandos found guns and other 'paraphernalia' on board. The Ministry of Defence said it was unclear whether the Yemeni who died had been shot by the Marines or was wounded from a previous incident involving the pirates.

The Russians claimed a helicopter based on their own patrol ship *Neustrashimy* had also taken part in the battle, though the Royal Navy said they knew nothing about it. 'The pirates fired on the Danish craft with automatic weapons and tried twice to seize it,' said a spokesman for the Russian Navy. The *Neustrashimy* had been escorting another Danish vessel when it was called to help.

The Turkish ship *Karagöl* was not so lucky. On 12 November, she was hijacked 16 miles off the coast of Yemen near the Horn of Africa with 14 crew aboard. The second Turkish vessel to be hijacked in two weeks, it was reported to be carrying 4,500 tons of chemicals, en route to Mumbai. The vessel was released on 13 January 2009.

Soon afterwards, British private security guards claimed to have repulsed a Somali pirate attack on a chemical tanker. Former army pilot Nick Davis, who started in the company Anti-Piracy Maritime Security Solutions in 2008, said he had three-man teams of ex-Special Forces personnel working on six vessels in the Gulf of Aden. Their first clash with the pirates took place more than three hundred miles north of the Somali coast and just 18 miles off the coast of Yemen. This put it inside the Maritime Security Patrol Area established in August 2008 by an international coalition of navies.

'There was a direct approach at high speed towards our ship,' he said. 'We then activated our procedures. The ship started evasive manoeuvres, all the hoses were on full power. Then we used the magnetic acoustic device. They closed to within five hundred metres and then turned away to a ship that was due south of ours by approximately five miles. Based on intelligence from our team leader on board, there was intent to attack the vessel and clearly, if no one [from the company] had been on board, we do not know what the outcome would have been today.' As a result, the company was inundated with inquiries and planned to open offices in Aden and Salalah, Oman.

On 14 November, the Chinese fishing vessel *Tianyu No 8* and its multi-national crew of 24 were seized by Somali pirates off the coast of Kenya. She was released on 8 February 2009 and escorted from the area by the Chinese Navy. Despite the presence of foreign warships, pirates struck again on seizing in the Japanese chemical tanker

MV *Chemstar Venus*. She was released on 12 February after a ransom was delivered by tug boat. The following day, Somali pirates hit the headlines when the *Sirius Star* was taken.

Some Somali pirates now had a huge prize on their hands, but others continued plundering the high seas. On 18 November, they captured the Iranian cargo ship MV *Delight*, carrying 26,000 tons of wheat, near the coast of Yemen. The same day, a distress call was received from a Thai boat, saying it was being chased by pirates, but then the communication stopped. The *Delight* was released on 10 January 2009 but the Thai boat, the FV *Ekawat Nava 5*, was not so lucky. She had been en route from Oman to Yemen when she was approached by pirates in two speedboats. They had boarded her and were in the process of seizing control when the INS *Tabar* arrived. She mistook the *Ekawat Nava 5* for a pirate mother ship and ordered her to stop. The pirates opened fire and the *Tabar* fired back, sinking her. One of the crew, a Cambodian, was found alive six days later; he had been adrift in the Gulf of Aden before being rescued by a passing ship. Another crewman was known to be dead and the other 14 crew members were listed as 'missing'.

The Puntland security forces took a hand again when pirates seized the MV *Adina*, a Yemeni ship carrying steel, on 19 November. They asked for a ransom of $2million, but Puntland officials were eager to maintain good relations with Yemen and prepared to use force. 'We will release the hijacked Yemen ship forcibly if they do not release it without a ransom because we have good relations with Yemen,' said Ali Abdi Aware, state minister for

Puntland. 'Now we are preparing our troops.' The pirates released the *Adina* at Eyl on 3 December. No ransom had been paid.

Early in the morning of 28 November, the MV *Biscaglia* came under heavy fire from pirates and called for assistance from nearby NATO forces. She had guards from Anti-Piracy Maritime Security Solutions on board and the three ex-British service men tried to fight off the pirates by using 'sustained non-lethal resistance'. For 40 minutes they held off the pirates with high-pressure hoses and the LRAD sonic cannon but, unarmed, they could not stop the attackers seizing control of the ship.

'I have spoken with my team leader on the phone and he informs me that the level of violence was significant and forced them reluctantly to leave the vessel after every effort was made to ensure the safety of the ship's crew,' said APSS director Nick Davis.

The pirates had continued firing after they had boarded and fearing for their lives, the three British guards had jumped into the sea. Even after they were in the water, the pirates kept firing at them. The trio were rescued and airlifted to safety by a German naval helicopter and flown to a French frigate. They were later transferred to a British Royal Navy ship. The *Biscaglia* was then taken to Puntland and released on 24 January.

Another cruise ship came under threat on 28 November 2008. The MS *Astor,* en route from Sharm-al-Sheikh in Egypt to Dubai, was approached by two pirate speedboats in the Gulf of Oman. However, while the skiffs were still three miles off, the German frigate *Mecklenburg-Vorpommern* steered into their path. Warning bursts of machine-gun fire warded off the threat without the 492 cruise passengers being aware of the danger.

Two days later the MS *Nautica* was attacked in the Gulf of Aden by pirates on board two skiffs that had hidden among fishing vessels in the Maritime Safety Protection Area. An officer on deck quickly spotted they were hostile and its captain, Jurica Brajcic, ordered the ship to make evasive manoeuvres and sail away at maximum speed. Eight shots were fired at the *Nautica* but she was able to outrun her pursuers, although one of the skiffs did get within three hundred yards. The 684 passengers and four hundred crew were uninjured, and the ship remained undamaged.

On 3 December 2008, another cruise liner had a narrow escape when pirates made three separate attempts to board the MS *Athena*. 'During a morning quiz, we looked outside and saw 29 small boats with up to six pirates in each boat,' said a passenger. Water cannon were used to repel the pirates and the ship was not boarded. 'We saw an Air Force Orion circling the convoy. This seemed to scare off the pirates.' However, the captain told them that the oil tanker behind had been attacked. No one on board the *Athena* was injured and the ship escaped without damage and continued on her voyage to Australia.

The pirates were even more out of luck when they tried to board the MV *Gide* on 13 December 2008. Three speedboats had surrounded it and had fired a couple of rounds, but the crew returned fire with small arms and sent out a distress signal. The Indian destroyer INS *Mysore*, which had taken over from the *Tabar*, was just 15 miles away and came to the rescue, sending a helicopter loaded with marine commandos. The commandos launched an attack on two pirate boats, which fled back to their mother ship, a dhow called the *Salahadin*. The helicopter gave chase. The dhow was boarded and 23 men – 11 Yemeni and 12 Somali – surrendered. A search of the dhow yielded a substantial cache of arms and equipment, including seven AK-47 and three other automatic rifles, 13 loaded magazines and a rocket-propelled grenade-launcher with rockets, cartridges and grenades, along with three outboard motors, a GPS receiver and other equipment. The pirates were taken into custody and the Indian Navy said they would be handed over to the appropriate authorities.

On 18 December 2008, a Malaysian tugboat, a Turkish cargo ship – the MV *Bosphorus Prodigy* – and a private yacht were all seized. This prompted a new UN resolution that allowed maritime nations to pursue the pirates on land as well as at sea. The *Bosphorus Prodigy* and its crew of 11 were released after seven weeks.

On 17 December 2008 the Chinese fishing boat MV *Zhenhua 4* was on her way back to Shanghai when she was attacked by nine Somali pirates in two motor launches. Captain Peng Weiyuan called for help while his crew of 30 fought off the pirates. After they had seen the raiders approaching, the crew had prepared a counter-attack with beer bottles, crockery and anything else that came to hand. Then they removed the access ladders and hid, ready to ambush the pirates with Molotov cocktails as they boarded. 'Everyone lit up hundreds of bottles containing an oil-based paint and threw them on to the deck,' said Captain Peng. 'We heard the pirates crying loudly.'

But the pirates were no push over. Three of them came

to the back of the living area and tried to break in. 'Three crew members did their best to guard the door,' said Captain Peng. 'If one latch was pulled open, we latched shut another one. If another latch was pulled open, we latched another back – this went on for about 15 minutes. Then the crew started to shoot at the pirates using the fire hydrant. They couldn't withstand that and ran off.'

Seven pirates had come on board, leaving two to guard their boats. Four had machine-guns, which they fired as they boarded, but the crew were uninjured. 'It was the first time we had ever seen such terrifying faces,' said Captain Peng. 'We are not trained or armed soldiers, so I would be lying if I told you we were not scared. But the crew did a very good job. Nobody withdrew during the whole battle.' The crew, who had been well trained and prepared, used anything they could be to battle the raiders. 'Thirty minutes later, the pirates gestured to us for a ceasefire.'

After calling a truce, Captain Peng told the pirates that as long as they left the ship, his men would cease attacking them. He also gave the attackers shoes so they could leave the ship without hurting their bare feet on the broken glass that littered the deck. However, the pirates resumed fighting and the crew started spraying them with fuel oil from the tanks. Eventually, a helicopter from the Malaysian frigate KD *Sri Indera Sakti* answered the distress signal, arrived and fired at the deck to scare them off. The pirates got back on their speedboats and fled. One of the skiffs sank, but not as a result of gunfire.

Speaking on China Central Television the following day, Captain Peng said, 'Looking back over yesterday's battle is like watching a brilliant shoot-'em-up film. Afterwards, everyone was a bit excited. Many of us failed to sleep at all last night – a little bit afraid and excited at the same time.'

Twelve hundred Chinese vessels passed through the Gulf of Aden in 2008. A fifth of them were attacked, and seven were hijacked. At the time of the attack on the *Zhenhua 4,* one Chinese fishing vessel and its crew of 18 were still being held. As a result of the *Zhenhua 4* incident, China decided to join the anti-piracy policing operation in the Gulf of Aden – the first time its navy had ventured beyond the Pacific since the Ming dynasty ended the empire's great days of exploration in the 15th century. Two destroyers and a supply ship were sent from China's southern naval base at Sanya, on Hainan island.

The pirates got the worst of it again on 1 January 2009. The cargo ship *Venus* was 50 miles off the coast of Yemen in the Gulf of Aden when small boats carrying pirates started to pursue her. The *Venus* sent a distress call to a nearby French frigate, the *Premier-Maître L'Her.* The frigate's approach scared off the pirates, but several hours later they approached the *Venus* again. This time, the French fired warning shots and launched their own Zodiac with a boarding party, arresting eight men. The captain of the *Premier-Maître L'Her,* Lieutenant Commander Alexis Beatrix, said the pirates were travelling in two skiffs, like those used by local fishermen, but they were carrying automatic rifles, rocket-propelled grenades, grappling hooks and rope ladders for boarding vessels. They spoke no English and only one spoke enough Arabic to answer questions. They carried no identification, but said they were Somali nationals. They were given food and medical care and then sent to Somalia for trial under the provisions of an agreement between France and Somalia's Transitional Federal Government.

However, pirates did succeed in hijacking the Egyptian cargo ship *Blue Star* and its crew of 20 the same day. Fifteen armed pirates boarded the cargo vessel, which was carrying six thousand tons of fertilizer, as she was coming out of the Red Sea into the Gulf of Aden. She was released on 5 March after $1million had been paid.

But on 2 January the Danish frigate HDMS *Absalon* caught five pirates in the Gulf of Aden after receiving a distress call from the MV *Samanyolu*, a cargo ship carrying the flag of the Netherlands Antilles. Its crew fended off the raiders with signal flares until the Danish ship arrived and sank the raiders' vessel, which the freighter's crew had set on fire with a distress rocket. Five suspects were captured and sent for trial.

At eight that morning, the captain of the cargo ship MV *Kriti Episkopi* saw pirates in three speedboats racing towards him and took evasive action. When this did not work, he sent out a distress call. Armed with machine guns and RPGs, the pirates twice tried to board but were driven off by high-pressure hoses. There was an EU naval mission in the area, which dispatched a warplane, frigate and helicopter to help. The air support held off the pirates until the frigate came to escort the ship to safety.

Later the same morning, the Indian tanker MT *Abul Kalam Azad* was attacked by pirates in two skiffs. One of the boats had seven men in it, all armed with machine guns. They unleashed a barrage of fire at the bridge and accommodation area of the ship, and continued firing while trying to board the tanker. However, the captain began taking evasive action and increased speed to the maximum. He also sent out a distress signal, which was picked up by Malaysian navy support ship KD *Sri Indera Sakti* about 17 miles away. Her commanding officer, Captain Mohamad Adib Abdul Samad, despatched a Fennec military helicopter that reached the tanker in less than ten minutes. The helicopter carried a general-purpose machine-gun and a sniper from the Paskal naval commando unit was also on board. It was joined by a Dauphin helicopter of the Saudi Arabian navy, and the two of them scared off the pirates. The captain of the *Abul Kalam Azad* then asked to join the Malaysian I convoy escorted by the *Sri Indera Sakti*, but later accepted an offer from a Saudi Arabian naval ship to escort it to its destination.

Captain Vinayak Anant Marathe, who had commanded the slow, heavily laden bulk carrier through the Gulf of Aden, outlined the problem he faced in these waters, even when following the narrow corridor of the Maritime Security Patrol Area (MSPA).

'As a bulk carrier master, I am a sitting duck doing just 12 knots while the pirates can just circle around us at a speed of 25 knots,' he said. 'We followed the courses through the MSPA corridor, which is patrolled by the naval fleet. It was a very tense 40-hour passage. We witnessed an attempted attack just ten miles behind us, one successful hijacking and another two attempts just close – indeed, good enough to turn anybody a nervous wreck. The stress of sailing through the area is unbelievable. I was a casual smoker before, but then I smoked eight packs in 48 hours... The only thing I can do is to zigzag and try to hit them, but if I do and they turn out not to be pirates then I might lose my licence. Unless we employ a convoy system then it will never be safe.'

Even convoys do not guarantee the safety of shipping. The pirates managed to take the liquefied-gas tanker MV *Longchamp* when it was some 60 miles off the coast of the Yemen. After passing through the Suez Canal, she waited a day for naval escort but was some distance from the patrolling ships when she was attacked. She sent a distress signal and helicopters were sent, but they arrived too late: seven pirates had boarded and had taken control of the ship. The captain was allowed to communicate briefly with his company. He said the crew of 12 Filipinos and one Indonesian was safe, even though a gunshot was heard over the ship's radio. The ship was tracked by satellite as it was taken towards Eyl, and the hijackers asked for a ransom of $6million.

However, the task force was beginning to make its presence felt. On 2 January the French Navy captured eight pirates who had attacked a Panamanian-registered ship. Three days later the frigate *Jean de Vienne* came to the aid of a Croatian cargo vessel and another Panamanian ship, capturing 19 pirates who were handed over to the Somali authorities.

On 11 February the US Navy arrested seven pirates carrying automatic rifles and RPGs who had tried to board the merchant ship *Polaris* from a skiff. A team from the cruiser USS *Vella Gulf* intercepted a small skiff matching descriptions given by the crew of the *Polaris* on which a US Navy search team found weapons. The following morning the *Vella Gulf* responded again when the Indian tanker *Prem Divya* reported being fired at. A pirate skiff attempted to escape after warning shots were fired, but the USS *Mahan* intercepted it and the boarding party discovered weapons, including an RPG. Nine men were arrested. All 16 suspects from both operations were transferred to a temporary holding facility onboard a US naval supply ship until 5 March, when the US Navy handed them over to the Kenyan authorities who had set up a new court system to try and punish the pirates.

On 3 March, the German frigate FGS *Rheinland-Pfalz* responded to a distress call from the German merchant ship MV *Courier*, saying she was under fire from pirates armed with bazookas and machine guns. According to the shipping firm, the pirates fired bazookas at the vessel but missed. The frigate dispatched a helicopter, which, together with another chopper from the USS *Monterey*, fired warning shots that stopped the attack. The US helicopter then returned to its ship while the *Rheinland-Pfalz* steamed the 57 miles to the area. They boarded the pirates' vessel and took nine men into custody. They would be sent to Germany to stand trial.

The Russian Navy has also struck a blow against the pirates in the Gulf of Aden. A Russian helicopter from the nuclear-powered cruiser *Petr Velikiy* spotted armed pirates on two speedboats chasing an Iranian fishing boat. At the sight of the helicopter, the speedboats turned back to their mother ship, which the Russian cruiser then intercepted. They arrested ten pirates and seized automatic rifles, grenade-launchers and landmines, along with five hundred grammes of a 'narcotic substance'. The pirates were handed over to the Yemeni authorities.

Meanwhile, two journalists who had been working on a

piracy story were released in good health nearly six weeks after being kidnapped. Reporter Colin Freeman of the *Sunday Telegraph* and Spanish freelance photographer José Cendon had been abducted on 26 November. The Telegraph Media Group would not say whether a ransom had been paid.

Marshall County Public Library
1003 Poplar Street
Benton, KY 42025

CHAPTER 9

PORTRAIT OF THE PIRATES

So who are these modern-day pirates? Most seem to have begun as fishermen who were driven out of business in the 1990s by the large industrial trawlers that came from all over the world to fish off the coast of Somalia. Their traditional fishing methods were no match for the factory ships raiding their waters and with no government, Somalia had neither the might nor the diplomatic clout to keep them out. Other ships came to dump industrial wastes, further depleting fish stock. 'Illegal fishing is the root cause of the piracy problem,' said Abdulkadi Mohamed, a resident of Garowe, the regional capital of Puntland.

The former fishermen are considered the brains of the operation because they know the sea. They have been joined by ex-militiamen, who provide the muscle. The militiamen learned their trade fighting for various Somali warlords during the inter-clan wars of the 1990s. Then there are the technical experts with the know-how to operate the hi-tech equipment by twenty first century pirates – satellite phones, GPS and military hardware.

The three groups share the ever-increasing illicit profits from the huge ransoms paid in cash by the shipping companies. By 2009 the average ransom had reached $2million and it is estimated that the pirate groups were bringing in over $30million a year. This is an enormous haul in one of the world's poorest countries, where 73 per cent of the population survive on under $2 a day. Almost half the population lives on food aid after 19 years of non-stop civil war.

Most of the pirates are aged between 20 and 35. Although it is feared that militant Islamists might take their terrorism to sea, most pirates are in it solely for the money. In a land full of starving people, the pirates live a lavish lifestyle. 'Piracy in many ways is socially acceptable,' said Abdi Farah Juha, another inhabitant of Garowe.

'They don't call themselves pirates,' added Abdulkadi Mohamed. 'They call themselves coastguards.'

Somalis are flocking to the coast to join in the gold rush. Soon after the hijacking of the *Sirius Star*, Mohammad, a 40-year-old father of six who had spent the past 20 years living in a crumbling ruin in Galcaio, received money from 'friends of friends' to fund his journey to Hobyo, where he was hoping to take part in the next attack. 'Everyone knows that piracy is the only activity round here that pays well,' he said. Young men are particularly attracted by the pirates' lavish lifestyles.

Pirate bands have grown large. While the initial attack on a ship was still usually made by a team of seven to ten men, about 50 would occupy the vessel once it had been seized. Another 50 would wait on shore in case anything went wrong.

Not only does piracy bring money, it brings respect. Membership of The Coast Guard is regarded as a prestigious badge of honour among many in Somalia. It provides instant credit with traders and a free pass at checkpoints. The pirates have even become the heroes of a popular cartoon strip in which beautiful women snub the militiamen in favour of these new lords of the sea.

'They have become fashionable,' said Abdi Farah Juha. 'They have money, they have power and they are getting stronger by the day. They wed the most beautiful girls, they are building big houses and they have new cars, new guns.'

But one shopkeeper in Eyl said, 'There is no truth in the stories that the pirates build big houses and marry beautiful girls. They just use Eyl as a launching pad and a hiding place. Most of the people can't stand the actions of bandits, but if the whole world can't stop them, how can we?'

He was right, up to a point. A journalist who visited Eyl towards the end of 2008 reported that the old tin-roofed shacks remain. Much of the money had been spirited away either to the home villages of the pirate crew – which can be hundreds of miles inland – or to overseas bank accounts. Another journalist who travelled to Eyl expecting to find a boom town reported dolefully, 'There are only Kalashnikovs, goats and khat here.'

There were few signs of opulence in Hobyo either, or in any of the dusty little towns and villages along the Somali coast. However, several new restaurants had opened, and new 4x4s were seen racing dusty lanes. Gunmen proudly showed off gleaming new weapons and middlemen in smart suits punched numbers into the latest mobile phones. They wore ties, carried laptops and talked in English and French, as well Swahili, Arabic or Somali. Oozing bravado, they would not look out of place in a Western nightclub. Then there were the moneychangers who carried huge wads of new US dollar notes, the only currency that matters in a country that has been in chaos for almost two decades, and clan elders who were on hand to sort out problems between young turks.

The pirates do not build big houses in Eyl, but along the coast and in Garowe, where they spend most of their money. Palatial villas more usually associated with the oil-rich Gulf states are under construction. Although piracy is estimated to have pumped $35million into the economy in 2008, Puntland remained so poor that for seven months it went without paying its police force. Consequently, pirates carrying large sums of money were welcome in Garowe. 'I very much support the pirates,' said one woman resident. 'Nobody else gives us anything.'

Once a pirate has made his fortune, he often takes a second and third wife. Usually these new wives are very young women from poor nomadic clans, who are renowned for their beauty. Such trappings of success naturally proved a great attraction for the youth of Puntland, who had little hope of establishing an alternative career in war-torn Somalia.

The pirates reportedly get most of their weapons from Yemen, which is only 90 miles across across the Gulf of Aden at its narrowest point. They also buy weapons from the dealers in Mogadishu who supply the warring clans there. An order is placed via a *hawala* company – an informal money transfer system based on the honour of those involved. Militiamen then drive the arms north and deliver them to the pirates in Puntland, where they are paid the balance.

The militiamen saw the money that could be earned and hundreds of armed men moved north to join the pirates. This caused its own security problems, but there was little infighting. The promise of large sums of money kept the peace. Wounded pirates were seldom seen and residents of Puntland's coastline rarely reported finding bodies washed ashore. Given Somalia's history of clan warfare, this was remarkable. Talk of a shoot-out on the MV *Faina* was quickly quashed when the hijackers' spokesman Sugule Ali told the BBC Somali Service, 'Everybody is happy. We were firing guns to celebrate Eid.'

The downside to the vast sums of money pouring into the impoverished region is that life has become more expensive for ordinary people. The huge amounts of US dollars pumped into the local economy resulted in fluctuations in the exchange rate and rich young men abandoned the traditional drug khat for hashish and alcohol.

Thirty-nine-year-old Yassin Dheere was a typical pirate. When interviewed in Garowe in 2008, he was dressed in expensive-looking traditional robes, chewed khat and stroked his AK-47. He had taken to piracy five years before and had made a fortune. A large man, he towered over his bodyguards.

'I was born in Eyl town and I used to be a fisherman,' he said. 'I was forced to hijack foreign ships after the central government collapsed. No one was monitoring the sea, and we couldn't fish properly because the ships which trawl the Somali coasts illegally would destroy our small boats and equipment. That is what forced us to become pirates.'

The first time he hijacked a ship was in 2003. He thought the vessel was Arabian – there were 18 Yemeni crew on board. 'It was a big fishing ship that destroyed our boats several times,' he said. 'We surrounded it with our boats and seized it at gunpoint at night. We did not know these modern methods of using hooks and ladders, so we got near with our boats and climbed on.'

Dheere and his pirate band held the ship for two weeks, then some Somali and Arab mediators stepped in to negotiate. Dheere was surprised when they were offered $50,000 as compensation for their fishing equipment. It was a huge amount for poor fishermen. 'That inspired us and gave us an appetite for hunting ships,' he said. 'At that time we had no idea what we were doing. We were very worried about what would happen. Two of my friends backed out because they were afraid.'

But Dheere continued and since then he has made more money than he thought he would ever see. In one incident alone he got $250,000. This changed his life completely. However, he stressed that piracy is not easy work. Some of his fellow pirates have died, lost at sea when their boat capsized. His own life has been endangered. 'The worst experience I had was when a US warship attacked us while we were hunting a ship,' he said. 'It fired on us and captured some of us unexpectedly. We escaped with our speedboats while bullets buzzed over us.'

In 2006, his band drew up alongside a ship they were intending to hijack. One of his friends jumped on board, but the ship escaped. He has not seen or heard of his friend since and does not know whether he is alive or dead. But Dheere remained philosophical. At sea there were always losses as well as benefits. There was a constant danger they would be attacked by warships, and there were other risks in his new profession. Once, he had been jailed in Garowe, but his family attacked the jail and killed two of the policemen. During the exchange of fire he broke out with other prisoners. After that he decided that he would no longer risk either his life or his liberty and went into management.

'I have employees doing the business for me now,' he said. 'I am a financier. I get my money and I don't have to leave Eyl.' So while his pirate band went to sea, he stayed on dry land, managing their finances and buying the speedboats, weapons and other equipment they needed. He also had to keep up to date on the latest strategies, especially as so many warships were now plying the Indian Ocean. Still his band had the latest satellite equipment to show where the warships were. There were few disagreements among his men, but after they took the *Carré d'As*, there was a difference of opinion over whether to keep the Delannes at Hobyo or take them to Eyl. The pirates lost men in that operation, but Dheere was sanguine. 'At the moment we have a new, active young generation which wants to take part in piracy,' he said. 'They mostly like money.'

Nor was he worried about the UN resolution that allowed foreign nations to chase the pirates on land as well as sea. 'That will only lead to death of innocent Somalis,' he said. 'They cannot differentiate us from ordinary

Somalis – we dress alike. Piracy will not stop unless we get a government.'

Another pirate who spoke out was Shamun Indhabur, leader of the band that captured the MV *Faina*. He, too, had been a fisherman before he turned to piracy. He had been a crewman aboard a small fishing boat that fished for lobster and shark, but foreign ships had robbed them of their income. 'One of the few sources we have had is fishing, and the superpowers and Asian countries sidelined us in our own sea,' he said. 'So at first we started out just to counter illegal fishing, but international forces started to protect them.'

With no government – and no chance of foreign investment – there was high unemployment in Somali. Without fishing there was no alternative source of income and the young men grew increasingly desperate.

He claimed that foreign navy vessels escorted illegal fishing boats and ships dumping toxic waste. This was the pirates' justification for attacking merchant shipping. 'If they are escorting fishing boats, they can't escort all commercial shipping, and if we are forced to avoid fishing our waters, then those ships are all our fish.'

He even justified attacking luxury yachts. After all, the pirates were only after money and if they captured a luxury yacht they stood to make a fortune.

According to Indhabur, the pirates are not afraid of being apprehended. 'They can arrest us if they find us out at sea,' he said. 'They've arrested our friends several times, but that will never deter us from this business. The only thing that can stop piracy is a strong government in Somalia.'

The Americans, he said, were considered the 'most

friendly forces in Somali waters. They arrest us and release us, because they know we are not going to hurt them. But the French and the Indians treat us badly and sometimes they don't know what they're doing.' He cited the case of the Thai fishing boat *Ekawat Nava 5* that was sunk by India's INS *Tabar* on 18 November 2008, claiming there was not a single pirate on board when the *Tabar* opened fire.

Nor were the pirates intimidated by the arrests made by French special forces. 'French nationals will pay for that,' he said. 'If we get a ship with French nationals, we will punish the crew and they will pay double ransom.'

The French action after the ransoming of *Le Ponant* did not scare them, he said. Now they were alert to the possibility of being attacked on land. Indhabur also dismissed ships' attempts to defend themselves by employing guards and carrying LRAD sonic cannon, claiming to have hijacked ships even after the sonic weapon was used. 'When we go to sea we are drunk,' he said, 'and we are like hungry wolves running after meat. We don't even know what we are doing until we have boarded.'

The Islamists were no threat either. Indhabur explained that the pirates had a memorandum of understanding with them. While the Islamists condemned piracy in public, that was not their true position. They were only trying to send a message to the Arab nations that funded them. Besides, the Islamists were not a homogenous group. They fought one another and Indhabur could not see them getting back into power. Even if they did, they would still have to restore law and order, and create jobs. That was the only way to stop piracy.

The pirates themselves were much better organised. Although there were separate factions, these fell under the auspices of two main umbrella groups – one in Puntland and Indhabur's group in south and central Somalia. 'I am a member of the seven top committee members in south and central,' he said. 'We are a group of men with norms and terms, and we respect them.'

One pirate commander who claimed to be a friend of those who seized the *Sirius Star* said, 'If anyone tries to take back a ship by force, the hostages will face bad consequences we don't wish on them. We have the confidence to take on anyone in the world.'

Another pirate interviewed in a dingy bar in Eyl explained how easy it is to hijack a ship. 'We had two small boats and the first attacked the ship,' he said. 'We climbed about and demanded the captain to stop. We put the crew in one room and we brought the ship over here to Eyl and held the crew for about two months. We gave them nice food and we understood each other. When we got our money, we divided it up. I got a little, about $20,000, and then we released them and left the ship.'

But there were dangers. 'Sometimes when we are going to hijack a ship we face rough winds,' he said, 'and some of us get sick and some die.' However, they were still on the lookout for European ships because they get bigger ransoms.

Shamun Indhabur explained how the ransoms reached the pirates. 'We get the money two ways,' he said. 'A boat takes the money from Djibouti, then a helicopter takes the money from the boat, then it drops the money in waterproof cartons on assigned small boats. Then we collect it, check if it is false or not, then we release the ship. The other way we get the money is a boat from Mombasa.'

There are dangers in carrying large amounts of money in such a lawless region, as the pirates are split into competing groups. In Puntland they have also had problems with the middlemen, some of whom have been killed. But putting the world's navies off shore is no deterrent. 'We know the EU and NATO forces are coming, but that is not the solution,' he said. 'The solution is to restore peace in Somalia so that we can have a better life and more job opportunities... Sending forces will not stop us going into piracy.'

Forty-two-year old Asad 'Booyah' Abdulahi claimed to head a group of pirates with boats operating in the Indian Ocean and the Gulf of Aden. He finished high school and aimed to go to university, but his family did not have the money to send him. Instead he followed his father into fishing in Eyl. He still dreamed of working for a big company, but there was no chance of that after the Somali government collapsed in 1991 and the country descended into anarchy. Soon the fishermen were confronted at sea by foreign fishing vessels. Some had no licences. Others had obtained permission from the authorities in Puntland but did not want competition from the locals.

"They would destroy our boats and force us to flee for our lives,' said Abdulahi. By then he had nine children to support. 'I started to hijack these fishing boats in 1998. I did not have any special training but was not afraid.'

The first ship he hijacked was ransomed for $300,000. The money was used to buy small speedboats and AK-47s. Since then he claimed to have hijacked around 60 ships.

'To get their attention we shoot near the ship,' he said. 'If it does not stop we use a rope ladder to get on board. We count the crew and find out their nationalities. After checking the cargo we ask the captain to phone the owner and say that we have seized the ship and will keep it until the ransom is paid.'

Abdulahi claimed that they had no hostile intent when it came to the crew. They made friends with the hostages, telling them that they only want money and would not kill them. Sometimes they even sat down to eat rice, fish and pasta with them. Once the money was delivered to the ship, they would count it, then let the hostages go.

When they got back to Eyl, friends would be waiting to welcome them. Then they would travel by Land Cruiser to Garowe where the money would be divided up. Out of a ransom of $1.8million, say, $380,000 would go to their financial backer who had funded the mission. The rest would be split between the pirates themselves.

Abdulahi admitted that even the local community thought getting money that way was illegal, but pirates do not see it that way. 'We consider ourselves heroes running away from poverty,' he said. 'We don't see the hijacking as a criminal act but as a road tax because we have no central government to control our sea.'

When ships began avoiding Somali waters, the pirates had no alternative but to go further out. 'We went into the deep ocean and hijacked the unarmed cargo ships,' Abdulahi said. 'For the past three years, we have not operated near the Somali coast. We have operated at least 80 miles out, in international waters... There is no law that allows us to hijack travelling ships. But what motivates us is life, since we are the people who used to work at sea. We work together and our ranks grow because there is more hunger and more skills. That is why there is more piracy. Piracy is growing faster, it is not something that it lessening. The world can do nothing about it.'

The foreign warships on patrol did present difficulties, Abdulahi admitted. But the pirates responded by getting new boats and weapons and they were willing to take any risk. 'The pirates are living between life and death,' he said. 'Who can stop them? Americans and British all put together cannot do anything... It is possible because the Indian Ocean is vast and huge and the foreign warships who say they will protect the oceans cannot do so. No ship has the capability to see everything. We will not stop until we have a central government that can control our sea.'

Opinions among the Somali authorities are divided. Some, such as the governor of Eyl, are dismissive. 'In most cases these pirates are nothing more than unemployed youth, mostly armed with AK-47 assault rifles,' he said. 'They want to get their hands on easy money. I don't know why Americans and NATO aren't dealing with it. I don't know why warships with planes and helicopters and thousands of marines can't stop a few bandits armed with AK-47s.'

But the governor of Garowe saw the pirates' point of view. 'Even if thousands of ships assembled here, there is nothing they could do about it,' he said. 'The only effective way is to wage a land war, to attack their camps and bases on the mainland.'

In that case, with the Islamist militants in play, the US or NATO might be faced with another costly, unpopular and open-ended campaign such as those in Iraq and Afghanistan. Foreign intervention in Somalia does not have a distinguished track record.

As if to illustrate the point, when the French began pinpointing Eyl as the centre of pirate activity, many of the pirates moved out of semi-autonomous Puntland to another stretch of coast in the self-proclaimed state of Galmudug. The rule of law did not operate there either. Its capital, Galcaio, was a battleground for rival militias trying to control water wells and the main route towards Bosasso, a key port on Somalia's northern coast.

Galcaio quickly became the new operating base for those who supplied the pirates with food and khat. Several times every week, lorries and trucks carrying supplies, arms or the familiar speedboats could be seen heading from Galcaio to Eyl, Hobyo or Haradheere. The authorities are powerless to do anything about it. Behind the vast desk in his office in Galcaio, Mohammad Warsame, president of Galmudug, could only shrug his shoulders. As far as he was concerned, the pirates were untouchable. He had only 40 policemen at his disposal. They were paid about £60 a month, a pittance compared to what the pirates were raking in, so the battle was lost before it had even begun. Meanwhile, the pirates were attaining the status of folk heroes. These days they dressed in fashionable military fatigues.

The 'blame' for the pirates, Warsame said, lay with the authorities in Puntland. He also condemned the international community for being 'a bunch of amateurs' who fuelled the pirate trade by paying millions of pounds in ransom.

Although few in Galcaio actually take part in the hijackings, piracy is a tribal business, with relatives facilitating negotiations, dealing with foreign currency transactions and carrying out building or other work. Others in the clan are paid to provide Western food to the seamen held captive by the pirates. It is all paid for from the vast sums of money flowing into the war-ravaged area.

Again, the millions of dollars paid in ransom to the pirates have not turned the impoverished fishing villages of Galmudug into dens of luxury. However, some of the pirate chiefs have built themselves lavish walled compounds and drive round in Toyota 4x4s. Twenty-seven-year-old pirate Ali Ahmad build a vast residence in Galcaio with his £70,000 share of the £1million ransom for the French yacht *Le Ponant*. The money also purchased a 4x4 truck, kilos of khat and a second wife, along with guns and a new speedboat which were rented out to a group who carried out a raid on the *Yasa Neslihan*. His profit on this was £20,000 – 'a good transaction'.

However, the hijacking of food-aid shipments, upon which 40 per cent of the country depends, was beginning to hit the pirates' status, as was the impact that the huge influx of US dollars was having on a region of so many have-nots.

Those not involved in piracy have other worries. Ex-Somali Army Colonel Mohamed Nureh Abdulle, who lives in Haradheere – the nearest major population centre to where the hijacked *Sirius Star* was moored – advises the town's elders on security matters. 'Some time ago we had our own problems of piracy in our town, but that has not happened lately,' he told the BBC. 'The people who have been hijacking these ships in our seas are not from our region. We do not know any of the guys on the supertanker and they haven't made any contact with us. But, you know, our problem is not piracy. It is illegal dumping.'

While the attention of the world was focused on the *Sirius Star* and the other hijacked ships, the real problems of the local people, such as the dumping of toxic waste in their waters, had been ignored. 'These problems have been going for some time and the world knows about it,' said Abdulle. 'The Americans have been here in the region for a long time now. They know about the pollution. Instead, no, the world is only talking about the pirates and the money involved.'

For years, he said, foreign ships had taken advantage of the state of anarchy in Somalia to use their waters as a tip for industrial waste. 'It is dumped in our seas and it washes up on our coastline and spreads into our area,' he said. A few nights before the *Sirius Star* turned up, some tankers had come in from the high sea, leaking waste into the water and air. 'The first people fell ill yesterday afternoon. People are reporting mysterious illnesses. They are talking about it as though it were chicken pox, but it is not exactly like that either. Their skin is bad. They are sneezing, coughing and vomiting.'

Although people had suffered before, this was the first time that people had been so acutely ill. 'The people who have these symptoms are the ones who wake early, before it is light, and herd their livestock to the shore to graze,' Abdulle said. 'The animals are sick from drinking the water and the people who washed in the water are now suffering.'

With no government in Mogadishu, the people of Haradheere can expect no help. 'We are people who live in a very remote town and here, we are isolated' Abdulle said. 'We only rely on God.'

The former military man echoed the protests of pirates when he complained that the people's livelihood was being taken from them. 'Our community used to rely on fishing, but now no one fishes,' he said. 'You see, a lot of foreign ships were coming and they were fishing heavily – their big nets would wipe out everything, even the fishermen's equipment. They could not compete. So the people here began farming and keeping greater numbers of livestock. Like in any other Somali town, all one can do is rely on oneself. But now we have these medical hazards. What can we do about it?'

There seems to be some truth in Abdulle's allegations. The United Nations Environment Programme (UNEP) said the huge wave that battered Puntland after the Asian tsunami on Boxing Day 2004 stirred up tonnes of nuclear, toxic and medical waste that had been illegally dumped offshore in the 1990s. Rusting containers were washed up on the shore and broke open, scattering their contents. UNEP reported many unusual illnesses in the region following the event.

Abdullah Elmi Mohamed, a Somali academic studying in Sweden, said European companies charged 'approximately $8 per tonne for dumping off Somalia, while in Europe the cost for the disposal and treatment of toxic waste material could go up to $1,000 per tonne'. UNEP also said European companies were involved in the dumping trade, but because of the high levels of insecurity on shore and off the Somali coast, there was never any accurate assessment of the extent of the problem.

CHAPTER 10

THE STRAITS OF MALACCA

The coast of Somalia has taken over the dubious honour as the world's pirate hot spot from the Straits of Malacca. A key trade route, the Straits have been a famous hunting ground for pirates since the 14th century. Piracy particularly flourished in the 18th and 19th centuries with the growth of the spice trade and the beginnings of colonisation. In one gruesome 19th-century case, British Captain James Ross was forced to watch as his young son was lashed to an anchor and drowned by pirates who believed that Ross had a stash of silver coin hidden on his ship. They then cut off Ross's finger joint by joint.

The Straits are a 550-mile channel between the Indonesian island of Sumatra and the mainland of Malaysia, and the gateway from the Indian Ocean to the South China Sea. At its narrowest, the main channel is just 30 miles wide. But at the southern end, off Singapore, lie the Sunda Islands, which divide the straits into smaller channels just ten miles across. The mangrove swamps around the islands there have long given pirate vessels plenty of places to hide and the islands are still home to pirates today.

In the twenty-first century, around 70,000 merchant vessels pass through the Straits each year. They carry a fifth of all seaborne trade, among it a third of the world's crude oil shipments. This includes 90 per cent of the oil needed by Japan. Between 2002 and 2007, there were 258 pirate attacks in the straits and the surrounding waters, though the International Maritime Bureau (IMB) reckons that at least half of attacks go unreported.

The pirates of the Malacca Straits are much more ruthless than the Somalis. Indeed, so many sailors were being killed that in June 2005, Lloyd's of London classified the area a war zone. The classification was lifted in August 2006, after Singapore, Malaysia and Indonesia had stepped up security in their waters.

Pirates in the Malacca Straits began simply boarding ships to rob them of any cash they had on board, rather than holding them to ransom. In 1992, the *Australia Star*, a 35,000-tonne container ship carrying arms and cars, set off from Singapore for New Zealand. After guiding the ship through the Straits of Singapore, Captain Peter Newton left the bridge and headed to his cabin to unpack. They were 12 hours into the voyage and about 20 miles off Bintan, the largest of the Greater Sunda Islands.

'I had only just gone back to my cabin at that time,' said Newton. 'The first I knew of the pirates boarding was when they came in my cabin door wielding swords. They were dressed in black clothing and they were wearing balaclavas... It was terrifying.'

Newton had only been a captain for six months at the time. 'My first thought was that it was the crew committing mutiny,' he said. 'Then it became quite obvious their intention was to rob me.' He later learned that the pirates had boarded the ship over the starboard quarter, a blind spot in most vessels.

'The first thing the pirate leader did was come up to me and strike me,' said Newton. 'He made it absolutely clear to me that his intention was that, if I behaved myself, I would live to tell the tale. If I didn't, they would kill me.'

The pirates located the ship's safe and told Newton to open it. However, it was fitted with an alarm and they were afraid it would go off. 'So they put me on my hands and knees, and the pirate captain put his sword to the back of my neck and said to me, "If the alarm goes off, Captain, I will kill you immediately." I was particularly frightened.'

Fortunately, the alarm had been disabled by the previous captain and Newton had not had time to re-activate it. While the other four pirates kept a look out, the pirate captain took $24,000, which was to have been the crew's pay. Newton then had his hands tied behind his back and was marched out onto the deck at sword-point.

'The only thing I could think of was that their intention was to throw me over the side,' Captain Newton. 'I thought they were going to kill me.'

Instead, the pirates left the ship by a rope ladder. The last one gave the captain a push, indicating he should make his way back to the accommodation block, while they got back onto the small craft and sped away. Relieved that his ordeal was over – and grateful that he had survived – Captain Newton raised the alarm to alert other vessels.

As with other seafarers, his experience with pirates did not put him off going to sea again. But Captain Newton has tried to raise awareness of the problem, which he thought was not being taken seriously enough by the authorities or the shipping companies. Most cargo ships have small crews of 22 to 25 unarmed men. They are of different nationalities, have no particular allegiance to the ship and see no reason to risk their lives.

'Pirates know there is absolutely no risk,' said Newton. 'Once on board, there is no risk whatsoever. They know the civilian crew is not armed. The only defence is trying to stop them getting on board.'

The reason that piracy was not taken seriously, Newton said, was because the money robbed from the safe was insured. Besides it was 'peanuts' compared with the $2million in fuel it takes to sail from Singapore to New Zealand. 'But it is not peanuts if one of the crew or the captain gets killed,' said Newton.

Just three weeks later, another British captain, John Bashforth, was killed in a pirate attack. The same year, 1992, pirates caused an even greater disaster and loss of life. On 19 September they boarded the *Nagasaki Spirit*, which was carrying 40,154 tonnes of Khafi crude, as it was going through the Malacca Straits. They put the ship on autopilot and left, taking the captain who they intended to hold for ransom. The massive tanker was left sailing down one of the world's busiest waterways at full speed with no one at the wheel. At 11.20pm, the *Nagasaki Spirit* ran into the 27,000-ton container ship *Ocean Blessing*, which was travelling at 21 knots. The prow of the *Ocean Blessing* ripped a hole in the side of the tanker and 12,000 tonnes of oil spilled out into the sea and caught fire, engulfing both ships. The fire on the *Nagasaki Spirit* burned for six days, but the *Ocean Blessing* burned for six weeks. Everyone on the *Ocean Blessing* perished; there were only two survivors from *Nagasaki Spirit*. In all, 44 people died.

The last message from the *Nagasaki Spirit* said, 'Have been fired upon and now have fire in numbers five and six and central tanks. Abandoning vessel immediately into two 16-man life rafts and will activate EPIRB [Emergency Position Indicating Radio Beacon] in latitude 04.33 north, long 98.43 east at 1623 GMT September 19. No time to report further as abandoning vessel.'

It was thought that the *Ocean Blessing* had also been attacked by pirates. An observer on another ship said that she was changing speed and moving from side to side as if the deck watch officer was employing evasive manoeuvres to avoid being boarded.

The most notorious hangout for pirates in the area was Batam, the island next to Bintan. It is just ten miles across the water from Singapore, where the Malacca Strait feeds into the smaller Singapore Strait. More than a thousand ships a week pass between Singapore and Batam. Most do business in Singapore, which is one of the world's pre-eminent free ports.

In the 1980s Indonesia tried to turn Batam, which is just a 15-minute ferry ride away, into the mirror image of Singapore. The jungle was cleared to make way for hotels, casinos, golf courses, shopping malls and office blocks. A tariff-free zone was established, and maritime brokers, who hire sailors for shipping companies, moved in. However, Batam did not enjoy the strict rule of law that applied in Singapore. Corruption quickly took hold. Gangsters moved in and Batam became a marketplace for weapons, stolen cars, illegally felled timber and other contraband. The local pirates called Batam 'Happy Happy' for its cheap drugs, hostess bars, strip joints, prostitutes and brothels.

Many local Indonesian seamen turned to piracy because they could not get work. They lacked the qualifications to work on commercial ships as they could not afford the expensive training required. In the past, they would have got round this by having older seamen to show them the ropes, after which they would have bought counterfeit credentials. However, the shipping companies clamped down on this, leaving many experienced Batam seamen unemployed. To survive, they turned to piracy.

However, while most pirates were in it for the money, others liked the excitement. 'It is fun,' said one, 'an adventure, like James Bond.'

Their run-of-the-mill attacks on cargo ships were known as 'shopping'. Even the smallest tanker or cargo vessel carries large amounts of cash to pay the crew and buy provisions. Using small wooden boats known as *pancungs* with powerful outboard motors, they would stalk a passing ship at night and scale its sides. Sometimes they colluded with members of the crew, who would turn a blind eye. When asked how the attackers got aboard undetected, one pirate said, 'We use magic. We cast a spell to make the crew stay asleep. We can be invisible, bulletproof.'

These pirates would start their attacks from small islands, often within sight of the skyscrapers of Singapore, their *pancungs* hidden among the mangrove swamps. They would attack from the rear, speeding up to the stern next to the rudder, out of sight of crewmen on the deck above. To get aboard, they would use a simple piece of equipment: a hooked mangrove root lashed to a long bamboo pole. Once under the stern, they would hook the root over the ship's rail, then climb the pole. Not for nothing were these attackers known as 'jumping squirrels'. A skilled band of pirates could get aboard in a matter of minutes. To attack taller ships, they simply lashed a number of poles together.

Grabbing the first crewman they saw, they would hold a *parang* – a sharp machete-style knife – to his throat and ask him where the money was. Once they had the cash, they would slide back down their bamboo poles into the *pancung* and speed off. The most important man in the pirate band was the boatman. He had the difficult task of holding the *pancung* steady in the turbulent water above the churning propeller and he got the biggest share of the money. Once they had made their escape, the pirates would speed back to 'Happy Happy' where they would spend the stolen money on beer in karaoke bars or in strip joints where you can eat sushi off the belly of a naked girl. Today, others squander their ill-gotten gains on ecstasy and crystal meth, or marathon sessions with prostitutes.

While some of the pirates were content with such smaller hauls, others became more ambitious – and more dangerous. At three o'clock on the moonless morning of 26 March 2003, a pirate boat pulled up to the stern of the 3,900-ton chemical tanker *Dewi Madrim* off the coast of Sumatra. A dozen men threw grappling hooks and ropes up onto the deck and swarmed aboard. Wearing black with their faces obscured by balaclavas, they were armed not with *parangs* but automatic weapons. They smashed the windows of the bridge, and one of them held a pistol to the head of the officer on duty and asked him where the rest of the crew were.

The captain, Surahmat Johar, was asleep in his cabin. Roughly awoken, he was herded into another room with the rest of the crew. 'They tied our hands tight behind our backs with a white, plastic wire – the kind that tightens even harder if you try to loosen it,' he said.

The captain grew concerned that no one was on the bridge and he asked to be allowed to take the helm. The pirates told him to shut up. 'Don't worry, our commander is fully capable of taking care of your tanker,' one of them raiders said.

Later the captain was escorted up to the bridge and discovered that the pirates really did know what they were doing. 'Someone was expertly steering the vessel, reading the radar very well,' said Surahmat. 'I remember thinking, My God, he can handle the ship better than I can.' Until then he had thought that pirates were just a bunch of petty robbers who jumped onto a ship, robbed the crew and disappeared. 'But these pirates were totally beyond my imagination. They were professionals.'

After disabling the ship's radio and steering the ship for more than an hour, the pirates left with some cash and two of the crew, who were still missing six months later.

Later that year, a pirate named Nurdin and 13 other modern-day buccaneers seized the *Luen Fatt*, a 1,270-tonne tanker registered in Taiwan, as it sailed past Batam. Within hours, its cargo of diesel oil had been pumped out, the ship renamed and repainted, and sent on its way to maritime brokers.

By this time, these brokers had broadened their remit to hiring pirates for Asian crime syndicates. One of the hiring grounds on Batam was a café called HQ. With its corrugated iron roofing, bare concrete floors and red plastic tables and chairs, it looked like just another place to drink beer and eat noodles. However, the clientele were Indonesian sailors looking for work and they were not too fussy whether it was legal or illegal.

These pirates would steal to order. Sometimes they were asked for a ship of a certain type, size or capacity. On other occasions a client was after a particular cargo – known in the parlance of the pirates as the guts. The fabric of the vessel was called the skin.

'When the big boss only wants the skin, we'll try to find a vessel with no cargo, but if he wants just the guts, we'll find another buyer for the ship,' said Nurdin, who looked down on men who simply raided ships for the cash, regarding them simply as thugs. He and his men were above that sort of thing. 'We aren't pirates,' he said. 'We're professionals.'

A typical case was the hijacking of the 4,595-tonne tanker *Suci*. She was six hours out of Singapore with a cargo of diesel oil bound for Sandakan on the island of Borneo when armed men scrambled on board. In a smooth operation, the gang took over the bridge, tied up the crew, painted out the ship's name and daubed the funnel in new colours. The next morning, the crew was forced into a lifeboat and the renamed *Glory II* sailed off. The crew were soon rescued but the tanker vanished.

Then there was the 5,590-tonne *Marine Master*, registered in Panama. On the bright moonlit night of 17 March 1999, she was hauling soda ash through the Straits of Malacca when she was pursued by a twin-motor speedboat. At around 2am the pirates caught up with her and some 20 men, dressed in army fatigues with automatic rifles, scrambled up a rope ladder, catching the crew of 21 by surprise. Four days later, the pirates put them in nine inflatable life rafts and set them adrift. Six days later they were picked up by a Thai vessel, but by then the *Marine Master* would have had a makeover. The soda ash would have been sold and the ship – with a new name, new flag, new coat of paint and new crew – would have been chartered out. The International Maritime Bureau (IMB) drew comfort from the fact that no one was killed.

Though the number of attacks was dropping, 162 crewmen were assaulted, maimed or killed in 1998, and all but one of the 67 reported murders in pirate raids had taken place in the Straits of Malacca or the South China Sea.

By 2004, the IMB reckoned that there were five criminal syndicates operating in the area. Based in Malaysia and Indonesia, they were responsible for large-scale hijacking in the Malacca Straits. While there were still plenty of locals who boarded ships armed with machetes to steal some cash and mobile phones, the syndicates were gradually taking over.

'Previously, attacks were isolated and mounted from one or two boats,' said IMB director Pottengal Mukendan. 'But now they are much more coordinated, with pirates using five to six boats in their attacks. They are also increasingly heavily armed, with some even using rocket-propelled grenades.'

Fearing a terrorist attack after the Bali bombing of 2002, Singapore had upgraded its radar tracking of ships and stepped up patrols and spot checks. There had already been one terrorist attack on a merchant vessel. On 6 October 2002 the French oil tanker *Limburg,* carrying 397,000 barrels of crude from Iran to Malaysia, was attacked in the Gulf of Aden. Her attackers were not pirates, nor did they board the ship. Several miles off the coast of Yemen, a dinghy rammed into the tanker's starboard side, detonating its load of explosives. The ship caught fire and some ninety thousand barrels of crude oil poured into the Gulf of Aden. One crewman was killed and 12 were injured.

Al-Qaeda claimed responsibility. Osama bin Laden issued a statement saying, 'By exploding the oil tanker in Yemen, the holy warriors hit the umbilical cord and lifeline of the crusader community, reminding the enemy of the heavy cost of blood and the gravity of losses they will pay as a price for their continued aggression on our community and looting of our wealth.'

Thirteen members of al-Qaeda were convicted for the bombing, including Jamal al-Badawi who had masterminded the attack on the USS *Cole.* However, they escaped from jail in the Yemen, but Fawaz Yahya al-Rabeiee, who was sentenced to death for the *Limburg* attack, was later shot and killed by Yemeni security forces.

Some seamen were not reassured by increased patrols in the Straits of Malacca. One of them was British tanker master Captain Allan McDowall. He did not believe that the naval forces in the area could be trusted. When pirates attacked his VLCC off Sumatra in 1992, he was somewhat surprised to see that the armed, hooded men who boarded his supertanker from inflatables wore the dark, camouflage battle dress of Indonesian marines.

'I knew there was an Indonesian warship in the area, because we could hear them talking on radios,' said McDowall. Although others reported similar experiences, he could never prove his suspicions and the Indonesian authorities denied the existence of any such rogue military units.

As it happened, McDowall's attackers left empty-handed, outfoxed by doors that would not open from the outside and a steam whistle so loud 'it scrambled the brain and prevented talking,' according to McDowall. Captains would do well to improvise such defences, he said. Civilian cargo ships make soft targets for pirates who have upgraded their weapons while their victims have been disarmed. 'In the old days, pirates carried cutlasses but you did, too,' he said. 'Now we are forbidden to carry weapons on board.'

In the autumn of 1999, the 370ft *Alondra Rainbow* – a Japanese-owned Panama-registered general cargo ship – was tramp trading around southeast Asia, picking up any cargo she could find and shipping it primarily between the Malay peninsula and Japan. She was a conventionally designed container ship, with a raised bulwark at the bow, two main cargo holds and a superstructure aft that rose five floors above the deck. The bridge spanned the top of the aftcastle. It was 64 feet wide and extended over the side of the ship so that waters close to the ship were in view. The ship was worth around $10million.

The crew comprised 15 Filipino seamen and two Japanese officers – 68-year-old Captain Ko Ikeno and 69-year-old Chief Engineer Kenzo Ogawa. Both had been life-long seamen. Ikeno had graduated from the Tokyo University of Fisheries when he was 25 and assumed his first command 11 years later in 1967. Since then he had mastered cargo vessels in all the waters of the world.

In early October, the *Alondra Rainbow* made an uneventful crossing of the Java Sea, arriving with an empty hold at the outer anchorage of Kualatanjung on Sumatra, where the port is dominated by a giant aluminium smelter. It took five days to load 6,972 tonnes of aluminium worth another $10million. Captain Ikeno's job was to steer ship and cargo some 3,300 miles across open water to Omuta on Japan's southern island of Kyushu. It would take about a week, and Ikeno took on extra fuel as it was typhoon season. None were currently charted, but if one blew up the *Alondra Rainbow* would have to skirt it, adding many miles and several days to the voyage.

In the late afternoon of 22 October, the *Alondra Rainbow* was ready to sail. The sun set at 6.06pm and two hours later, after manoeuvring to clear the dock, she got under way. It was night before she cleared the outer anchorage and headed off down the Straits of Malacca.

The sea was calm and the lights on the bridge were dimmed so the officer on watch could see out over the bright moonlit water. As the *Alondra Rainbow* made moderate speed down the straits, Captain Ikeno remained on duty with a helmsman and the third officer, occasionally ordering a minor correction in course. All eyes looked forward as they watched for small islands, coastal craft and other ships plying the channel. Knowing they were in danger from pirates, Captain Ikeno increased the speed to 13 knots before telling the helmsman to switch to autopilot. Then, after reminding the third officer to keep an eye out for marauders, he went below to take a bath and draft a telex to the ship's owners, telling them that they had left Sumatra. A few minutes later the ship was under attack.

The pirates who boarded the *Alondra Rainbow* were not fishermen looking for a bit of cash. Three weeks before, a 'recruiting agent' named Yan Makatengkeng, a man on the run from the authorities in Malaysia, had visited a certain coffee shop in Batam. There he had met two men. One was a Sulawesian from eastern Indonesia named Christianus Mintodo, who held a master's certificate either from Belize or Honduras. The other was a local man, a ship's engineer named Burhan Nanda. Both were middle-aged, short and slight but hardened by years at sea. Both had been involved in piracy before. At the meeting a phone call had come through from a man simply known as The Boss – possibly Chinese. Makatengkeng handed the phone to Mintodo and Nanda so The Boss could speak to them. The call would have seemed quite innocent to anyone overhearing it. A ship-owner was simply welcoming two new officers into his employ.

Mintodo and Nanda then flew to Jakarta on the northern tip of Java. There the port service boat ferried them to an old freighter in the outer anchorage. This was the *Sanho*, a pirate ship owned by The Boss and his syndicate. The master, Marnes Zachawarns, was another fugitive from justice. As the *Sanho* took on fuel and provisions, a crew of 35 cut-throats slowly assembled. Most were Indonesians, but there were also Chinese, Thais and Malaysians. Some were skilled hijackers who would assault the target ship at sea. The others were experienced seamen who could control the ship once they had taken her.

On 16 October, a call came from Makatengkeng giving the go-ahead. The *Sanho* was soon under way and heading for Kualatanjung on Sumatra. She arrived there on 21 October but instead of going into the harbour, she lingered in the outer anchorages. The next day, word came from an informant in the port that the *Alondra Rainbow* was leaving that evening. There is speculation that one of the pirates went ashore and disguised himself as one of the hawkers who sold electrical goods and trainers, usually stolen from other ships, to the crews of ships tied up there. It would have been easy for the pirate to join the other traders as they scampered up the gangway of the *Alondra Rainbow* and hide himself on board while they haggled.

As the pirates knew from their informant which way the *Alondra Rainbow* was bound, the Sanho upped anchor first. She was one of the darkened hulks in the straits that Captain Ikeno had taken care to avoid. Once the *Alondra Rainbow* had sailed by, the *Sanho* deployed a speedboat carrying an assault team that sped up to the cargo ship from behind. Once it reached the ship, the pirates boarded, shinning up bamboo poles or climbing rope ladders secured by grappling hooks.

Captain Ikeno was at his desk drafting his telex to the owners when he heard a thump on the deck above, followed by a few garbled shouts over the intercom. He ran up to the bridge to find that the door had been barricaded from the inside. He pushed at the door, which opened far enough for him to see knives and pistols. The door was then yanked open and a pirate grabbed him and threw him against the bulkhead. The raider then held a knife to his throat and warned him, in broken English, not to resist.

There were about ten pirates on the bridge, armed with guns, knives and machetes. Their faces were covered with ski masks but Captain Ikeno noted that they were barefoot and wearing loose clothing. From the language they used and their general demeanour, he thought they included both Indonesians and Malays. Both the helmsman and the third officer already had their hands tied behind their backs, and as the pirate bound Captain Ikeno's hands, he began to worry that the *Alondra Rainbow* was now steaming down a busy waterway at 13 knots with no one on watch and no one at the helm. But he did not say anything, fearing the wrath of the pirates.

The captain was then forced to lead the pirates to the crew's cabins. His men were roughly pulled from their beds, blindfolded and bound, and pushed into the mess room where they would be held. Chief Engineer Ogawa tried to resist but was quickly overpowered. Next Captain Ikeno was pushed into the engine room, where the third engineer was ordered to reduce speed. Then he, too, was blindfolded, bound and taken to the mess room.

Now that all 17 crew were accounted for, the captain was led back to his cabin, where he was forced to open the ship's safe. Inside were several thousand dollars, along with a bundle of yen. The pirates grabbed the money, along with the crew's papers and passports and a spare watch belonging to the captain. After the pirates had ransacked the other cabins, they took the captain to the mess room, blindfolded him like the others and warned them all that they would be killed if they made any trouble.

This was no empty threat, as the crew well knew. At around midnight on 27 September 1998, a small Japanese freighter named the *Tenyu* and its crew of 15 had disappeared after leaving Kualatanjung carrying around three thousand bars of aluminium. It was on its way to Korea but vanished a day after leaving port. The ship's engineer, Park Ha Joon, had promised his family he would be home in a month. The 40-year-old South Korean had made this kind of trip hundreds of times before, so when he said goodbye to his wife and two daughters, nobody was upset. 'Be healthy,' he had said to his wife, 'and take care of the kids.' Park had then boarded the 2,642-tonne *Tenyu* in the southern port of Ulsan and sailed for Indonesia. Over the phone, Park's 11-year-old daughter had asked him to bring her some dolls. Once in Kualatanjung, Pak had supervised the loading of the cargo, then the *Tenyu* had sent off for Inchon – and vanished.

In mid-October there was an unconfirmed report of an unidentified vessel that might have been the *Tenyu* crossing the South China Sea. The ship was found three months later up the Yangzi river in the Chinese port of Zhangjigang. Its name had been changed to *Sanei 1* and it was now sailing under the Panamanian flag. The Chinese authorities had grown suspicious when they noticed that the 14-year-old vessel had only been repainted in a few places – specifically where the name had been – and they had informed the Piracy Reporting Centre in Kuala Lumpur. A lawyer for the owner of the *Tenyu* went on board disguised as a Chinese border guard and confirmed that the ship was the *Tenyu* from the serial number on the engine. However, both the cargo and the original crew were missing. It was assumed they had been killed.

The new chief engineer and another crewman promptly disappeared, but the rest of the crew was arrested on suspicion of being pirates. However, they claimed to have joined the ship legitimately at Rangoon and used airline tickets and Myanmar visas issued in Singapore to back up their story. As there was no evidence they were pirates and had committed no crime in China, they were released. The story of the *Tenyu* had circulated widely and the crew would have known it. What they did not know was that at least one of the pirates on board the *Alondra Rainbow* had been among the men released by the Chinese.

The crew of the *Alondra Rainbow* were held in the mess room under guard and were not allowed to talk. Beneath them, they could feel the vibration of the ship. They soon noticed the engine's speed and that it was changing course. It was plain the ship was in experienced hands. Although it was hard to keep track of time, Captain Ikeno reckoned that several hours had passed before the engine's speed began to slow again. Then there was a sharp bump and a pump started up.

Now the men were led one at a time from the room, still blindfolded and bound. They were taken down the corridor, through a door and out onto the aft deck. Standing next to the railings, the crewmen feared that were going to be thrown into the sea. Instead their blindfolds were removed. Below them was a freighter, riding high in the water with her holds empty. She was rusty and poorly maintained, and Captain Ikeno would refer to her simply as 'the dirty ship'. It was probably the *Sanho*.

Captain Ikeno and his men were then ordered to jump down onto its deck. They were led below and put in two separate cabins. There they were blindfolded again and ordered to lie on filthy mattresses on the floor. Again, there was to be no talking, and they were warned that anyone standing up or attempting to look outside would be killed. All they could do was listen out for the clues given by the sound of machine, bumps and thumps, and the occasional shout. From what they could tell, the two ships lay together for an hour or more, then went their separate ways.

The pirate ship then headed back up the Malacca Straits and into the Andaman Sea. For nearly a week Captain Ikeno and his crew remained blindfolded and bound in sweltering cabins below decks. They were fed only twice and rarely taken to the head [toilet]. The foul drinking water they were given came from a can marked Esso, which Chief Mate Voltaire Lapore glimpsed from beneath his blindfold.

As the journey went on, the blindfolds loosened. The pirates did not realise this, as they came into the cabins unmasked. Perhaps they did not care as they were intending to kill their captives as they had continually threatened. Either way, Ikeno got a chance to study the pirate captain, who was around 5ft 8in and muscular, though potbellied. His dark skin and features led Ikeno to think he was either Indian or Pakistani.

On the seventh night of their captivity, the engines stopped. Captain Ikeno and his crew were taken outside and made to lie on the deck. Again they feared for their lives. Less than a year before, on 16 November 1998, a 17,273-tonne bulk carrier called the *Cheung Son* had been carrying slag from a steel mill in Shanghai to Malaysia when she was seized in the South China Sea by pirates dressed as Chinese customs officers. They stole 970,000 yuan in cash and later sold the contraband for $300,000, but the crew of 23 had been killed and slung overboard.

However, shortly afterwards fishermen in Shantou found a corpse in their nets. Its mouth had been taped shut and it was bound to a metal weight. Over the next few days they brought up several more. According to autopsy reports, one had died of drowning – he had been alive when they threw him over the side. The rest were riddled with machine-gun bullets. The suspects were arrested but they might have got away with it, had not the Chinese authorities discovered some photographs that showed the pirates partying among the dead. As it was deemed that the crime had taken place in Chinese territorial waters, the accused were tried in China. The court determined that the plot had begun in August 1998, when the gang had started buying guns and boats. All 13 – including an Indonesian citizen – were found guilty and executed. On their way to the execution grounds, drunk on rice wine, they sang: '*Alé, alé, alé!*' – 'Go, go, go!' – the refrain from the Ricky Martin pop song 'The Cup of Life'. But the boat and its cargo were never found.

The pirates holding the crew of the *Alondra Rainbow* were not the sort to care one way or the other about the fate of their captives. But rather than sully their own hands with the blood of their victims, they cast them adrift in a life raft purloined from the *Alondra Rainbow*. After the men had been forced to crawl on board, the rope was cut and the pirate ship sailed away into the night. Neither it nor its crew were ever found.

The crew were now free, but their situation was little better. They were adrift in an overcrowded rubber raft on the vast expanse of the Indian Ocean with no effective form of propulsion and little idea of where they were. They had no navigation equipment and no radio to summon help. On board were some meagre provisions – a little fresh water and some tinned food. Along with that, there was a first-aid kit, knives with buoyant handles, a couple of paddles, two bailers, ten signal flares and a pamphlet on survival. It was written in English and warned readers to stay out of the sun – an impossibility – and not to drink sea water – that much they knew already.

Ten ships sailed by but all ignored the crew's waves and flares. After ten days, all ten flares had been fired and the water was running low, but they managed to catch some fish and drink the moisture they squeezed from them. Morale slumped; men began to pray and cry. As the only two Japanese on board, Captain Ikeno and Chief Engineer Ogawa feared the Filipinos would turn on them, so the captain ceded command, particularly of the water ration, to the Filipino first mate, Voltaire Lapore.

After ten days, a small commercial fishing boat came in sight. The crew of the *Alondra Rainbow* took off their shirts and waved them frantically. The boat approached but seemed hesitant. In these waters, pirates had been known to lure their victims by pretending to be marooned sailors. Eventually the fishing boat, which was flying a Thai flag, came within shouting distance. One of the stranded men shouted out in English, saying that they were two Japanese and 15 Filipino sailors who had been attacked by pirates. If they were not rescued they would die. The fishermen seemed unconvinced and asked to see their passports, but these had been taken by the pirates. One crew member had an old cancelled passport in his pocket, but still the fishermen were not convinced.

After a good deal of negotiation, the fishermen allowed Captain Ikeno on to their boat. He spoke no Thai, but wrote down his name and the name of his ship. One of the fishermen got on the radio and relayed the details to his company. The reply reassured the skipper and he allowed the rest of the crew aboard. The following day, the fishermen dropped them off on the holiday island of Phuket. It was 9 November, 18 days since they had been attacked. The Filipinos were flown back to the Philippines, while Captain Ikeno and Chief Engineer Ogawa flew back to Tokyo, where they retired.

The *Alondra Rainbow* had not finished its days at sea, though. Once in command, Christianus Mintodo had sailed her down the Straits of Malacca, through the Singapore Straits, into the South China Seas and along the coast of Sarawak to the Malaysian port of Miri. On the way, the pirates had spent a day painting the hull black and renamed her the *Global Venture*. All other distinguishing marks were removed.

At Miri three thousand tonnes of aluminium – nearly half the *Alondra Rainbow*'s $10million cargo – was transferred to a freighter named the *Bansan II*. This took several days. The *Bansan II* then headed off to Subic Bay in the Philippines. When she arrived she was the *Victoria* and carried the necessary documents to account for her cargo, which was quickly sold. The insurance company eventually traced the cargo to the Philippines, but their attempts to get it or receive compensation got tied up in the courts. Similarly, the police investigation of the *Victoria* was gathering dust.

Mintodo still had nearly four thousand tonnes of aluminium on his hands, so he set sail again. At sea the *Global Venture* now became the *Mega Rama*, home port Belize. She headed westwards into the Indian Ocean, possibly travelling once more through the Straits of Singapore.

A week after the hijack, the owners of the *Alondra Rainbow* realised she had not turned up in Omuta and contacted the Piracy Reporting Centre in Kuala Lumpur. An alert was sent out with a detailed description and a reward of $200,000 was offered. Ships and planes scoured the waters, but the 300ft *Alondra Rainbow* seemed to have vanished.

On 13 November, however, the captain of the Kuwaiti freighter *Al-Shuhadaa* sailing in international waters off the southwest coast of India, reported seeing a suspect vessel. It was evening and in the fading light he could not read her name, but she appeared to be freshly painted. He gave her location and said she was steering north-northwest and travelling at eight knots. The Piracy Reporting Centre contacted the Indian coastguard, but they were reluctant to intervene. The *Alondra Rainbow* was a Japanese ship registered in Panama, hijacked in

Indonesian waters, and had no Indian citizens on board. However, under the Law of the Sea, a treaty passed by the United Nations in 1994, nations were given the right to stop pirates on the high seas, no matter where their crimes took place, and old colonial laws left by the British obliged them to act.

Accordingly a coastguard cutter named the *Tarabai* headed out of the south Indian port of Cochin with 24 men on board. Early the following night, they located the suspect vessel by radar. It was 13 miles ahead. The *Tarabai* closed on it and when its lights came into view, they hailed it by VHF radio, ordering the ship to slow down and identify itself. There was no response. The Indian coastguard then flashed its lights and fired two yellow flares. Again this elicited no response – except that the ship picked up speed and veered to port. The *Tarabai* had a Bofors gun mounted on her deck and the coastguards then put six warning shots across her bow. It made no difference. The ship did not slow or alter course, so the coastguard pulled up behind her and settled in for the night.

In the morning, they inspected the huge ship through their binoculars. On the stern they could see her name *Mega Rama* and the flag stated Belize. Later the *Tarabai* was joined by a patrol plane, a German-built Dornier turboprop. It hailed the ship and ordered it to stop. This time someone on board answered. He identified the ship as the *Mega Rama*, bound from Manila to Fujairah in the United Arab Emirates. She had a cargo of aluminium and a crew of 15 Indonesians on board.

It was clear from the description of the *Alondra*

Rainbow that they had found the right ship, despite the name change, and the Indians again ordered her to stop. She refused, saying she was in international waters and had a schedule to keep. The patrol plane was equipped with a self-loading rifle and put some warning shots across the ship's bows. When that did no good, it made five strafing runs, but the Dornier's puny gun had little effect on the huge vessel. Low on fuel, the patrol plane turned for home.

But the *Tarabai* stayed on station. For the rest of the day, the coastguard fired 40mm rounds at the ship, taking out her windows and putting holes in her superstructure and hull. The pirates had taken refuge in the engine room, below the water line, where they thought they would be safe. They had left the ship on autopilot, heading for Pakistani waters. If they made it, the Indian coastguard would have had to abandon their chase. But the Indians were not going to let their prey escape so easily. The Indian Navy sent the INS *Prahar*, a corvette armed with missiles. They gave the *Alondra Rainbow* a pounding with its AK-630 cannons and 76.2mm main gun, and soon after dawn on 16 November the ship slowed to a halt. The chase had covered 575 miles and lasted 35 hours.

By this time, smoke was belching from the ship's bridge and superstructure. Fifteen pirates, waving their shirts and holding their hands aloft, stood on the deck. A larger coastguard ship, the *Veera*, had turned up and teams from the two cutters climbed aboard and handcuffed the pirate crew. Among them were Burhan Nanda and Christianus Mintodo, who had met in the Batam coffee shop six and a half weeks before. They were transferred to the *Veera* to be delivered into the hands of justice.

The smoke from the ship, it turned out, came not from the shelling but from a small fire started by the pirates. They had been burning documents. They had also opened the sea cocks (valves in the hull of the vessel, below the waterline) before they gave themselves up in an attempt to scuttle the ship and send the evidence to the bottom of the sea. By the time the Indian coastguard boarded her, she was going down by the stern. However, the Indian Navy sent divers who went down into the flooded engine room and closed the cocks. Emergency pumps were then set up on deck to pump out the engine room and the *Veera* towed the ship the 345 miles to Mumbai. During this four-day trip, the suspected pirates were interrogated and one suffered a gunshot wound. The results of these on-board interviews were not presented as evidence in court. The men were charged with armed robbery, attempted murder, assault, theft, forgery and fraud – even entering India without a valid passport, though they had done so in shackles. Fourteen stood trial; the other man had died in jail before the case came to court.

Throughout their trial the men maintained that they had not hijacked the ship. They said they had been recruited as sailors in Jakarta, then flown to Manila where they took over the ship. The captain also maintained that he had run from the Indian coastguard fearing they were pirates – despite their uniforms. But neither Mintodo nor any of his crew took the stand. There were no witnesses for the defence and no evidence that they had joined the ship in the Philippines was presented. They were convicted on all counts, except for the passport violation, and sentenced to seven years, three of which they had already served.

An appeal was lodged on the grounds that Captain Ikeno had failed to identify any of the 14 men as being part of the ten-man team who had originally taken over the *Alondra Rainbow*. The defence continued to argue that the defendants were a new crew put on during the lay-over in the Philippines after the ship had been repainted and renamed, and were therefore not guilty of piracy. On 18 April 2005 the High Court in Mumbai overturned the conviction and the defendants were acquitted.

The fact remains that the men captured on the *Mega Rama* were not the assault team that had hijacked the *Alondra Rainbow*. They were still at large. This was all the more worrying as they were part of the gang that had taken over not just the *Tenyu*, whose crew were missing presumed killed, but also the *Anna Sierra*, a freighter carrying twelve thousand tons of sugar – worth between $4million and $5million – from Ko Si Chang in Thailand to Manila in the Philippines in 1995.

The *Anna Sierra* was sailing off the coast of Thailand on 13 September 1995 when she was attacked by a gang of between 25 and 30 men in a motorboat. Once the pirates, who were hooded and armed with machine-guns, were in control of the ship, they handcuffed the crew and imprisoned them in the engine room for two days. Meanwhile the ship was repainted and renamed the *Arctic Sea*. The crew were then brought up on deck and told they would be killed if they did not hand over their valuables. The pirates also robbed them of their clothes. The crew were then forced overboard onto rafts and cast adrift without navigation equipment or provisions, but proved to be luckier than the crew of the *Alondra Rainbow*: they were rescued by Vietnamese fishermen after one day.

The pirates then piloted the *Anna Sierra* into the Chinese harbour of Beihai, not far from the Vietnamese border. At this port the authorities were presented with false papers: the ship was supposedly registered at Kuala Lumpur under a Honduran flag with bills of lading claiming the cargo of sugar came from Santos in Brazil. The pirates managed to sell the sugar in Beihai, to a Chinese company that been defrauded of $800,000 in April 1995 by a gang in Hong Kong. As recompense, the sugar was sold at a discount of that sum.

Meanwhile a large reward had been offered through the International Maritime Bureau (IMB). This prompted a reported sighting of the vessel in the harbour at Beihai from an employee of the China Ocean Shipping Company to his head office in Beijing, and the pirates – two Malay, 12 Indonesian – were arrested. On investigation, the ship's Honduran registration proved to be false, the ship's papers forged and Thai labels showed the bags of sugar had not come from Brazil. The company in Hong Kong claiming to be the owner of the *Arctic Sea* immediately presented a second set of documents. These too were forgeries. Then another company sprang up with new documents claiming that they were the owners, but the legal battle became sandbagged. Two years later ten of the pirates were released without charge and returned to Indonesia. The fate of the other four is unknown. All this time the *Anna Sierra* remained in the harbour at Beihai. The Chinese authorities demanded $400,000 in docking fees, which both companies claiming to be the owners refused to pay. The ship eventually began to list and was towed away and beached nearby. Officially declared unseaworthy, it has since been broken up.

Along with the 15 nabbed on the *Alondra Rainbow*, more of the gang have now been rounded up. Four South Koreans are facing trial in their home country for involvement in the *Tenyu* case. According to a Korean TV documentary, a former ship's captain reportedly recruited the Indonesians who replaced the original crew through a Singaporean company. The captain was arrested in Singapore and extradited to South Korea, where he was charged with selling the cargo of aluminium to a Chinese company for $3million. The Korean prosecutor thought another Singaporean had masterminded the operation, but was frustrated by slow speed of investigations in Singapore, China, Indonesia and Hong Kong.

Another Korean, Kim Tae Kuk, who was jailed in Hong Kong for smuggling aliens, was also thought to be part of the gang. Kim was the former head of the *Tenyu* owner's office in the Chinese port of Dalian and had once been captain of the *Tenyu* himself. Korean prosecutors, who suspect he was involved in the hijacking, tried to get him extradited. Then there was Chew Cheng Kiat, a Singaporean also known as Mr Wong, who stood trial in Batam for other hijackings.

The Chinese authorities, for their part, denied involvement in piracy, though Beijing launched a major crackdown on corruption to wipe out the trade. As the investigation of the *Tenyu* drags on, Kim Mae Ja, the wife of ship's engineer Park Ha Joon, struggles on without her husband. The ship's owner stopped paying her husband's salary, but the insurers, with no proof of death, refuse to pay up. The Chinese released the suspected pirates they found on board, though it has long been assumed that the original crew members had been murdered. Kim Mae Ja said of her missing husband, 'I want to believe he is alive, but my faith is waning.'

According to Noel Choong, director of the IMB's Piracy Reporting Centre, attacks in the Straits of Malacca have become increasingly violent and pirates have been abducting crewmen for ransom. In January 2004, four crewmen were killed off the coast of northern Sumatra after negotiations between the pirates and the ship's owners broke down.

No one was safe. In June 2004, 30-year-old Malaysian fisherman Teh Chor Joo was out fishing for shrimp and squid with his brother a few miles off the western coast of peninsular Malaysia when his 30ft wooden fishing boat was approached by men toting rifles. At first, Teh thought they were policemen. 'They fired some shots in the air and told me to get on their boat,' he said.

The pirates were young, about 25 years old, and grim-faced. Some of them were wearing bandanas around their heads. They looked like a gang from a movie, Teh said. All of them were carrying rifles and some had grenade launchers. Teh feared for his life when they told his brother to take their boat back to their village and wait for a phone call.

Teh was then taken to what he believes was Sumatra, 130 miles away on the other side of the Malacca Straits, and held there for eight days. Each night he was moved from one jungle clearing to the next. During the day, he was hidden away in the thick forest. Finally he was bundled onto a boat at gunpoint one morning and dropped off on a passing fishing vessel that took him back to

Malaysia. Teh and his family insist that no ransom was paid, but the story of his kidnapping spread fear in his village of Kuala Sepetang.

'This is the first time one of our fishermen was taken,' said Chua Tiong San, a local politician. 'It's like having a baby snatched from the front room of your house.' The other fishermen were too scared to go out and their boats remained moored in the murky green waters of the Sepetang River. 'We are at the mercy of the pirates,' said Chua.

The following year, 2005, Johan Ariffin was one of a band of pirates who attacked the *Nepline Delima*, a tanker carrying seven thousand tonnes of diesel fuel worth $3million, in the Straits of Malacca. The plot had been hatched, he said, in a coffee shop on Batam. Ariffin had been approached by a Malaysian shipping executive and an Indonesian sailor named Lukman. Ariffin, 44, had been at sea since he was a teenager and had served alongside Lukman as a mechanic. Both of them had been being struggling to find work recently. Lukman told Ariffin that they planned to hijack the *Nepline Delima* and steal the fuel she was carrying.

'All we had to do was board the tanker, tie up the crew and sail to open sea,' said Ariffin. They would meet another tanker coming from Thailand, transfer the fuel and abandon the *Nepline Delima*. It would be easy, Lukman said, as one of the tanker's crew was in on the job. Ariffin was offered $10,000 to man the tanker's engines after they had hijacked her.

As a young man, Ariffin had been on a ship that was attacked by pirates. They had waved *parangs* and threatened to kill everyone, but they only took cash and food. Despite, or perhaps because of, this brush with pirates, he agreed to go along with Lukman's plan. 'It is very hard for Indonesian seamen,' he said. 'We all need money.'

Ariffin, Lukman and two other seamen from Batam set out posing as tourists and pretended to snap photos as they took the ferry up the straits to the Malaysian port of Pinang. There they met six other men Lukman had recruited from Aceh, Sumatra's northernmost province. 'They weren't seamen,' said Ariffin. 'We needed their muscles.'

After stealing a fibreglass speedboat from a nearby beach and painting it blue, they loaded it with petrol, a GPS device, food, water, two cell phones and five freshly sharpened *parangs*. After midnight on 16 June, they set off into the straits. Meanwhile, the inside man on board the tanker was texting the *Nepline Delima*'s position course and speed. Once they had located the ship, all they had to do was wait for their man to take his turn on watch.

In the early hours of the morning, the other pirates slipped onto the tanker, their faces covered with ski masks, while Ariffin stayed below guarding the speedboat. He heard a crewman cry out '*Lanun!*' – 'Pirates!' – as the *parang*-wielding gang tried to round up the crew, who put up some resistance. Meanwhile Lukman and two others quickly took over the bridge. The tanker's distress signal had already been disabled. They flicked on the public address system and started beating the captain, forcing him to order the crew to surrender. 'Please, they are killing me,' he shouted.

The crewmen then surrendered. They were blindfolded, tied up and locked in a cabin. Some were bleeding. There were sixteen of them, but the pirates had the ship's manifest and they knew one was missing. They scoured the ship for 30 minutes, but could not find the seventeenth crewman. There was no time to continue the search, so Ariffin tied the speedboat to the ship's rail and clambered on board to man the engines. The pirates set a new course for the open sea where the Thai tanker was waiting, but an hour later Ariffin got a frantic call from Lukman on the bridge. Their speedboat was gone. The missing crewman had taken it, stranding them on the tanker.

Ariffin cranked the *Nepline Delima*'s engines up to full throttle in a desperate attempt to reach international waters. But even at top speed the tanker could make only about ten knots. Within hours the Malaysian marine police had cut off their escape from the straits. There was nothing they could do. Ariffin went up on the deck, lit a cigarette and waited for the authorities to board.

The missing crewman was 27-year-old Mohamed Hamid, who had been asleep in his cabin when the pirates had boarded. Awoken by the ship's siren, he had hidden while the rest of the crew were being rounded up. He was under the bunk in his cabin when the pirates came in. 'Their torchlight caught my knees and chest, but for some reason they didn't see me,' he said. 'I was terrified.'

Later Mohamed moved out of his hiding place. He watched surreptitiously as the pirates beat other crew members and his terror turned to anger. 'My colleagues were getting hit really badly,' he said. 'I had to do something.'

Then he heard the captain's pleas over the Tannoy. He was making his way to the bridge to surrender when one of the pirates grabbed him and put a *parang* to his throat. 'I though this is my death,' said Mohamed. Instinct took over. He hit the pirate with his elbow and slipped from his grasp. Jumping down three flights of stairs, he scurried under some pipes on the main deck and lay there, reciting Muslim prayers and trying to compose himself. Then he saw the rope tied to the railing leading to the pirates' speedboat.

As he slipped over the ship's side, he caught his foot on the rail, but landed in the pirates' boat. He had a blunt penknife in his pocket and it took several agonising minutes to hack through the thick rope that tied the motorboat to the ship. Once he was adrift, the tanker quickly disappeared into the night. In total darkness, Mohamed groped around for the ignition switch, feeling his way along the wires from the motor. In the distance he could still hear the sound of the captain's cries over the ship's Tannoy as the pirates beat him. Mohamed had never piloted a speedboat before but after ten minutes he managed to fire up the engine and roar away.

With little idea of where the shore was, Mohamed now found himself lost in the middle of a rainstorm. 'I prayed to Allah. "You brought me this far, please show me the way,"' he said.

After five hours the fuel ran out, but Mohamed found a spare tank. The following morning he struck lucky. He spotted a group of fishermen, who directed him to a nearby marine police station. Six police boats headed out and caught up with the *Nepline Delima*. After a six-hour standoff, the gang freed the crew and surrendered.

Aggressive patrolling in the Straits of Malacca cut down on the number of pirate attacks for a while, but few raiders had been arrested and it was feared that they were just lying low. On 2 July 2006, a Japanese cargo carrier heading for Aceh province in Indonesia was attacked. The pirates stole cash and construction materials belonging to the UN's World Food Programme. Two days later a speedboat was seen approaching another UN-chartered cargo carrier. Its crew used high-pressure fire hoses and floodlights trained on the pirates' boat to repel them, but were still chased for about five minutes before the pirates vanished. These two attacks took place not far from each other and it was thought that they may been carried out by the same band.

On 13 August 2007 the tug boat *Brantas 15* was attacked while towing the barge *Singa Besar* from Penang to the port of Belawan in northeast Sumatra. Ten pirates boarded the tug some 35 miles north of Belawan and destroyed all the communications equipment. They then stole the crew's personal belongings and the ship's documents and left, taking the captain and chief engineer with them. The two men were released two weeks later.

Malaysia's marine police had some success on 16 February 2009, when they captured a group of seven Indonesian pirates who had been attacking vessels in the Straits of Malacca. The pirates fired three grenades at the police boat but could not make their escape because the police had damaged the engine on their boat. One of the captured pirates was wounded by the police gunfire, but three of them managed to get away. They were thought to be part of a gang that had stolen $111,000 from ships over the previous year.

Three days later two crewmen were taken from a Singapore-registered tug and barge. The tug MLC *Nancy 5*, towing the barge *Miclyn 3316*, was attacked by 12 armed pirates at 2.30pm – broad daylight – in the northern part of the Straits. The tug's communication equipment and some personal effects were taken, and the captain and chief engineer were abducted. The second officer and the seven remaining crewmen headed for Penang 90 miles away to report the kidnapping to the authorities. Four days later the two abductees were released, but it was not revealed whether a ransom had been paid.

CHAPTER 11
THE SOUTH CHINA SEA

Beyond the Malacca Straits, pirates are active in the area around the Anambas and Natuna Besar islands in the South China Sea. Some stray further south into the Karimata Strait off Borneo, the gateway from the Java Sea.

On 11 December 1992 the *Baltimar Zephyr* was about 30 hours from Singapore, on her way from Freemantle to Kolkata (Calcutta) A 300ft-long mixed cargo carrier with a gross registered tonnage of 2,854, she was fully laden with containers and riding low in the water. There was a stiff breeze and a six-foot swell but her speed of 12 knots and just six feet of freeboard would present no obstacle for pirates.

The commanding officer, Captain John Bashforth, was British. The Chief Officer, Teodolfo Pereja, was a Filipino. For the moment, they felt safe. They were far from the Straits of Malacca. Their cargo was mining equipment and tractors, which were too bulky to be offloaded at sea, and they were too far from shore to be pestered by small-time crooks after the contents of the safe and the crew's meagre possessions. The only danger came from Indonesian navy personnel eager to supplement their wages with a little thievery.

It was a moonless night and on the bridge with the captain and chief officer was Able Seaman Charlito de Vera. Around 30 years of age, he had joined the ship in Hong Kong the previous month before it had sailed for Australia. Captain Bashforth remained on the bridge discussing company business with Pereja, and de Vera said later that he overheard the chief officer tell the captain he had a stash of cash hidden where no pirate would find it, as he intended to spend $2,000 on a computer when they reached Singapore.

To the aft of the accommodation block was an external stairway that led up to the bridge. This gave access to the three cabin decks, but only through watertight doors. Inside each one was another wooden door. At around 9pm, de Vera had checked that all the doors leading to the accommodation block were locked. Anyone trying to gain access would have to force these doors, though in some cases pirates have been found to have a set of master keys. In this case, one of the locks was later found to have a piece of metal jammed in it. This could have been done by a pirate or it could have been sabotaged earlier by a disaffected crewman.

At around 10.45pm, Captain Bashforth went below, somewhat later than usual. He left Pereja working under the muted lights of the chart room, adjoining the bridge. The radio room was also next to the bridge, but it was kept locked to prevent crewmen making unauthorised calls home. Other communications equipment included a VHF radio, Inmarsat satellite phone, telex and mobile phones capable of making international calls. There was also an internal telephone system linking the bridge to each cabin.

De Vera was on watch. The seven large windows gave him a panoramic view of the containers on the deck below and the prow of the ship cutting through the water. He also kept an eye on the port and starboard radar screens. However, these left a blind spot to the stern. As this is the quarter most pirate attacks come from, some masters mount a dedicated watch to stern when in pirate waters, but as they were not yet in the Straits of Malacca, de Vera was only told to check to aft every 20 minutes. When the man on watch went out to check the stern, he had to unlock the door from the bridge and step out onto the external walkway, then scan the ship's wake for small craft. That night de Vera saw nothing. He was also insistent that he had remembered to lock the door to the bridge each time he returned from making an inspection.

While the rest of the crew relaxed in their cabins below, Pereja and de Vera went about their business on the bridge. Then, around midnight, de Vera said he heard a noise and turned to see Pereja with his hands in the air. A man wearing sunglasses with a bandana around his face was holding a gun to his head. He did not know how the pirate had got on board. He might have approached from the aft in a rubber dinghy that could remain unseen in the turbulence of the wake, and for 18 minutes out of every 20, no one was checking the stern. Otherwise a boat might have approached from the side. A boarder could easily have cleared the rail on the crest of a wave and remained hidden from the lookout on the bridge by the containers.

The pirate indicated that both men should lie on the floor, then went over to the radio room and tried to get in. Pereja and de Vera made it clear that they did not have a key. The pirate then smashed the starboard radar screen. It was thought that he did this so he could escape back to the mother ship that had brought him from shore without being detected. Next he tried again to get into the radio room. When he failed, he slashed cables of the VHF radio on the bridge and the internal telephone system.

The pirate now put a gun to de Vera's head and asked, 'Officer? Officer?'

De Vera looked at Pereja. The gunman then pulled Pereja to his feet and pushed him through the internal door to the cabins. About five minutes later de Vera heard a shot. Pereja's body was later found in the captain's day room. He had been forced to kneel, then shot through the back of the head. The safe was open, but the *Baltimar Zephyr*'s Danish owners did not think there would have been much money in it. On the table lay US$153, AUS$150 and HK$240. It is thought that this belonged to Captain Bashforth. Pereja's cash was never found.

The body of the captain was found two floors below. It seems that he had tried to escape, but he had broken his toe in an accident the previous week and was not as agile as he would normally have been. He had tried to barricade himself in the toilet on A Deck below, but the gunman had caught him, putting a shot in his thigh and chest. This had hit his heart and killed him.

De Vera did not hear these shots, but they woke the

ship's cook Manuel Agravante. He looked out of his cabin and saw the captain lying on the floor. Beside him was a gunman wearing a ski mask. Agravante ducked back inside his cabin and locked the door. Someone tried to get in, but gave up after a few minutes.

Able Seaman Igano also heard the shots but remained in his cabin. After about 40 minutes he began a low conversation with Able Seaman Roswell in the next cabin. They were unsure what to do. Were a murderous gang of pirates still on board? Or were they risking their lives leaving the bridge unattended? The pair squeezed out of the portholes in their cabins and hid in a crane until they could be sure there were no more pirates about.

On the floor above, the chief engineer and second engineer heard voices talking in a language they did not recognise. Second Officer Gueverra also heard the shots and stayed in his cabin, eventually sounding the alarm by holding his cigarette lighter under the smoke detector. The rest of the crew emerged from their hiding places to find that the bridge had been unmanned for 90 minutes. Gueverra put out a distress call. A lookout spotted a speedboat and Gueverra ordered the crew to prepare Molotov cocktails. In the distance they spotted what might have been the mother ship, but no further attack was made.

The owners of the *Baltimar Zephyr* told Gueverra to continue heading for Singapore. A new captain would be sent out to them. However, when the cargo ship met the cutter bringing the new captain, they were intercepted by the Indonesian Navy and the *Baltimar Zephyr* was taken to the Indonesian port of Tanjung Uban. There the crew were interrogated and beaten for four or five hours a day. The Indonesian authorities concluded that the crew had mutinied and killed the captain and first officer.

'They told us we were in mutiny,' said Charlito de Vera. 'I know it was pirates. I saw a man in our ship. I saw a gun.'

Nevertheless, de Vera said he and the rest of the crew had admitted to mutiny, signing a document in a language they did not understand, before they were released. The Indonesian investigators produced no evidence – or even a credible motive. Both Captain Bashforth and First Officer Pereja were popular with the men. De Vera only volunteered that he had heard of Pereja's stash of cash later. If he had taken it, he need never have volunteered that information at all. Eric Ellen, director of the IMB said that one of the crew had been threatened with death if he told what he knew. The implication is that the pirates were, again, from the Indonesian Navy.

Accusations of piracy have also been made against the Chinese authorities. On 21 June 1995 the 1,606-tonne freighter *Hye Mieko* left Singapore, carrying a consignment of cigarettes and camera equipment worth $2million to the port of Kas Kong in Cambodia. She was due to dock on the 24th, but before she reached her destination she was stopped by what appeared to be a Chinese customs cutter. The Chinese authorities denied any knowledge of the cutter, so it was assumed that it was manned by pirates.

Although the *Hye Mieko* broadcast her plight to the world, not a single vessel came to her aid. Her owner, William Tay, hired a small plane and spotted her sailing across the South China Sea, miles off course. In the end she was forced to sail more than a thousand miles through international waters to Shanwei in south China. There she was impounded. The cargo was sold and Tay charged with intending to smuggle cigarettes into China, where contraband is a problem. According to the IMB's Eric Ellen, 'Navies were reluctant to intervene because of the power of China.'

The Chinese Foreign Ministry said 'it was not justified' to accuse members of China's armed forces of hijacking the ship and stated that no report of the incident had been received in Beijing. But Tay described the incident as 'pure daylight robbery'. This was not the first time that Chinese security officials had been accused of acts of piracy. The previous year, the *Alicia Star* was carrying cigarettes out of Singapore when she was hijacked by men in green uniforms and carrying AK-47s. The *Alicia Star* also turned up in the port of Shanwei.

Between 1990 and 1994, Hong Kong's Security Branch said there had been 81 reported instances of unauthorised incursions into Hong Kong waters by Chinese military vessels. Although these were not technically classified as acts of piracy, many of these incursions involved 'maritime theft'.

In April 1998, the Singapore-owned tanker *Petro Ranger* was attacked while sailing from Ho Chi Minh City to Singapore with a cargo of oil and kerosene. The heist was organised with military precision. Twelve pirates wearing balaclava hoods came alongside in a speedboat and climbed aboard. They dragged the terrified Australian captain and crew to the bridge, strapped the captain to a chair and held machetes to his groin and throat, threatening to kill him if he did not cooperate. They then called nearby Hainan island, a southern Chinese territory known for smuggling and corruption scams, by cell phone.

Four days later a lighter flat-bottomed barge pulled up and started to unload the *Petro Ranger*'s $1.5million cargo. Chinese Border Defence officials then showed up and escorted the ship into port, where they held the pirates and crew for 30 days of interrogation before they were released. The captain, Kenneth Blyth, was convinced that the Chinese authorities were part of the operation. He thought that the attack had been staged in order to smuggle the ship's cargo into China – and that the ship's owners were involved.

'What on earth would we have to gain?' said Tan Cheng Meng, executive director of Petroships, the company that owns the *Petro Ranger*, who denies any involvement. However, like Blyth, Petroships officials suspect that the Chinese authorities – who never prosecuted the case – were involved. 'What the Chinese did was totally irresponsible and deplorable,' said Tan. 'They let the pirates go despite overwhelming evidence. They got their money and want to wash their hands of the whole mess.'

Blyth also claimed that the pirates knew the names and address of his family in Australia. 'I was supposed to be disposed of,' he said. 'In the fishermen's nets – that's where I was supposed to be.' He has now given up the sea.

The Chinese simply said there was no proof of piracy in this case.

A similar incident occurred in October 1997, when pirates dressed in battle fatigues chased the *Vosa Carrier* in speedboats, boarded her just south of Hong Kong and then brought the ship to the tiny Chinese port of Huilai. According to the IMB, the local authorities forced the crew to sign confessions saying they were smuggling before they were released. The police then used the confessions to confiscate the $2.5million cargo.

It is thought that syndicate bosses were behind the heists. In some Chinese ports, they need only to buy off a few harbour officials. 'These guys get a big dinner and a handful of cash, and they don't ask why the documents don't look right,' said Clay Wild, an investigator who worked on the *Tenyu* case.

In November and December 1998, the Indonesian Navy arrested a number of alleged syndicate members on Batam. One of them was Chew Cheng Kiat, aka Mr Wong. He was said to have confessed to five hijackings, including that of the *Petro Ranger*, in the previous two years, though he argued that he was charged without a proper arrest order and that the arresting officers demanded 50,000 Singapore dollars. Indonesian intelligence officers alleged that he ran a hijacking syndicate that worked the waters between Indonesia and Singapore, and that he operated from a small tanker named the *Pulau Mas*, which stayed in international waters most of the time. When Indonesian authorities boarded Wong's tanker in November, they found 15 pairs of handcuff, 14 ninja-style masks, 15 automatic weapons, three knives, immigration and ship's stamps, false ships' documents, paint and various ships' flags.

Perhaps the Chinese authorities got their act together after the Thai tanker *Siam Xanxai* was hijacked on 8 June 1999 off the Malay coast not far from Singapore by 12 armed men. The 17 Thai crewmen were set adrift in a small boat and rescued near the coast of Indonesia. On 17 June, the *Siam Xanxai* was found, freshly painted and carrying two thousand tones of diesel fuel, in the Chinese port of Shantou. The ship was returned to Thailand while the suspects were charged with smuggling, a crime that carries the death penalty in China.

It is not just large merchant ships that run into trouble in these waters. Small operators pick on yachts. In 1993 Bobby Ernst and Gernot Bernot from Frankfurt in Germany began a round-the-world trip in their yacht, the *Nisos*. They took their time, making extended stays at Cartagena, Salinas in Ecuador, the Galápagos and the Marquesas Islands in French Polynesia. Perhaps ironically, they decided to stop at Mopelia, the last island in the latter archipelago, where the 'Kaiser's pirate' Count Felix von Luckner had lost his ship *Seeadler Sea Eagle*. Having slipped though the Royal Navy blockade on Germany in 1916, he attacked numerous engine-powered, metal-hulled merchant ships with his three-masted windjammer in the Atlantic and Pacific. He claimed it was a tsunami that wrecked the *Seeadler* on Mopelia on 24 August 1917. American prisoners vessels who were with him at the time said the vessel had drifted onto a reef while the prisoners and most of the crew were on the island having a picnic. The wreck can still be seen.

The *Nisos* was sheltering in the lagoon there when a hurricane hit. When the storm abated, the yacht was on land, marooned on a stack of fallen palm trees. It took two months to make her seaworthy again, after which she was towed back into the lagoon on a sled. A tug then towed her to Raitaea, also in French Polynesia, for more repairs.

When the pair set sail again, they knew they were entering a danger zone. Pirates had been reported off Honiara, the capital of the Solomon Islands, off Vanuatu to the south, and around Port Moresby in Papua New Guinea. After that they would be moving on to the Philippines and Indonesia, where piracy had been a traditional occupation for hundreds of years. But the couple were nothing if not adventurous. On 9 November, they left the Java Sea to sail through the Karimata Straight between Borneo and Belitung Island, and into the South China Sea. They would then head directly for Batam, where they planned to clear Indonesian customs.

However, at around 4.30am on the night of the 10th, when they were in the South China Sea, Bobby woke Gernot, telling him that a boat was approaching. She had been watching it on the radar for some time. The boat lay ahead, about one nautical mile to starboard, but was showing no navigation lights. The only thing that was visible was a dim glimmer from the windows of the deck house. Then she suddenly altered course and Gernot had to give the *Nisos* full throttle and turn hard to port to avoid her.

Although the ship had almost run them down, it could have been an honest mistake. Under normal circumstances, the *Nisos* would be required to give way. But they were perfectly visible. The other ship must have seen them and instead of going under her stern, it had aimed straight for their bow. 'Instantly, the situation became clear,' said Gernot. 'They meant to board us.'

From what they could see in the light of their powerful searchlight, the other vessel was a low wooden boat about

30 to 35 feet long. It had a low deckhouse and a wooden roof over the cockpit. Inside they could see men crouching.

The other vessel closed on them again. Gernot grabbed the flare gun and when they were within 50 yards, shot off a red flare and sounded the horn. The vessel veered away, then turned onto a parallel course, pacing them. Ahead the couple saw a red light.

'Another one,' said Bobby. But Gernot was not so sure. It might have been a fishing buoy like the ones they had seen in the Java Sea. But Bobby looked at the radar screen and saw a boat moving in towards them from the port side. Gernot fired another flare – and a shot from his pistol. In the *Nisos*'s spotlight, he saw a motor launch only yards away. It was speeding across their bow, and on the prow was a man holding a torch.

As it seemed likely they were going to be boarded, Bobby went down into the main cabin and hid their money and valuables beneath the floorboards. She pulled on a track suit and hid her long blonde hair under a knitted cap. When she returned to the cockpit, she checked the radar screen and saw that the first boat had vanished. The other held its course about a mile away until daybreak.

In the morning, they saw three large motor vessels running a parallel course. Gradually they got nearer and it was possible to make out that they were crab ships starting their day's work. One of the fishermen waved and flashed his torch. Then the motor vessel dropped to stern and the *Nisos* headed on for the Straits of Malacca.

Gernot Berner and Bobby Ernst had had a narrow escape – from the first ship at least. Others had reported being menaced in these waters. Herbert and Diane Stuemer from Ottawa, making a round-the-world trip in their cruiser *Northern Magic* with their three sons, said they had been pursed in the South China Sea. Single-handed yachtsman Peter Högel also reported being chased by pirates when he sailed through on his yacht *Pandarea*.

The *Nisos* passed on through the Straits of Malacca without further incident, but 230 miles off Sri Lanka they were becalmed and had to continue under engine-power, chugging along at five knots. After the busy shipping lanes of the Malacca Strait, the Gulf of Bengal was practically deserted. On 7 February, Gernot heard a voice over the radio calling to the sailing ship off its port bow. Gernot went out to look around but could not see another vessel. Later, he heard the same voice again. This time when he went out on deck, he saw a boat on the horizon. He got on the radio and asked whether the call was for the *Nisos*. There was no reply.

Gernot now began keeping an eye on the radar. The other boat was gradually approaching and by 1pm it was within three-and-a-half miles. Gernot tried to raise it on the radio twice more, but got no reply. However, a third call was answered. The captain of the other vessel said his boat was called the *Daringi* out of Madras. She was line-fishing and had 18 men on aboard. He asked Gernot how many men were on board the *Nisos*. Gernot said four.

While the conversation was going on, the *Daringi* was pulling ever closer and gradually getting ahead of them. Then Gernot realised that there could not be 18 men on board the *Daringi* – it was too small. He opened the throttle to speed up. The *Daringi* did the same. Gernot changed course. The *Daringi* followed.

Gernot grabbed the flare gun, his pistol and the fire extinguisher, ready to repel boarders. Bobby grabbed the video camera, eager to capture footage of the pirate attack before she hid it. Gernot switched on the boat's Galaxy Inmarsat, scrolled down the menu and hit 'pirate attack'. This transmitted their speed, position and course automatically.

The *Daringi* had now turned and come up astern. A man was standing on the bow ready to board. Gernot sent out a mayday and swung ten degrees to port. The man on the *Daringi*'s forecastle was holding a coil of rope and relaying instructions to the helmsman – one of four men Gernot could see in the cockpit. As the *Daringi* came alongside, the man prepared to jump, aiming to make a soft landing on the *Nisos*'s bimini sunshade. Gernot feared that the rope would then be made fast to the mizzen mast and other pirates would shin across. All he could do was keep steering to port, making the jump impossible.

As the *Daringi* closed again, Gernot fired the flare gun, narrowly missing the man on the forecastle. But he was shaken: the *Daringi* broke off. Gernot now steered away from their intended landfall at Galle on the southern tip of Sri Lanka, as that was where he feared the pirates were headed. The authorities there showed little interest. Radio Colombo did not even reply to his call. Twenty-four hours later the chief of the harbour police at Galle had been informed of the incident, but still nothing was done. Gernot sent some pictures they had taken of the pirates to the Sri Lankan Navy. They sent a patrol boat out to Little Basset Reed, 35 miles from where the attack had taken place, but that was the end of it.

Herbert and Diane Stuemer also escaped from pirates in the South China Sea, and they, too, met more on their way home. It had been a long-held ambition of the Stuemers to sail around the world, so in 1997 they purchased a 40-year-old steel-hulled ketch and filled it with all the latest electronic equipment. They were sailing between the Indonesian island of Lombok and Borneo when they stumbled into one of the world's hotspots for piracy. They were convinced they were being chased, and again the craft that menaced them followed them at night. Diane believed she scared the pursuers off by the simple ruse of putting on a husky voice and broadcasting the message: '*Futuna, Futuna*, this is Northern Magic. Situation sixty-eight. Situation sixty-eight...' There was no *Futuna*. Indeed, there was no other yacht within a hundred miles, but the bogus message seemed to do the trick.

A year later, they were sailing from Kenya, up a thousand miles of lawless coast and around the Horn of Africa. They were well aware of recent attacks that had taken place there and marked the position of each incident with an X on the map. They removed their radar reflector, turned off their VHF radio and decided to run without lights at night in an attempt to make themselves invisible. They would keep in contact with a friend via short-wave radio, which is more difficult to get a directional fix on, and use code when giving their position. All their valuables, including their wedding rings, were safely stowed away, though a little cash was left out in case they need some to give boarders.

Although the International Piracy Reporting Centre in Kuala Lumpur warned them to stay away from the coast, the northerly current there was stronger and the trip would be shorter. So they decided on a course just 60 miles from the coast. On the sixth night out, they were almost run down by a huge tanker because they were not showing lights. Then they were picked out by the tanker's spotlight and switched on their masthead lights, so the ship could see they were a yacht, not a small powered pirate boat.

On the ninth day out, the Stuemers reached Socotra at the mouth of the Gulf of Aden. They then had to decide whether to go round the east of the island and risk meeting a cyclone in the Arabian Sea, or round the west side nearer to the coast of Somalia. They went west. That night, in the midst of the danger zone, there were problems with the engine and a pump failed. By morning, they had made it to the Gulf of Aden, but there was not a breath of wind and they were running low on fuel. They cut the engine speed to save fuel, and then gradually a gentle breeze began to blow. They reached Aden after 13 days – just in time to witness the attack on the USS *Cole* that left 17 American sailors dead.

That was not the end of their problems. They were in the middle of the Gates of Sorrows, the narrow entrance to the Red Sea, when Herbert noticed that a speedboat was heading for them. To the east of them was Yemen; to the west Djibouti. But neither was close enough to get to before the speedboat reached them. When it caught up with them it circled, then came to an abrupt stop astern. The fishing lines the Stuemers were trawling behind the *Northern Magic* had wound their way around the speedboat's propeller, leaving it dead in the water while the couple made their way to the comparative safety of the

Red Sea. Their fishing lines had proved an effective anti-pirate device.

But perhaps not all pirates are bad guys. There is a tale told of an Australian named Paul who was hauling some tropical hardwood back home. He was sailing across the Sulu Sea off the Philippines when his yacht was boarded by pirates. They asked him for his GPS. He said he did not have one. They asked for his radio. He did not have a radio either. Then they ask him for his compass. He did not have a compass. Then they demanded money, but were out of luck there too. He had just a few coins in his pocket, which he handed over.

Then one of the pirates said, 'Wait a minute.' He went back the pirate ship and returned with a GPS, a compass, a torch and some food. As he handed over the stuff, the pirate said, 'Be careful.'

CHAPTER 12
BRAZILIAN BRIGANDS

New Zealander Peter Blake was knighted in 1995 for his services to yachting. He had won the Whitbread Round the World Race in 1989 and the Jules Verne Trophy in 1994, circumnavigating the world in 74 days, 22 hours, 17 minutes and 22 seconds in his catamaran *Enza*. (The record has since been beaten five times.) He also led the New Zealand team that won the Americas Cup in 1995 and 2000.

He then went on to become an environmentalist, heading the Cousteau Society, an environmental group founded in 1973 by the undersea explorer Jacques Cousteau. In 2001 Blake was named special envoy for the UN Environment Programme and led an expedition up the Amazon in his 119ft yacht *Seamaster* to monitor global warning and pollution. He spent two months in the upper Amazon and Rio Negro, where he met nothing but 'friendly, warm, hospitable people'. On 6 December 2001, he was anchored off Macapá, Brazil, not far from the tiny fishing village of Fazendinha at the mouth of the Amazon delta (some 1,800 miles north of Rio de Janeiro), where the *Seamaster* waited to clear customs. The next day Blake and his 11-man crew planned to make their way out into the Atlantic via the Canal do Norte – the northern channel.

That evening, they were moored around two hundred yards off the riverbank and the entire crew went ashore for a meal. It had been a long trip. Before their months spent exploring the upper reaches of the Amazon, they had visited in the Antarctic in March, then refitted in Buenos Aires before making the long haul north.

When the group returned to the ship at around 9pm, they strung up hammocks on deck. It was impossible to sleep in the cabins in the sweltering heat, though Leon Sefton, son of Blake's partner, and a young English student named Charlie Dymock ventured below. The rest of the crew downed a few more beers under an awning at the aft of the schooner and turned on some music, dreaming of the cold Atlantic trade winds they would enjoy the next day.

Ashore, whatever port security there was, was stood down. Harbour master Claudio Roberto Pareira Lira was watching football in his wooden shack. The night was pitch black when, at around 10.15pm, a dinghy approached the *Seamaster*. In it were six members of the gang known as the *Ratos de Agua* (Water Rats), who were notorious for attacking cargo vessels in the Amazon delta. Their leader was Rubens da Silva Souza and they were armed with sub-machine-guns, shotguns and pistols.

The *Seamaster* was ablaze with light and must have looked like a glittering prize, alone on the dark waters.

Music rang out across the water making it more seductive. The gringos on board were having a party and were not expecting an attack. *Estrangeiros* rarely put up a fight. No one noticed when the pirates, wearing balaclavas and crash helmets, slipped aboard. As one approached the aft deck where the crew were drinking, Blake stood up and said, 'Get the fuck off my boat.'

The pirate brandished a pistol. Alistair Moore, the father of Roger Moore, another crewmember, rushed forward and threw his beer in the pirate's face. The pirate struck back with the butt of his pistol and Moore sank to his knees. Meanwhile Blake shouted, 'This is getting serious!' and ran below.

Leon Sefton heard the mêlée above and came out of his cabin to find out what was going on. Through the door to his stateroom, he saw Blake grabbing a weapon. As Leon headed topside, he saw a pirate above him on the companionway, later identified as 27-year-old Isael Pantoja da Costa. He pointed a gun at Leon, who instinctively raised his hands. At that moment, Blake came out wielding a rifle he had used on a previous trip to ward off polar bears. At the sight of him, da Costa fled. Blake charged up the companionway after him and shots rang out.

Leon now took refuge in Blake's stateroom. Another gun was lying on the bunk, so he grabbed it, along with some ammunition and headed back topside to help Blake. They were going to need all the firepower they could muster. At that point Leon believed that they were all going to be killed.

As Blake emerged onto the upper deck, he was confronted by da Costa. He fired, knocking the pistol out of the pirate's hand. The bullet hit da Costa's fingers, severing one of them. It then entered his arm and came out of his elbow. Blake was trying to reload when Leon arrived from below. Leon handed Blake some ammunition, but he waved it away. Instead, he told him to go and open the forward hatch, so they would have an escape route if the situation deteriorated. Leon did as he was ordered.

Alerted by da Costa's howls of pain, 23-year-old Ricardo Colares Tavares turned to see Blake framed in the brightly lit companionway. His gun was jammed. Tavares took aim with his .32 pistol and shot Blake twice in the back. One bullet passed his heart, ripping away the aorta and killing him. When Leon returned, he found Blake lying sprawled face up on the deck with his head on the companionway ladder. He was not moving. It was clear that he was already dead, but for 15 minutes, Sefton and the other crewmen tried vainly to revive him.

By this time, the fight was over. The pirates had taken over the schooner. They were threatening the crew with their guns and shouted, 'Money! Money!' The pirates then began ransacking the yacht, grabbing anything of value – money, cameras, lenses, watches. They even took the Omega off Blake's still warm arm. Stealing one of the *Seamaster*'s dinghies, they made their escape, firing wildly back at the schooner. A bullet hit crewman Geoff Bullock in the back, though he lived to tell the tale.

During the attack, the boarders had injured two other crew members with knives, but the remaining seven were unhurt. All of them except Peter Blake recovered.

The Brazilian authorities were less than sympathetic. 'It is certain that Sir Peter Blake was the first to shoot,' said

Manolo Pasana, the chief homicide investigator. 'He would probably still be alive if his gun had not jammed.'

Nine men were arrested in connection with the murder. The man who actually fired the fatal shots, Ricardo Colares Tavares, was sentenced to 36 years and nine months, but under Brazilian law will probably serve no more than 30. Five others received sentences ranging from 26 to 35 years. Three were given suspended sentences.

More than thirty thousand people turned out for Peter Blake's memorial service in New Zealand, though he was buried in the small English village of Warblington, where his family had settled in the 1970s.

Pirates in Brazil prefer to attack ships in port. At first they usually targeted the money in the captain's safe and the watches, money and jewellery of the crew. Then in the 1990s, they began to go after cargo, seeking out electronic products and other expensive goods that could be worth millions of dollars per container. They knew which ships to hit by obtaining copies of the manifests, and by 1998, Brazil was rated the fifth worst nation in the world for pirate attacks. But as the port improved efficiency, getting ships in and out quicker, less time was left for the pirates to steal. Ports also improved security.

The security chief at Santos, the port of São Paulo, Percival de Araujo Costa, had been trained at Quantico, Virginia and the Marine Corps jungle warfare school at Camp Lejeune, near Jacksonville, North Carolina. On a hot summer night in January 1998, Araujo and six of his officers faced down a gang of four pirates as they patrolled the piers. It was Uzis against pistols. One of the officers ran out of ammo, but another did not hesitate. He raced through the darkness and dodged bullets, crates and other port paraphernalia to get close enough to let go another round. 'If you think, you don't go,' said Araujo.

By the time the shooting was over, one pirate had been killed and two crew members of the British-flagged oil tanker *Isomeria* wounded. Araujo was confident that this shootout had ended organised dockside attacks at Santos, one of the busiest ports in South America. However, attacks were still on the increase in Rio de Janeiro, though many were not reported. 'Some pirates get aboard a ship in Rio,' said the top regional executive of a leading shipping line serving Brazil. 'If no one has been hurt, we don't report anything.'

Captains were also ordered to keep quiet. It was not considered good business to be seen as a patsy of the pirates. Besides, shipping lines cannot afford to have ships tied up while officials conduct their investigations. 'What's 24 hours to do an investigation?' said Araujo. 'We need to talk to the crew members, we need to get descriptions.' Consequently few pirates are caught or prosecuted.

Other yachts had been attacked too. On 5 August 2001, the South African yacht *Macanudo* was boarded by pirates off the north coast of Brazil. The 45ft catamaran had only been delivered to her owners Russ and Gail Covey in Cape Town the previous year. The couple were in their fifties and had been sailing around the coast of South Africa for more than 30 years. Now that Russ had taken early retirement, they had decided to spend more time on the sea. In their first trip on their new boat, they ventured further afield, sailing to the Seychelles. They had intended to sail on through the Red Sea and the Suez Canal into the

Mediterranean, but as the Gulf of Aden was reportedly swarming with pirates, they headed back to Cape Town.

In April 2001, they set sail again. This time they were heading across the Atlantic to the Caribbean. They passed the island of Fernando de Noronha, two hundred miles off the easterly tip of Brazil, then made landfall at Fortaleza. They spent the next three months leisurely exploring the coast and gradually moving northwards. On 1 August they anchored in the lee of Lençóis Island, a well-known ecological haven. Their next stop was to have been the former French penal colony of Devil's Island, but they were so enamoured of the scenery of Lençóis, they stayed on.

A fisherman came out to them to sell prawns and invited them to visit his village, which was no more than a mile away. Russ was a Spanish speaker and could make himself understood by the Portuguese-speaking fishermen. The villagers had a collection of boats, from dug-out canoes to 30ft vessels with diesel engines.

On the fourth day at the anchorage, the Coveys decided to do some bird watching in the nearby mangrove swamp. Taking a camera and binoculars, they set out in their dinghy for the next cove where the mangroves came to the water's edge. As they were looking for a place to land, Russ glanced back at the catamaran. He saw two men on board, turned the dinghy around and raced back to the yacht. As they drew near, he could see that the two men looked like locals. They were barefoot and wearing worn and ragged clothing. The engines were running and they were trying to prise open the main hatch.

As the Coveys got back on board, the men protested that they were just looking, but this did not explain why they had switched on the engine. Several things had been removed from the cockpit, but the door to the companionway that led down to the cabins was locked. Russ ordered the two men off his boat. When they ignored him, he let out a stream of invective in Spanish. This did the trick. They got back into their dugout and paddled away.

As the sun set that night, the Coveys feared that the men might return, perhaps bringing others with them. The fisherman they had met before paddled out with his family. The intruders, he said, had not come from his village. They were probably from Belém, the other side of the Amazon delta from Macapá.

Just after midnight, the Coveys had already retired when they heard movement on the deck above. Russ crept up into the cockpit. Intruders were helping themselves to the outboard motor of the dinghy. As Russ turned a high-powered spotlight on the men, one of them leapt over the side and the other paddled off in a dugout. Russ kept the spotlight trained on him and Gail sounded the foghorn. This scared the second man so much that he too leapt into the water and swam for safety among the mangroves.

There were other boats out that night, but none came to the Coveys' assistance. One picked up the two intruders, who were plainly part of a gang. For the rest of the night the Coveys kept watch. In the morning, a larger boat came menacingly close, but by then the *Macanudo* had weighed anchor and was heading for Trinidad and Tobago. Later the Coveys sailed through the pirate-infested waters of Venezuela, but this time they sailed in convoy and stayed in touch with other cruisers.

In 1995, a German couple, Jürgen and Hannelore Boehnke, made a similar trip along the coast of Brazil in their 30ft cruiser, *Rike*, which Jürgen had built himself. On 24 April, they set sail from Salvador de Bahia heading for Recife, some 420 miles up the coast. As the wind dropped, Jürgen switched on the engine. They were also assisted by a current that drew them northwards towards the Caribbean.

On the second night they had reached the town of Piaçabucu. It was around midnight and they could see the navigation lights that marked the mouth of the Rio São Francisco. It was then that they noticed the navigation lights were moving. Then, around 1.45am, the lights suddenly disappeared. Soon afterwards the Boehnkes heard a crunch. They had run aground. A large breaker turned the boat on its beam end, but that was the end of their buffeting. The tide was running out fast and they were left high and dry.

Jürgen turned off the running lights, switched on the Emergency Position Indicating Radio Beacon and inspected the boat. Despite the impact, the hull was intact. There was some sand and water inside the boat, but that had come in through a hatch that had not been tied down properly. The couple then made a distress call on the emergency frequency, 2.182 Mhz. Radio Araçuçu replied. The Boehnkes gave their position and explained what had happened. They were told to do nothing. Other distress calls garnered garbled responses. An amateur radio enthusiast in Norfolk, Virginia contacted them, but was in no position to offer any help. They even tried calling on aircraft distress frequencies. Above they could see two planes alter course but that was no help either.

In the morning, they inspected the boat again. The keel was slightly bent and the rudder had been broken. A man approached and took them to a nearby farmhouse which had a phone. The owner could speak English. He told them that he would send two boats to pull them off the beach.

By the time they returned to their stranded yacht, a crowd had gathered. People were climbing all over it, but the Boehnkes had locked the companionway. The two fishing boats turned up, and they refloated the *Rike* and towed her back to Piaçabucu. They were stuck there for two weeks while a local blacksmith made a makeshift rudder out of metal sheeting and an iron pipe. Every night they were menaced by small boats. The Boehnkes scared them off with infra-red acoustic warning devices that went off every half-hour. A Frenchman who ran an ice factory there told them that eight yachts had been robbed in the vicinity in the previous year and later they heard that four motor cruisers had disappeared 70 miles up the coast in Maceió.

Eventually the auxiliary rudder was ready, but Jürgen was not happy with it. He requested a tow to Maceió where they could have the boat fixed properly and called the harbour master to say they were coming. As the steering was still not working, they would need an extra man on board with a steering oar to make the trip. He was not someone they had seen before, nor were the men on the fishing boat that arrived to give them a tow. A bag of white powder changed hands.

The tow boat had turned up two hours late, so it was after dark when they set off, hoping to make Maceió by daybreak. Once out to sea, the Boehnkes followed their position on the GPS. After a few hours, they noticed that they were being towed towards some cliffs and shoals. They tried to alert the man with the steering oar, but he ignored them. Then they tried to raise the fishing boat on the VHF radio. Fearing for her life, Hannelore grabbed the flare pistol and pointed it at the man with the steering oar. He fled to the bow and shouted to his mates in the fishing boat.

Ahead they could see the lights of Maceió, but there were more lights to the side of them. A boat was running a parallel course about a mile to starboard. Then an unlit boat appeared dead head. The crew shouted to the men on the fishing boat and pointed at the *Rike*. The large boat then moved in behind them and shone a spotlight on the *Rike*. Jürgen now turned on the engine, reckoning they could make it to Maceió under their own power if necessary. Hannelore got on the VHF radio and got through to another Brazilian station, but it told them, again, to do nothing. Finally, at their wits' end, the Boehnkes cut the towline and fired off two red distress flares.

Then, over channel 16 the couple heard a welcome voice from an officer aboard the *Görlitz*, a German vessel, and were rescued. Later they discovered that the bag of white powder was sugar. It had been poured into their diesel tank in an attempt to make the engine seize. But the sabotage had failed as the fuel intake pipe was two inches above the bottom of the tank.

CHAPTER 13

PIRATES OF THE CARIBBEAN

One of the most enduring mysteries of the Caribbean is what happened to the 55ft, custom-built, steel-hulled sloop, the *Nordstern IV*. After her distinctive tomato-red hull with a yellow stripe was last seen slipping out of English Harbour, Antigua, on 18 March 1977, vanished. On board were German skipper Manfred Lehnen, his girlfriend Christine Kump and four German charter guests. The guests were never seen again and have been officially declared dead. However, the German police file on Lehnen and Kump remained open as the authorities in Düsseldorf, the home port of the *Nordstern IV*, believed that they were investigating an extraordinary case of piracy.

Manfred Lehnen was a butcher by trade. In 1976, at the age of 42, he sold his thriving business in Düsseldorf and left his wife and two young children. He took a large loan – more than 130,000 Deutschmarks, about $80,000 – to purchase the *Nordstern IV* and moved to the Mediterranean to start a new life as a charter skipper. It did not work out. He was not attracting enough clients to pay the bank back. By the end of the season, it became clear that he could not make a living in the charter business in Europe, so he decided to try his hand in the more lucrative charter waters of the Caribbean. In December 1976, the *Nordstern IV* set off from Spain and crossed the Atlantic.

But the Caribbean was no bed of roses either: Lehnen did not get his first customer until late February 1977. The client later told the German police that when he left the ship at the end of the month, Lehnen became quite emotional. He talked of quitting the charter business altogether and just 'taking off'. Early the following month Lehnen was joined in Antigua by his girlfriend Christine Kump. A Swiss national, 39-year-old Kump was a scientist with a PhD in chemistry. She had met Lehnen while he was sailing in the Mediterranean and had now left her family and children to begin a new life with him at sea.

By then Lehnen had a new charter booking. The clients were four Germans who had planned and paid for the cruise of a lifetime: they wanted to cross the Atlantic from Antigua to Lisbon under sail. The crossing would take six weeks, with a stop at the Azores. Lehnen would then have to sail back to the Caribbean, possibly without passengers, but he needed the money. The fee was four thousand Deutschmarks – around $2,500.

In the middle of March, Lehnen's four passengers arrived from Germany. They were 44-year-old engineer Hugo Rosel, 34-year-old surgeon Helmut Kuhn, 33-year-old Jürgen Gross and 22-year-old medical student Ulrike Müller. By all accounts they were delighted when they saw the *Nordstern IV* and were excited about the trip.

But that was the last their family and friends were to hear from them.

They were last seen by catamaran owner Rudolph Wagner, who told the German police that he had seen the *Nordstern IV* with Lehnen, Kump and all four guests aboard leaving English Harbour in the late afternoon of 18 March 1977. When the *Nordstern IV* failed to turn up in the Azores and no word was heard from either the crew or the passengers, the police were alerted in both Antigua and Germany. It was initially thought that the *Nordstern IV* had been lost with all hands in a storm at sea. Then the press began running stories that the sloop had been seized by pirates. Later it was claimed she was being used to run drugs from South America into the United States. The story became so big that the German news magazine *Stern* sent a reporter to the Caribbean.

The police, the families of the missing passengers and the journalist from *Stern* quickly concluded that the *Nordstern IV* had not been lost in a storm. There was no record of any bad weather in the area at the time. Other possibilities were examined. No collisions had been reported. The *Nordstern IV* could have been lost in a fire or some other freak accident, but Lehnen and Kump were experienced sailors and it was thought that any plausible scenerio would have been survivable. Indeed, there was clear evidence that Lehnen, Kump and the *Nordstern IV* had survived.

Just two days after the sloop had been seen leaving English Harbour with her passengers, Lehnen and Kump were back in Antigua. They had collected and signed for a replacement sail at the airport. This in itself was a puzzle.

Why would you start out on a six-week charter if you knew a new sail was about to be delivered?

Three days later, on 23 March, the *Nordstern IV*'s distinctive red hull and broad yellow stripe were seen 175 miles to the south in Fort de France, Martinique, by businessman Heinz Müller, a guest on another charter boat. In May, the boat was seen again at Dominica, then off Bequia in the Grenadines to the south, where its striking colours and classic lines were noted by local historian Nolly Simmons, among others. In June and July, harbour pilot Mike Forshaw and boat builder Ray Smith both remembered seeing the boat in different locations and at different times around Grenada. But Smith recalled that the colour had been changed. The hull was now white with a blue stripe.

Dr Antje Kuhn, the wife of missing passenger Helmut Kuhn, spent months in the Caribbean after her husband's disappearance circulating pictures of Lehnen, Kump and the *Nordstern IV*'s four guests. The *Stern* reporter then followed up, interviewing witnesses. All of them positively identified Lehnen and Kump as the only two people they had seen with the boat. No one had seen anyone else. The four passengers had disappeared.

Antje Kuhn and Brigitte Hardert, the girlfriend of another missing passenger, unearthed other anomalies about the trip. Lehnen had never obtained clearance to leave Antigua, something almost unheard of if one is setting out on an Atlantic crossing. Eyewitnesses also reported that they had not taken enough stores on board to feed six people on such a long journey.

In July Kump was again seen in Bequia, this time alone

and apparently without a boat. German yachtsman and illustrator Peter Frey met her at a party. He recalled little of the conversation that evening, but remembered the woman clearly. 'You could not forget that face,' he said. After this last confirmed sighting, the trail went completely cold and remains so to this day.

In the years since the disappearance, there has been much speculation about what happened on board the *Nordstern IV*. Both the police in Düsseldorf and the families of the missing guests believe Lehnen and Kump were responsible for the deaths of their four passengers. Lehnen was depressed and deeply in debt, and faced the possible confiscation of his boat on his return to Europe. The widely held theory is that he planned to disappear together with the boat and start yet another new life with Kump. To do that he would have to fake an accident in which the boat and all hands appeared to have been lost at sea. If they killed their passengers and threw them overboard, their disappearance would be reported to the authorities and eventually it would be concluded that the *Nordstern IV*, along with her crew, had sunk.

However, it seems that they assumed that news of the missing passengers would only spread slowly through to the sailing community of the southern Caribbean. It would also have taken a little time for them to arrange to have their sloop repainted. Fearing they had been seen, the police believe that Lehnen had fled south to Venezuela, where he returned to work in the meat trade. The couple separated and it was rumoured that Kump was living alone on a small Caribbean island.

Yachtman and journalist Klaus Hympendahl, who has

looked into the case, has his own theory. Back in 1977, he was a young man looking for a berth on a sailing boat in the Caribbean. Two advertisements in *Yacht* magazine caught his eye. One was for a berth on the *Nordstern IV*; the other was for an Italian ketch called the *Muenster*. After weeks of deliberation, he chose the *Muenster*. 'That probably saved my life,' he said.

After investigating the case for his book *Pirates Aboard*, Hympendahl concluded that the *Nordstern IV* had been pressed into service by drug smugglers trafficking between Colombia and the south coast of the United States, and that Lehnen and Kump had later been killed. He quoted Dieter Timm, the Caribbean expert of *Yacht* magazine, who said, 'If, after its scheduled departure date, the *Nordstern IV* was still actually seen over there, it can be assumed that the German crew was no longer on board. In that case, this steel sloop, which could easily have been sunk by contract, was hijacked by pirates. The island group of the Grenadines has become a major trade centre for drug smugglers.'

But the mystery persists. For years, Lehnen's wife lived in poverty in a dingy one-room apartment in Düsseldorf as the repayment for her husband's outstanding debt for the purchase of *Nordstern IV* was still being deducted from her welfare cheque each month. Lehnen's two sons had never had any contact with him after he left for the Caribbean, but firmly believed their father was capable of murdering his charter guests and probably did.

The disappearance of the *Nordstern IV* had other unintended consequences. The mother of Ulrike Müller, despairing at her daughter's death, later took her own life by drowning. Creepily, when the *Nordstern IV* was sold to Lehnen, it already had a sinister history. Someone had been murdered on board. However, no one has posited a satisfactory supernatural theory. According to Düsseldorf Police's crime file No. 111/5 Js300/77, the disappearance of the *Nordstern IV* is a case of piracy by its own crew.

Normally piracy in the Caribbean is a much more straightforward affair. When Jochen Winter, a travel consultant in Germany, married in 2001, he wanted to take his wife Regina on a Caribbean cruise that she would never forget. They flew to the French island of Martinique and picked up the yacht *Agatikan* at Le Marin, at the southern end of the island. An agent for the charter company Sunsail showed them around the boat and everything seemed shipshape. On board, along with the customary bottle of rum, the newlyweds found a bottle of champagne. Jochen had been sailing in the Caribbean the previous year, but the agent still ran through a series of tips and warnings. One of them was to avoid Cumberland Bay on St Vincent, where a number of outboard motors had disappeared recently. Instead, the agent said, they should put in at Wallilabou Bay.

The next morning they left Martinique, heading southwards for St Lucia. The sun was up, the sea was calm and a cool breeze sped them through the water. At St Lucia, they put in at Rodney Bay, clearing customs there. Then they sailed on around the Great Horseshoe Reef and into Marigot Bay, where they were greeted by friendly boys in boats who came out to sell them fruit and local craft work. Mooring there for the night, they had dinner in a bar and restaurant that over looked the bay, and then one more cocktail back on the boat before turning in. Everything seemed idyllic.

The next morning the Winters set sail for St Vincent, heading for Wallilabou Bay. There was an immigration office there, where they could clear customs. On the way, they passed Cumberland Bay, where a number of yachts lay at anchor. Jochen was surprised by this, after the advice the Sunsail agent had given, but nevertheless they pushed on.

The sun was setting as they entered Wallilabou Bay. A boat boy rowed out to them and directed them to a mooring. It was then that they noticed they were the only boat in the bay. But the mooring was directly opposite the local restaurant, the sun had gone down and it was too late to move on that night.

After mooring, they rowed ashore, but the customs office was already closed. They ate in the restaurant, then rowed back to the yacht for the night. The boat boy was on hand to see they were OK and asked them whether they would give him a T-shirt. They said that they did not have a spare, but gave him EC$15 and bid him goodnight. They had one more cocktail on the deck and enjoyed the starry sky before making for bed around midnight.

But Regina and Jochen did not sleep easy that night. The boat heaved at its moorings. Then Jochen thought he heard someone clambering aboard. He got up and peered through the hatch. No one was there. Then suddenly, at about 1.15am, they heard loud footsteps on the companionway. Someone was coming down the ladder. Before they were fully awake a bright light shone in their faces.

'Police!' barked the intruder. There were a number of men on board and the Winters found themselves looking down the muzzles of at least two guns. They sat up in their bunk and raised their hands. It was soon apparent that the intruders were not the police. 'Got any drugs?' they asked. 'Where's the money?'

Jochen denied having any money. In fact, he had a roll of notes in his trouser pocket, which the intruders had not noticed. Eventually, fearing for his life, he handed it over. The pirates then ordered him to get up and start the boat's engine. To do that, Jochen would have to find the ignition key. It was somewhere in the main cabin, which had already been ransacked by the pirates. Trawling through the wreckage, Jochen managed to find the key and start the engine. He assumed they were being kidnapped.

The pirates were thirsty and wanted beer, so Jochen went to get some. One of the pirates followed him and when he opened the fridge, grabbed the newlyweds' bottle of champagne. The pirates then stole the gold chain that Jochen wore around his neck, after which they packed all their booty into the couple's suitcases and shopping bags, and loaded everything onto their small boat. Their leader then warned Jochen not to say anything to the authorities and never to come back to the island. Then he opened the throttle and steered the boat directly towards some nearby shoals.

When the pirates jumped into their small boat and made off, Jochen grabbed the wheel and turned the boat away from the shoals. As he looked back across the bay, he saw that people in the restaurant had witnessed the entire incident. However, when they were questioned later nobody admitting seeing a thing.

Once they were headed safely out into open water, Jochen checked that his wife was OK. She was scared but unmolested. The pirates had cut the microphone cord of the radio so he could not contact the police, and they had also taken the distress flares. The GPS was gone, but they had left the compass. And while the pirates had taken all their cash, they had left Jochen's credit card and the couple's airline tickets for home. The pirates had also left two bottles of beer in the fridge, which the couple gratefully consumed.

In the morning they made for the nearest marina and called Sunsail. The company representative turned up with the police, who scoured the yacht but found no fingerprints. The pirates were professionals and had worn gloves. Curiously, as they packed to leave the boat, the couple found that a T-shirt was missing and wondered whether the boat boy at Wallilabou Bay had been working with the pirates.

A week after the *Agatikan* incident, another yacht was attacked by pirates in Wallilabou Bay. On 8 September 2001, round-the-world yachtsman Ruud Braams put in there. He had avoided Cumberland Bay since an American sailor had been killed there in the 1970s. He had also been warned off Wallilabou Bay but being an adventurous sort, that made it all the more attractive. He had with him two Danish charter customers – 50-year-old Charlotte Curden and 46-year-old Claus Oversen, whom he had met in Turkey the previous year. He had picked them up in Martinique and then sailed to St Vincent where he had friends. After tying up in Wallilabou Bay they went ashore for dinner, but were back on board and asleep by 11pm.

Around 1.45am, Claus awoke to find a gun in his face and a man ransacking his cabin. The noise woke Ruud who went into the saloon, where he saw a man with a torch. Ruud punched the intruder, who fell against the refrigerator. Another man came in from the deck with a torch and a gun. Ruud whacked his gun hand, then kicked him into the cockpit where he hit his head hard against the wooden bench. The third pirate decided that discretion was the better part of valour and jumped overboard. The first man got up so Ruud hit him again. Then he too jumped overboard, followed by the last man who took his pistol with him. They made off, leaving their dinghy behind.

The pirates had taken Claus's Discman and CDs, and Charlotte's money and credit cards were gone. Ruud's binoculars, camera, watch, money and chart-plotter were also missing. Again the pirates had slashed the radio's microphone cord. They had also cut the mooring line, though it was a calm night and the boat had not drifted. Ruud shouted for help and a police car turned up, but Ruud did not feel he could trust them, so he sailed round to the next bay where his friend Papa Taxi lived and woke him by sounding the foghorn.

The next day, they reported the matter to the police together. By that time, one of the suspects had already been apprehended. Claus and Charlotte were not keen to take to the sea again and moved into a hotel in Kingstown, the capital of St Vincent, before making their way back to Martinique. Local journalists were reporting that Ruud had been seriously wounded, so he phoned his family in Holland, then spoke to the Dutch newspapers to make sure that they got the story straight before continuing his voyage by himself. All three pirates were eventually arrested, convicted and sentenced to three years in prison.

When former fighter pilot Brad Salzmann retired from the US Air Force, he went to work flying civil aircraft for US Airways. In his spare time he liked to relax by sailing, usually on Cedar Creek reservoir some 50 miles from his home in Dallas, Texas, but also in the Caribbean when he felt a little more adventurous. He had planned a trip there with a few friends in October 2001, but when they dropped out, Brad saw no reason to cancel his holiday and decided to go alone. He flew to Grenada and picked up a yacht in Secret Harbour, a sheltered bay at the southern end of the island. From there he set out for the Tobago Cays. When he reached there on 9 October, there were already 15 yachts in his favourite anchorage between Petit Bateau Island and Baradal.

After he had moored the yacht, locals came out selling lobsters, mussels, fresh bread, souvenirs and T-shirts, and offering diving excursions around the nearby reef from their boats. Most of the vendors had made the 30-minute trip from Union Island and went home at the end of the day. Some, however, stayed overnight in their boats or in makeshift shelters on the islands.

When it grew dark, Brad noticed that a French couple had moored close to him. Fearing a collision if they drifted at night, he moved, dropping anchor near Horseshoe Reef. That evening, he sat out on the deck under the stars sipping a cocktail. Around 9.30pm he went in to make himself another one and change the music. He was on his way back topside when he saw men in the cockpit and on deck. For a moment, he thought it was locals having a joke with him, but soon realised this was no joke. The raiders forced him back into the cabin and demanded to know where his wife or his other shipmates were. Once they had established that he was alone, they demanded he hand over any money he had.

Brad had $400 with him but only parted with $350. The pirates were not impressed. One was nervous, jumpy. He pressed the muzzle of his .22 pistol against Brad's right arm and pulled the trigger. The bullet passed through Brad's arm into his side, through his kidney and diaphragm, and lodged in his lung. Brad did not feel any pain, but slumped over the galley table. One of the pirates said they ought take him to the hospital on Union Island. The other man disagreed. At this point, Brad heard the engine start up and a windlass running. When the two men came back into the main cabin, Brad pretended to be unconscious, but took a sly peek and saw them ripping cables out. That was all he remembered. Suddenly he felt as if he had been hit over the head with a baseball bat: his ears were ringing, he was dizzy and the world seemed to be spinning. In fact, he had been shot again, this time in the head. Blood was coming out of his ear. Seeing this, Brad thought he was going to die and reconciled himself to meeting his maker.

The pirates then left, but Brad decided he did not want to die below decks and somehow got himself back topside so he could die beneath the stars. On deck, he became very nauseous and began throwing up. By that time, it was plain none of the other boats had heard the gunshots or seen the pirates boarding his yacht. No one was coming to his aid.

Brad mustered enough strength to drag himself to the stern and lower himself down into the dinghy. He started the outboard motor and set out for Baradal Island. He knew a man named Alex there who took tourists snorkelling on the reef. For a moment, he wondered whether Alex might have been mixed up with the pirates, but put the thought out of his mind. There was, after all, no one else he could turn to. Later the police ruled Alex out of any involvement in the attack.

It was about 11pm by the time Brad neared the island. Alex was eating dinner with his brother when he heard his name being called. Alex grabbed a torch and the two of them waded out to the dinghy. After they had carried Brad up onto the beach, they examined his wounds. What they saw horrified them. They put Brad back in the dinghy and set out to the nearest yacht still showing lights. This is where Brad got lucky. There was a doctor on the yacht, along with an experienced crew. While the doctor treated Brad for shock, the crew quickly up-anchored and set out for Union Island.

Brad, who only had on his boxer shorts, was still retching but he had stopped bleeding. The bullets had lodged inside him but a .22 does not make a very big entrance wound. The crew radioed ahead for assistance and a pick-up truck met them at the harbour and took Brad to the local hospital. Once his condition had stabilised, he was flown to Kingstown on St Vincent. He was there within five hours of being shot.

Once his family back in Dallas had been contacted, colleagues at US Airways sent a Learjet air ambulance to pick him up. But there was a problem: Brad did not have his passport or any other travel documents. But again he got lucky. The following morning his yacht was brought into harbour on Union Island. The pilot who had flown Brad to St Vincent went on board, found his passport and sent it on the next flight to St Vincent. Brad got it just in time to head off back to the US.

Once back in Dallas, Brad spent a week in hospital while the bullets were removed. The shot to his head had shattered his cheekbone and lodged in his skull, but once again he had been lucky. The bullet had missed the carotid artery, but it cost him the hearing in his left ear.

Then news came that the pirates had been caught. The look-out of the pirate gang wanted nothing to do with an attempted murder and went to the police. The rest of the gang were arrested and sent to prison. The incident has not put Brad off sailing in the Caribbean. He believed the pirates did not set out with the intention of shooting him and that they were high on marijuana. However, next time he went sailing there, he intended to mooring closer to other yachts and be a little more wary of the locals. Most of them wished visitors no harm. Tourism was their livelihood and the activities of pirates were scaring trade away.

According to the International Maritime Bureau (IMB), the most dangerous coastline in the Caribbean belongs to Venezuela. Between October 1996 and February 1999, 90 cases of theft at sea or attacks on shipping were reported, particularly around the harbours of Puerto La Cruz and Guanta. Although the frequency of attacks has dropped off a little since then, the IMB still considers Venezuela to be a piracy hot spot and the attacks have become more violent. In 2002, a 35ft yacht with a Swiss family on board was attacked and sunk outside Puerto La Cruz. Two months later, after Leo Reichnamis had sailed the *Baltic Heritage* out of Bahia Redonda marina, both boat and sailor disappeared without a trace. Soon after, the freighter *Tropic Quest* was boarded by pirates who shot a crewman.

On 20 March 2001, pirates attacked a yacht three-and-a-half miles off the Paria peninsula. On board were Bo and Vivi-Maj Altheden from Bjarred in Sweden. A lifelong sailor, Bo had been in the merchant marines, while Vivi-Maj had been born on Åland Island, where the locals use motorboats as people use cars elsewhere.

In May 1999 the couple had set off from Sweden aboard the *Lorna*, a 44ft steel ketch, built in 1991. They crossed the Atlantic and sailed around the Caribbean. When the hurricane season began they sailed up the eastern seaboard of the United States to Maine, which reminded them of home. In November 2000 they returned to the Caribbean, stopping at Trinidad for repairs. Then, after the Carnival, they moved on.

Their plan was to visit the Venezuela resort island of Isla Margarita, and the national park of the Los Roques islands. However, they did not much care for Venezuela and headed back to Trinidad, from where they planned to travel home via Nova Scotia. They were just two miles off the Paria Peninsula National Park in northern Venezuela when they dropped anchor in San Francisco Bay, figuring that they would make it the 60 miles back to Trinidad the next day. Vivi-Maj was preparing a meal in the cockpit when Bo spotted a small boat approaching. He assumed the men on board were fishermen.

The boat approached within 25 yards of the *Lorna* and the men gestured as if asking for a cigarette. Bo shouted,

'No cigarettes, no smoke.' By now Bo was suspicious as the men did not appear to have any fishing gear. Suddenly they pulled guns out from under some rags and one of them fired, hitting Bo in the back. He tumbled down into the cockpit, bleeding profusely. The bullet had smashed through his hipbone, torn open the duodenum and lodged in the pancreas.

Three men quickly boarded the ketch, leaving one behind on their boat. One short man appeared dishevelled, but the others were clean and well dressed in T-shirts and shorts. One wore a mask over his face and appeared to be carrying an antique shotgun. As they stepped over Bo and entered the cockpit, Vivi-Maj retreated into the saloon. The short, thick-set man asked her for jewellery, money and guns, but she said they had none on board. Then they demanded alcohol. They leader, who appeared to be high on drugs, grabbed a kitchen knife and threatened to slit Vivi-Maj's throat. Then Bo squirmed with discomfort and all guns turned on him. When Vivi-Maj moved to tend to her husband, she was forced back by a gun stuck in her side.

The pirates then grabbed a sleeping bag and began shoving everything of value they could find into it – binoculars, life jackets, flippers, sandals, a torch, a compass, a Sony Walkman, a hand-held depth-sounder, credit cards. Again they demanded alcohol. She gave them three bottles of rum and said, '*Finito*,' making it clear that she wanted them to leave. But before they clambered back into their canoe with their stolen goods, she asked for her credit card back. After all, it would be no good to them back in their village. They obliged, but threw it in her face.

They then ripped out the microphone from the ship's radio but did not spot a small short-wave radio, which was left intact.

Vivi-Maj tried to get a good look at the pirates' boat as they made off, but they waved their guns at her, gesturing for her to sit down. Nevertheless she saw it was white with a green stripe down the side and had a large grey outboard motor. However, she could see no name or registration number.

Once the pirates were gone, Vivi-Maj made Bo as comfortable as she could. He told her how to activate the Emergency Position Indicating Radio Beacon. She tried to summon help on the short-wave radio, but got no reply. A Venezuelan trawler came alongside, but when she explained that her husband had been shot by pirates, it pulled away.

Finally Vivi-Maj started the engine, flipped on the autopilot and set a course for Trinidad. For the next few hours she continued making distress calls. Eventually she raised an amateur radio enthusiast on Trinidad who informed the authorities. However, the *Lorna* was still in Venezuelan waters, which the Trinidadians would not enter without permission. By then it was getting dark.

A Venezuelan coastguard cutter approached. It wanted to come alongside, but there was now a growing swell and Vivi-Maj insisted that they launch a rubber dinghy if they were coming aboard. But Bo had had enough of Venezuela. Though injured, he told Vivi-Maj to turn the boat away and continue making for Trinidad, and in another 15 minutes they had reached its waters. A Trinidadian coastguard now approached. Bo was put aboard the vessel and rushed to hospital on the island, where it took a five-hour operation to patch him up. The coastguard then helped Vivi-Maj sail the *Lorna* into harbour. It was a lesson learned the hard way. Next time he put to sea, Bo said, he would not sail so close to hostile shores where pirates could spot him, and he would stay close to other vessels.

Three years earlier, in February 1998, pirates had shot another yachtsmen off Venezuela. Peter and Maggie Mais had sailed down to the Caribbean from their home in Canada on their 46ft ketch, the *Scotia Pearl*. On board were their two young daughters – Kelsey, five, and Kayla, six. From Grenada they headed to Los Testigos, a nature paradise off the coast of Venezuela. Then they sailed on to Margarita Island, but were advised not to go ashore and began to grow apprehensive.

From Margarita, the family sailed on to Puerto La Cruz and berthed at Bahia Redonda next to their friends Harold and Diane on the *Sea Camp*. Together they sailed on to Caracas del Este where they went snorkelling, and then on to Bahia Manare in the Mochima National Park, sticking together as advised by travel guides. However, as Carnival was underway the anchorage was full and they had to drop anchor out to the west.

After a day on the beach with the girls, Peter and Maggie had drinks on the *Sea Camp* before taking the dinghy back to the *Scotia Pearl* around 8pm and turning in early. At around midnight, Peter was awoken by a loud noise. He looked out to see the outboard motor from the dinghy was missing and a small boat was sitting nearby in the darkness. Peter got Maggie to call the *Sea Camp* on the radio, while he went on deck with the flare gun. He fired a flare in the air, hoping that it would scare the pirates away. When that failed, he fired a second flare in their general direction. The pirates responded with two shots. On the brightly lit aft deck, Peter was an easy target. One bullet grazed his check, cutting open the flesh. The other passed through the flesh of his shoulder and came out of his back. Peter screamed in pain, waking the two girls. There was blood everywhere.

Maggie tried to staunch the blood with a towel and begged Peter not to die. The girls were awake crying, but stayed out of the way in bed. Meanwhile the pirates made off as Harold and Diane made their way over from the *Sea Camp*. They moved Peter below and gave him a shot of the synthetic morphine they kept in the first aid kit. A distress call was put out to the Venezuelan coastguard, but received no response. Eventually they raised the coastguard in Miami. They put a doctor on who gave what advice he could, then tried to contact the Venezuelan coastguards themselves.

No one came to their assistance. It was a moonless night and the *Scotia Pearl* had no radar, so there was nothing they could do but sit it out until daybreak. Soon after dawn, the *Scotia Pearl* raised anchor and headed for Puerto La Cruz with the *Sea Camp* following along behind. Before they arrived, they got on the radio and contacted friends there. Two of them – a retired surgeon and a nurse – were on the quayside to meet them and take Peter to hospital. He needed 14 stitches in his face, but otherwise he was left to heal up on his own as the bullets had missed all the vital organs. But the pirates had shot at his head: it was plain they had meant to kill him.

For German butcher Rudolf Nuss and his wife Isolde sailing had been a hobby, but when he retired they bought a yacht, the *Jan Wellem III*, and set off on a cruise they hoped would last the rest of their lives. At first the Canary Islands were the limit of their ambition but then they met the owners of the German yacht who were on their way to the Caribbean. The Nusses had friends in the West Indies and hitched a ride. As soon as they reached the Grenadines, they fell in love with the Caribbean and decided to make the trip on their own yacht. Once back in the Caribbean, they plied the waters between Trinidad and the Virgin Islands and for them, the whole area was an island paradise. But then they heard disturbing stories. Local men had tried to rape a Swedish woman while her husband was skin diving. She had resisted and the couple were later found with their throats cut. The men responsible had been arrested, the Nusses also heard tales about pirates.

After a trip home that winter, the couple returned to Trinidad in January 2001 to hear of attacks on Dutch and Swedish vessels. Trinidad was packed for Carnival, so the Nusses set off for Venezuela. At first they anchored off Los Testigos. There was a new military post there so Rudolf went ashore to show their passports, the ship's papers and his firearms licence. He was a trained marksman.

The Nusses cleared customs officially in Margarita where they heard that a dinghy had been stolen, so they kept theirs well secured. They also closed the companionway hatch at night and locked it from the inside. On 27 March 2001, they moored beside a Dutch vessel off the tiny island of Cayo Herradura, which was inhabited by a few fishermen whose boats could be seen tied up outside their huts. A young man with a badly swollen foot rowed out to them. Rudolf offered to bandage it, but the young man said he would prefer to do it himself, so Rudolf handed over the bandages and an antiseptic salve from their first aid kit. The couple then ate their dinner and went to bed at around 10pm.

At around 2.25am they woke to hear people moving around on deck. Through a small side window, they could see a small fishing boat tied up alongside and through a cockpit window they could see a man with a gun. They tried to raise the Venezuelan coastguard, but got no response. Then Rudolf switched on the deck lights in the hope that it would scare the men off.

'Open up!' a man shouted from outside.

'No way!' yelled Rudolf in response.

From the noise outside, it was plain that pirates were trying to break in. Fortunately the hatch to the companionway was made of steel, but one of the pirates managed to open a small portlight in the saloon which had not been locked. Rudolf then got out his gun – a 9mm pistol with a 14-shell magazine – and fired a warning shot. The pirates' response was a volley through the portlight. They also tried to fire through the hatch and put several holes in the dinghy. Bullets were hitting the deck around the Nusses and the situation was plainly desperate. Rudolf went to the portlight and emptied his entire magazine out of it. The pirates fired back briefly, then turned and fled.

Rudolf reloaded his gun but stopped shooting. He realised that if he killed or wounded one of the pirates as they made off, the rest would come back to get him. He handed the gun to his wife and, while the pirates continued to take pot shots at the yacht, Rudolf tried to raise the Venezuelan coastguard again.

Hours later, a boat turned up and shone a spotlight on the *Jan Wellem III*. The Nusses thought it might be the pirates returning, so they barricaded themselves in. The vessel circled then drew up alongside. The men on board identified themselves as the *Guardia Nacional* and told the Nusses to lay down their weapons and come out.

As the Nusses emerged onto the deck, men clambered on board. They were dressed in shorts and T-shirts, and looked more like fishermen – or pirates – than the coastguard. The men then went to the cabin, explaining they were searching for drugs. They took Rudolf's pistol and the Nusses' papers, at which point the Nusses then noticed that the Dutch vessel that had been anchored beside them had left.

The coastguard cutter departed but an armed guard was left on the *Jan Wellem III*. Apprehensive about having an armed man on his boat, Rudolf got on the radio again and contacted the German language service that broadcast weather reports and the latest news in the Caribbean. The story of their ordeal was then broadcast across the area, and the German embassy in Caracas and the German foreign ministry in Berlin were informed.

When the Nusses returned to Puerto La Cruz, Venezuelan officials offered their profoundest apologies and returned the Nusses' papers and their pistol. But after that the Nusses vowed to stay out of Venezuelan waters.

CHAPTER 14

BACK TO THE SPANISH MAIN

In the bygone days the richest spoils for the pirates of the Caribbean were Spanish treasure ships. Some sailed out of Cartagena in Colombia, carrying silver from Bolivia, while others loaded Inca treasure from Peru off the coast of Panama after it had been carried across the isthmus there. For mutual protection the galleons would then muster in convoys off Cuba before crossing the Atlantic. On the way they would pass Honduras and Nicaragua. Today, modern pirates ply those same waters.

Colombia in particular has the reputation of being a dangerous place. This is because the Colombian cartels run drugs from their country across the Caribbean and up the isthmus of Panama to the United States. In 1990, Edward Chadband left the Royal Canadian Mounted Police and his second wife. He bought the 32ft *Sol de Medianoche* in Kemah, Texas, and set out into the Caribbean. He planned to make the sea his home.

After reaching the Caribbean Chadband began to enjoy

the camaraderie of the sea. Over four years he visited many islands, including Trinidad for Carnival, where he enjoyed the parties, the rum and the women. In 1994, he headed west to explore Colombia and Panama. On Aruba, he bumped into an old friend, a retired Dutch merchant marine man who warned him to be careful around Punta Gallinas, the most northerly cape of Colombia. The three westerly bays there were the haunt of pirates who attacked any boat that came close to shore. The old sea dog told him to stay at least a hundred miles from the coast.

Chadband had intended to take this advice, but when he was off the coast of Colombia a sudden storm blew up and he was forced to take shelter off Punta Gallinas in the very bays he had been told to avoid. He had only been there for a few hours when he heard the sound of an outboard motor approaching. On board was an old man of around 60 and two teenage boys. They asked for petrol and US dollars. Chadband pretended he had not heard them, dropped his shorts and casually urinated over the side of the boat with his pants around his ankles. Then he told them that he had been taking a nap and asked them why they had disturbed him.

The old man repeated his demand for petrol and money. He had a machete in his hand. The two youths had clubs. A former Mountie, Chadband was not easily intimidated. He pulled the flare gun out of its locker and made a performance of loading it. Then he picked up his own machete, which was a good deal larger than the old man's. This took the smiles off the pirates' faces. The old man started up the outboard motor and took off.

Chadband next sailed on to Cartegena, where he stayed for six months, then across the Gulf of Darien towards Panama.

He landed on San Blas Island, where he lived with the Indians, then visited Portobello and Colón before sailing out to Roatán, off Honduras. There he was to meet up with Gary and Jackie Burke, an English couple he had met in Panama. On their way to Roatán, the Burkes' 34ft sloop *Starlight* had been attacked by pirates. After failing to heed advice to steer clear of the Mosquito Coast, an area disputed by Nicaragua and Honduras, they were chased near Pearl Lagoon by two large dugouts with powerful 50 horsepower outboard motors. On board were at least ten men who waved their arms and, when they came in range, loosed off AK-47s.

Unable to outrun their pursuers, the Burkes had no alternative but to drop their sail. The pirates came on board and knocked Gary down. They did not threaten Jackie, but demanded money and started ransacking the sloop, taking provisions and cans of fuel. Then they put the Burkes' diesel engine out of action and left. The couple were left with their sails, but they still had to negotiate the Honduran Banks at night when it was impossible to see the surf breaking on the reefs until it is too late. But they made it and finally turned up at Roatán, where all the police could do was offer their sympathy.

Three years later, in 1997, German couple Elke and Ralf Stieber were also attacked by pirates off Honduras. Like many amateur sailors they had promised themselves that when they retired they would sail around the world in their yacht, the *Wendy*. By 1996, they had reached Florida, where they decided to sail through the Panama Canal into the Pacific. The journey would take them though the Yucatan Channel and past the coast of Honduras.

In January 1997, they met Sigi Grigo and Peter Frahm on

the *Tranquillo* off Mexico's Isla Mujeres, and agreed to sail to Panama together. However, the two boats got separated off Honduras. The *Tranquillo* hugged the shore, while the *Wendy* stayed out to sea to avoid the reefs nearer the coast. They stayed in touch by radio and agreed to meet up again at Cayos Vivorillo, some small islands 60 miles off the Mosquito Coast, then sail on to the Panama Canal together.

On 19 February, the Stiebers dropped anchor in the calm water inside the reef at Cayos Bogus. In the distance, they could see one of the supply ships that bring provisions out to the fishermen and transport their catch to port. The couple had gone below for a drink when they saw two fishermen in a dinghy rowing up to the side. The men asked if they could come aboard, but Ralf said no. They then asked whether they wanted any coconuts from the island. Again Ralf said no, but before the fishermen went he gave them both a can of beer.

The Stiebers had learned to be wary. When they went back below, they locked the hatch to the companionway behind them. Later they heard the fishermen return, shouting that they had brought the Stiebers a present. Ralf unlocked the hatch and went out to thank them. But when he set foot on the deck, he found the fishermen were already on board. And they had not brought a present, but a nice shiny knife.

The fisherman cut Ralf, then pushed him back down the companionway. Elke found the bloodied body of her husband at her feet. Soon she was bound and gagged, after which the pirates carried the half-conscious body of her husband out onto the deck. They had brought stones with them and they tied them to Ralf's feet. Then Elke heard a splash as they threw him over the side. Now she feared for her own life. The two men demanded money. With her hands still tied, she managed to open her purse and give them its meagre contents. Then they started ransacking the cabins.

When it grew dark, the pirates ordered her to show them how to start the engine. They then began to head out to sea, towing their rowing boat. By this time Elke had managed to work her hands free and while the men were in the cockpit, she made her way to the aft deck, climbed over the rail and jumped into the water. In the distance, she could see the supply vessel and started swimming towards it. She knew that the sea around her was full of sharks and barracuda, and she feared that the men on the supply ship were in league with the pirates.

She was lucky. They were not. They helped the exhausted Elke on board and the captain, an American named Nick Guarino, radioed the Stiebers' son in Germany to tell him what had happened. He and his two sisters flew to Honduras but found the police there uncooperative, so they offered a $500 reward for the capture of the pirates. The following day a relative handed them over to the army. It was clear that they had intended to commit murder as they had brought stones and rope out to the Stiebers' boat.

The *Wendy* was spotted adrift by a Honduran aircraft, whose owner immediately asked to be compensated for the fuel used on the flight. The Honduran coastguard then had to be paid to tow her to port. When the family got the *Wendy* back, she had been stripped of all valuables. Some white powder was found on board and the police threatened to charge Elke with possession of cocaine. Even the judge had to be paid off when he threatened to confiscate the *Wendy* for his own use.

In March 2000 there was more trouble off the coast of Honduras when the *Hayat*, a 34ft steel-hulled yacht belonging to Jacco and Jannie van Tuijl, was attacked. The Dutch couple had built the boat themselves and, after sea trials, they set off around the world with their eight-year-old son Wilhelm. After two and a half years at sea they reached Guam, where Jacco was persuaded to take exams to get his amateur radio licence and buy an amateur transceiver. Later, off Kodiak Island, Alaska, the *Hayat* was dismasted and repairs – interrupted by the long winter – lasted a year. By the time the Hayat was seaworthy again, the van Tuijls were getting short of money and decided to head home. But first they wanted to relax, so they headed for Cayos Vivorillo, off Honduras, dropping anchor there on 28 March 2000. Two other yachts were moored there; one belonged to some friends from Panama so Jacco and son Wilhelm took the dinghy and paid them a visit.

While they were away four locals approached the *Hayat* in a fishing boat and asked for a drink. After going below to set some, Jannie handed their glasses over the side. Noticing there were nets in the boat, she asked, 'Don't you have any fish?'

The fishermen's reply was straightforward. They pulled assault rifles from under the nets, swarmed up over the side and tied her up.

From the other yacht Jacco could see something was wrong. He knew that Jannie would never invite anyone on board if he was not there, so he and Wilhelm set off back to the *Hayat* in the dinghy. The pirates saw them coming, and when they reached the *Hayat*, Jacco and Wilhelm were ordered to come aboard. Then they heard Jannie shout to them in Dutch, 'Get away!'

A pirate let off a warning shot but Jacco turned the dinghy around and made a run for it. The pirates fired wildly at them. Then one took careful aim and squeezed the trigger. The bullet ripped through the rubberised fabric of the side of the dinghy and hit Wilhelm in the stomach. The boy screamed, but his father could do nothing. He had to get as far as possible from the pirates before the dinghy deflated and sank. It was an impossible task. Before long, one compartment was empty of air and the boat flipped over, pitching the two of them into the water.

The pirates jumped into their boat and set off after them. When they reached father and son floundering in the water, they swung machetes at them. Jacco, who was holding Wilhelm afloat with one hand, yelled that they were murderers and kept on screaming until the pirates left. He then swam over to the *Hayat* with Wilhelm in one arm. By then the boy could no longer feel his legs.

Jannie had managed to get herself untied and helped Jacco get Wilhelm on board. They sent out a mayday message, and Jacco got the engine started while Jannie, who was a registered nurse, tended to their son on the deck. Then, with the transceiver he had bought in Guam, Jacco raised two amateur radio enthusiasts in the US. They alerted the American authorities and soon a naval vessel was despatched. More amateur radio enthusiasts got involved, relaying medical advice to the couple.

Jacco tried to head for Puerto Lempira, about a hundred miles away in Honduras, but the autopilot was not working.

Nor was the EPIRB, and the rolling of the boat caused Wilhelm pain. The yacht carrying their friends accompanied them, but both yachts kept their lights switched off in the hope that pirates would not see them. When they reached the coast the *Hayat*'s six-foot draft mean she could not sail through the shallow Caratasca Strait into Puerto Lempira and Wilhelm had to be transferred to an ex-US coast-guard cutter that had been given to Honduras.

The hospital at Puerto Lempira was ill-equipped and there was little they could do for the boy. He was rushed to the airport where a US Army Blackhawk helicopter whisked him off to La Ceiba, two hundred miles away. Throughout the journey Jannie feared her son was going to die. In the hospital, surgeons repaired Wilhelm's damaged kidneys, but found that the bullet had also damaged his spine. He was flown to the Children's Medical Centre in Dallas, Texas but nothing could be done. Wilhelm was now paralysed from the waist down and confined to a wheelchair.

Just north of Honduras lies Guatemala. The bay at the mouth of the Rio Dulce there has long been used as safe anchorage during a hurricane, and this provides modern-day pirates with rich pickings. In June 2000, the body of an American sailor named Steven M. Gartman was found on board his yacht, the *Sea Lion*, just a hundred yards outside a marina in Rio Dulce. He and his yacht had been shot up.

Then on 11 November, two yachts sailing in convoy were attacked. Four men approached one of them in a dugout and ransacked the vessel. The other yacht could see what was happening and tried to contact the skipper, who was held at gun point and could not answer the call. Half-an-hour later, the second yacht was boarded and looted. That year alone 14 yachts were attacked in Gulf of Honduras.

Keen sailor Dan Caruso had spent ten years building a boat, only to see it burn to cinders just weeks before it was due to be launched. This did not dampen the call of the sea. For the rest of his working life, Dan delivered boats for friends to keep up his sailing skills. Then in 1994, he retired and bought a 53ft catamaran, the *Sunshine*, and set off on a Caribbean cruise. His family and friends saw him off from Tampa Bay, Florida on 17 June. On board were his two teenage nephews, Paul and Ben. They passed Cuba and headed for the Yucatán Peninsula, then on to the Isla Mujeres. From there, they travelled from island to island down the coast. The kids went out in their kayaks. They snorkelled and fished and when they caught lobsters, had cookouts on the beach.

They were on their way to Belize, when the radio packed up, so they got no weather forecasts. One rough night, the kayak slipped over the side and broke away, and water got in through an unsecured hatch, soaking everything. One of their engines broke down and they only just made it into sheltered water when a storm broke.

They had trouble in Belize. The locals were threatening. One tried to board the boat and ashore someone threatened Dan's dog with a machete. There was more trouble in Belize City, so after Dan's wife Susan paid a visit, they headed down the coast to Guatemala. At Rio Dulce, Dan's catamaran had a shallow enough draft to pass over the sand bars at the mouth of the river and sail up into Lake Izabal beyond.

On 19 July the *Sunshine* dropped anchor in the Ensanada Los Lagartos, a small river at the other end of the lake that was surrounded by rainforest and wildlife. An hour before dark a dugout with three men on board came up the river. As it passed them, its engine cut out and they did not seem to be able to get it started again. They paddled over to the *Sunshine* and asked for a sparkplug spanner, which Dan gave them. He even gave them a hand with the engine, to no avail.

Then they asked whether Dan could give them a tow with his dinghy. He agreed, but when he went to get the tow rope, the three men got on board. One of them had a pistol, another a shotgun, the third a machete. The man with the pistol fired two warning shots in the air and forced Dan and his two nephews to kneel on the deck. Dan grew fearful. He had heard of visitors being shot or hacked to death with machetes in this part of the world.

While the man with shotgun kept guard on the prisoners, the other two pillaged the boat, dropping the TV, VCR and other valuables into their dugout. Then the man with the pistol took Dan into the main cabin, where he was sure the man intended to shoot him. This offered him a glimmer of hope. If they were going to kill him out of sight of the boys, that presumably meant they intended to let them go. The pirate ordered Dan to kneel. Dan refused. If he was going to die, he was going to die on his feet, not his knees.

The man grew agitated and poked Dan in the chest and head with his pistol. Dan was still certain he was going to kill him, but led the pirates to where he had hidden some money. On the way, they had to go through a narrow corridor. Dan considered tackling his assailants. He was certain that he could grab the pistol from the first pirate and use his body to shield him from the man with the machete. However, he feared the man with the shotgun would hear the ruckus and shoot the two boys.

Once they had the money – $10,000 in all – the pirates led Dan back up on deck, then started plundering the *Sunshine* again for anything they had overlooked. This time they took the outboard motor from the dinghy and cans of petrol. Dan then wondered whether he should jump overboard and hide in the undergrowth at the riverside, sure that they would never find him. But again there were the two boys to consider.

By the time the pirates left the *Sunshine* Dan had had the shirt stripped from his back and was black with mosquitoes. The pirates warned them not to call the police and now, convinced they were going to survive, they agreed. Once the pirates were gone, they weighed anchor and headed back out into the middle of the lake, where they spent the night. In the end they did report the matter to the police, who carefully drafted a report but showed no signs of acting on it. Dan was convinced that if he had been with two adults instead of two boys, the pirates would have killed all of them.

In the 16th and 17th centuries, pirates from the Caribbean would cross the isthmus of Panama or round Cape Horn to plunder treasure ships in the Pacific. Modern-day pirates prey on those waters too.

Dieter Lange had already travelled around the world in a camper van and a single-engined plane when he bought the 31ft *Ala Di Sabah* in Los Angeles to make his third circumnavigation, this time by sea. To learn the ropes he entered a race out to Santa Catalina Island. After that he headed south along the coast of Mexico, Guatemala, El Salvador, Honduras, Nicaragua, Costa Rica, Panama and Colombia. On 8 July 2001, the *Ala Di Sabah* was moored alongside his British friend Tim – with whom he had been sailing in convoy since Costa Rica – off the town of Sua, near Esmeraldas in Ecuador, 70 miles north of the equator.

That day Dieter invited on board an Ecuadorean family who were eager to see how his boat worked. There were 12 of them and they assured him that Sua was a safe haven; nothing ever happened there. As night fell at around 6pm, they started to take their leave. It took him some time to tidy up, then he made himself a bite to eat and turned in by 10.30pm. He was asleep when pirates climbed on board to rob him.

Dieter awoke to find a man standing over him. Although it was pitch black, Dieter knew his way around his boat. He managed to pin the man again the mast support, knee him in the crotch and break his arm. A second man, standing in the hatchway, shone a torch in Dieter's face, then there was a bang and a spurt of fire. Dieter felt a pain in his chest and knew he had been hit. But this only succeeded in making him mad. He tried to cling onto the first man's arm but the pain in his chest was too great. Again he tried to tackle the man as he escaped through the hatchway. Beyond him, the other pirate was ready to fire a second time, but could not without risking hitting his accomplice. The two jumped into their open boat alongside, a third man cranked up the throttle and they took off.

Dieter's strength was draining fast, but he managed to crawl to the cockpit and radio Tim before lapsing into unconsciousness. Minutes later he was roused by Tim, who could see by the light of a torch that there was blood all over Dieter's T-shirt. 'My God, what a mess,' said Tim. He told Dieter that he must not go back to sleep, but Dieter had reconciled himself to the thought of dying.

Tim then put out a distress call and three local men came to the rescue. They lifted Dieter into their boat and began rowing him ashore. The salt water stung as it splashed onto his wounds, but the sensation kept him conscious.

On the beach they gave Dieter mouth-to-mouth resuscitation and a car was requisitioned to take him to hospital. There an X-ray showed that a 9mm bullet had entered Dieter's chest: it had been fired directly at his heart but his breastbone had deflected it. The bullet remained lodged against his spine but the surgeon thought it too risky to try to remove it. (The bullet was finally removed after Dieter was flown back to Germany.) The police in Ecuador showed no interested the Dieter's story. Nor did the German embassy there but both the British and American embassies were keen to log a report.

Sua, it seemed, was not the law-abiding town Dieter's Ecuadorean friends had made out: the *Ala Di Sabah*'s dinghy was seen leaving Sua on a truck owned by the mayor. Undeterred, Dieter bought another one in Germany and took it back with him. After rigging up an alarm system connected to the deck lights, he and Tim continued on their journey.

The same year retired sea captain Robert Medd, a resident of Vancouver Island, had had trouble a little further to the north. In early 2000, he set off on a circumnavigation in his 34ft yacht *The Learning Curve* – affectionately known as *TLC* – by sailing down the Pacific coast. After wintering off Baja California, he began exploring the Gulf of California (or the Sea of Cortez). He was heading north from Santa Rosalia to Bahia de Los Angeles when at around 9pm he saw a small open boat with four men aboard. Robert was used to fishermen pulling up alongside and asking for water, so he went below to get some from the fridge. But one of the men got on board and followed him. When Robert turned from the fridge, he was confronted by a pirate holding his wallet and bread knife.

The man demanded money and when Robert said he did not have any, the pirate slashed him across the arm. A second pirate knocked Robert unconscious with a rock. The pirates then plundered the boat, slit Robert's throat from ear to ear and left.

Robert awoke to find himself lying in a pool of blood. There was a gash a quarter of an inch wide across his throat, but the main sail was still set and the engine was running. Then he lapsed back into unconsciousness. He was awoken again some time later by the sound of the hull hitting rocks. Somehow he clambered ashore, taking with him drinking water, a flare gun, a blanket and a torch. He found himself in the Desierto de Vizcaino, a desert that stretches some 60 miles down the coast, where the daytime heat goes up to over 100°F. By the time two Mexican fishermen found him the following afternoon and got him to hospital with the help of the Mexican Navy, he was hallucinating. With his yacht gone and his possessions pillaged, he had lost everything he owned. All he had left was his life, and a surgeon back in Canada told him even that had only been saved by his thick beard.

CHAPTER 15

SEA DOGS

These days nowhere on the high seas is safe. There are even pirates in the Mediterranean – a situation supposedly ended by Julius Caesar and the great Admiral Pompey more than two thousand years ago.

In May 1997, a British couple were placidly sailing their rented yacht around the Greek island of Corfu when masked men brandishing grenades and assault rifles suddenly boarded their boat. The gang stripped the couple of their possessions and the boat of its navigational gear. The couple's ordeal only ended when they were rescued by Greek coastguards. The tourist-conscious Greek government then began sending gunboats to discourage Albanian pirates from crossing the two-mile Corfu Channel to prey on yachts sailing around the island.

On 27 July 2000, skipper Aris Calothis and his charter boat the *Erato* picked up a Swiss family at the port of Navplion on the eastern Peloponnesus. As one of the party of five needed a wheelchair and they had a baby with them,

Aris got permission to moor the *Erato* next to the quay. That night a man climbed on board, slipped the moorings, started the engine and headed for the harbour entrance. Woken by the noise of the engine, Aris came up to the cockpit to find himself looking down the barrel of a gun. The intruder told him to get back down into the cabin.

Aris was puzzled. He wondered whether his charter client Andy Hagger was playing some sort of practical joke on him. The light in the cockpit was poor and he could not see the man's face. Nevertheless, he grabbed the radio microphone and reported the incident to the coastguard. Then he attempted to go up into the cockpit again. Again the man at the helm told him to get down.

Back in the main cabin, Aris bumped into Corinne Michelle, Andy's sister. She had been woken by the engines and wanted to know why they were already under way. When Aris questioned her about her brother, she opened the cabin door to reveal Andy still sleeping. Aris was staggered. He got back on the radio and contacted the coastguard again.

Then he went back to the companionway and asked the man at the helm what he intended to do. The pirate told him to stay in the main cabin and said he would be told everything he needed to know in 30 minutes. Making the best of a bad situation, Aris made himself a cup of coffee and lit a cigarette. Then he heard the pirate switch off the engine. He was trying to make sail, but could not manage it on his own and summoned Aris on deck. The skipper turned up with a cup of coffee and a lighted cigarette, trying to look as if nothing had happened. In fact, he was biding his time until the coastguard turned up.

Needing help to raise the sails, the pirate tried to be friendly. Speaking in English with a thick Eastern European accent, he explained that his name was Charlie and he was trying to get to Casablanca. Aris pointed out that the journey could take weeks.

'I've got time,' said Charlie.

Aris explained that they did not have enough fresh water and provisions on board to make such a trip. He had no charts of the water off North Africa and the coastguard would soon be after them because they had not requested clearance to leave port. The pirate said he was not bothered by this and ordered the skipper to make sail. Aris did what he was told, but slowly. First he made the deck shipshape, coiling the mooring lines and removing the bimini sunshade. By the time he had unfurled the main sail, the wind had dropped and the engine would not restart. The next day they covered less than a mile.

The yacht was contacted by the coastguards, who wanted to know if the situation had changed. Reporters who had got wind of the story hired power boats and headed after the *Erato* to shoot pictures from a distance with telephoto lenses. Then they began calling the boat's cell phone and shouting questions over the water. Friends of the family also began calling them on their mobile phones. Aris did his best to reassure everyone.

The pirate began to tell Aris his life story. He was a 38-year-old Czech who had served in the Gulf War. He had also been a mercenary, serving in Namibia. He had been badly wounded and spent a long time in hospital. Aris could see scars around his neck. In Casablanca he was hoping to get a new job, but he could not travel by conventional means as the police were after him. While Charlie and Aris got to know each other, the passengers sweltered below, where the temperature topped 100°F.

Frustrated by the slow progress they were making – two days out and they had not even cleared the Gulf of Argolikós – the pirate called the coastguard and demanded a faster boat, then a seaplane. The coastguard stalled.

Aris kept coffee on the boil, but the pirate refused both food and drink. Eventually, the *Erato* became completely becalmed and Charlie and Aris passed the time playing chess. They got to know each other so well that Aris suggested that they try and get closer to shore that night so that Charlie could slip ashore unnoticed and escape.

When a coastguard cutter approached, Charlie let Aris talk to it over the VHF radio, asking it to keep their distance. Charlie waved his gun to show that he was serious. The coastguards then spent their time shooing reporters' boats away. However, while appearing compliant, the coastguards were assembling a SWAT team. When Aris went below to get another coffee, there was a volley of shots and commandos swarmed aboard. The *Erato* was quickly secured and Charlie's body was found floating in the sea. Casablanca, once home to the Barbary pirates, would not be greeting its newest recruit.

There was more trouble off Albania in 2001. Two Austrians, Markus Sittinger and Georg Nigl, were used to taking regular sailing holidays in the Mediterranean on their little sloop *Rumtreiber (Layabout)* which they brought from Austria on a trailer. Over the years they had explored the Adriatic, the Riviera, the Balearic Islands and waters off Lipari, north west of Messina.

In May 2001, they returned to the Adriatic. This time they set off from Italy and headed for Corfu. To clear customs there, they had to land at the main port of Kerkira on the eastern side of the island. To reach it, they would have to sail round the northern side of the island and through the narrow Oranto Strait that separated Corfu from Albania. At its narrowest, the strait was just two miles wide.

By the evening of 14 May, they were 50 miles north of Corfu, some 23 miles off the Albanian city of Vlorë. They had planned to make landfall in Kerkira that night but had been becalmed, so they started their small 10 horsepower outboard motor. At around 10pm it was still light and they spotted a boat astern of them. It followed them for some time at a distance of around a mile. Georg could see through his binoculars that it was a fishing boat, but as other yachts and ships were in sight they attached little importance to it.

Once it was dark, Georg scanned the horizon again with his night-vision glasses. The fishing boat was still there. Georg and Markus did not fancy negotiating the Strait of Oranto in the dark, so they throttled back to a speed that would put them at the entrance to the strait just as dawn broke. Around 2am, Georg brought coffee up to the cockpit and they turned on the radio; the music and the chugging of the outboard now drowned out all other sounds. Suddenly the fishing boat loomed out of the darkness to starboard. While one man held the helm, two more were on the prow, ready to jump on board the *Rumtreiber*. Markus opened the throttle and swung the tiller to port.

Georg kept an emergency bag in the companionway. In it

was a Colt .45 and three magazines. In his rush to reach it, he spilt his hot coffee in his lap. Oblivious to the pain, he grabbed the gun. The fishing boat made a second attempt to board them, but again quick thinking by Markus foiled the attack. This time Georg brandished the .45 at them and the two men fled to the safety of their after deck. The would-be pirates then unleashed a volley of threats before their fishing boat disappeared back into the darkness.

Fearing that this might only mark a short respite in the attack, Markus and Georg switched off the lights on the sloop and pulled the plug on the radio. Running silent, they made a zigzag course until morning. Later they realised the pirates had not been planning a second attack. The two had left the radar reflector aloft, so the fishing boat could easily have followed them. George has now installed a VHF radio on the *Rumtreiber* so that he can call the coastguard in case of emergency. He also intends to carry a shotgun to repel boarders and a sniper's rifle to take out a pirate or an outboard motor at a distance.

There are also modern-day pirates operating off the Barbary Coast – the waters of North Africa from Morocco down to Libya, notorious for pirates up until the 19th century. On 23 October 1996, Franck Düvell was sailing a 45ft yacht from Gibraltar to Lanzarote when, around 30 miles off the shore of Morocco, he ran foul of drift net. It was ill-lit and practically invisible in the swell. He could not get clear of it under sail, and trying to pull the boat free using a dinghy and outboard motor did no good either.

The net was made of wire nearly an inch thick and Franck was about to set about it with bolt-cutters and a hacksaw when a small fishing boat carrying no navigation lights turned up. There were at least 12 people on board and they illuminated the scene with a powerful spotlight. Fortunately Franck was not travelling alone. His crew of seven assembled on the deck armed with boathooks and other tools. The fishermen demanded several bottles of whisky and a million French francs. After protracted negotiations, they settled for one bottle of whisky and $200. The net then seemed to vanish and they were allowed to go on their way.

Further south, the Cape Verde Islands have become a den of pirates. Refugees from Africa and impoverished locals have taken to attacking yachts that put in there, looking for cash and valuables. Some sailors are even more unlucky. In 1993 Monika and Uwe Reinders had had their 43ft fibreglass sloop, the *Muwi*, refitted in Roermond in the Netherlands and made their way to the Mediterranean via the canals of France. From there they sailed to the Cape Verde Islands, where Monika flew home and Uwe prepared to sail the Atlantic single-handed.

On the evening of 3 July, the *Muwi* was at anchor about 350 yards off shore in Tarrafal Bay on the northern peninsula of the southerly island of São Tiego. At around 6pm Uwe decided to go ashore for a couple of cool beers and something to eat. Knowing that thieves might target his outboard motor, he stowed it below and to avoid the freshly varnished companionway, climbed out of the saloon skylight, locking it behind him. He also made sure that the companionway hatch was locked before rowing the dinghy ashore.

After pulling it up the beach so it would not float away on a rising tide, Uwe had his dinner in a snack bar and then a couple of beers with a Swedish friend. At 10pm he returned to the beach to find his dinghy gone. He searched around but could not find it. It was now getting late so he decided to swim out to the Muwi, have a good night's sleep and worry about the dinghy in the morning. But first he found a convenient spot, dug a hole in the sand and buried his credit cards and cash – about $800 he had just got from the bureau de change. Then he plunged into the water and headed out into the bay, but when he reached where the *Muwi* should have been, she was not there. He swam over to a nearby fishing boat, but the fisherman said he had not seen a yacht anchored there.

Uwe swam back to shore, but could not find the money he had buried. Now he was wet, homeless, penniless and stranded. He walked to the police station, but they were little help. Fortunately, some fishermen put him up for the night. In the morning he borrowed some money and called Monika in Germany.

The following day, the dinghy was found to the south on São Tiego but the police said the yacht was nowhere to be seen. The insurance company thought it might have been sailed to Dakar in Senegal. Uwe and Monika met up there and hired a plane to search the coast. They found nothing and returned to Germany to pursue the matter with the insurers.

Two and a half months later, on 21 September, the Cameroonian freighter *Cam Bilinga* spotted the *Muwi* drifting off the Bijagos Islands, part of Guinea-Bassau. She was 620 miles southeast of the Cape Verde Islands, but the winds and currents would have made it impossible for her to have drifted there. She had been stripped of everything of value and was all but wrecked. The anchor and chain were missing and the rudder was jammed so far to starboard that she could not be steered. The *Cam Bilinga* tried to tow her but the seas were too high to pull a boat in that condition. Eventually the freighter hauled her on board using a cargo crane, causing more damage in the process, and delivered her to Nordenham, across the river from Bremerhaven in Germany, the *Cam Bilinga*'s destination. From there the *Muwi* was taken to Kiel for repairs.

Slowly investigators pieced together what had happened to her. They reckoned the pirates must have used Uwe's dinghy to get out to the yacht. They would then have cut the mooring lines, dropping the anchor and chain as hauling it in would have made too much noise. The pirates had not used the engine as the fuel levels when she was found were exactly the same as when she went missing. Nor had they sailed her: the socks Uwe had left to dry on the mainsail were still in place when the *Muwi* reached Kiel.

There was a streak of green paint down the side, indicating that a fishing vessel had tried to keep her tied alongside, towing her that way. But this would have been impossible if there had been any swell. A length of natural fibre was found tied to the mast. It seemed that the pirates had also tried to tow her that way, but with the rudder jammed over to one side, that too would have been impossible. The wheel had been taken off and the wheelhousing and chains dismantled, seemingly in an attempt to free the rudder. When all that had failed, the pirates plundered the ship. The padlock on the second hatchway was missing, giving them entry to the interior. They took the GPS, short-wave radio, radar, sonar, outboard motor, generator, life raft and anything else of value. Then they cast her adrift.

From where the *Muwi* was found, it was clear the coast of West Africa had been her intended destination. The natural fibre tied to the mast also indicated that the pirates were from the mainland of West Africa, rather than the Cape Verde Islands. Judging from the growth of mussels and algae on her hull, she had been in warm coastal waters for some time. Nevertheless, the insurance company contested the case. If the *Muwi* had not been taken by pirates, perhaps the Reinders had arranged the whole thing. The courts found in the Reinders' favour and the insurance company were forced to pay up. This was the first incidence of a yacht being stolen from the Cape Verde Islands.

Further south again in Nigeria, the IMB warn ships to be vigilant around Lagos and the mouth of the Bonny River. The pirates there are particularly violent. They have attacked and robbed vessels and kidnapped crews along the coast and rivers, and at anchorages and ports. There were more than 20 incidents off West Africa in 2008. And further afield pirates were also very active off Bangladesh, with a large number of attacks reported off Chittagong. Ships have also been attacked in Indian ports: tankers, cargo ships, even research vessels have been boarded.

On 13 February 2005, the USS *Bonhomme Richard*, an American amphibious assault ship, answered a bridge-to-bridge distress call from a Kuwaiti fisherman in the Persian Gulf. The fishing boat was being seized by a group of pirates in Boston whaler powerboats. The *Bonhomme Richard* pursued the pirates at top speed, chasing two pirate boats away from the fishing dhows.

'With 44,000 tons of combat power chasing after them, they got out of there in a hurry,' said the *Bonhomme Richard*'s commanding officer Captain J. Scott Jones. 'This proves again the deterrent capability of this ship and her sailors and marines. Just by being here, we were able to protect these fishermen.'

As his ship carried 48 helicopters and five Harrier jump jets, and was armed with machine guns and missile launchers, it was a sledgehammer used to break a nut. To be fair, however, the *Bonhomme Richard* was not solely on anti-piracy patrol. The ship's mission was to support maritime security operations around oil terminals vital to Iraq's economy, and to deter terrorism at sea. Previously, it had also delivered more than a million pounds of humanitarian supplies to Indonesian tsunami survivors, sent Marines ashore and chased pirate ships away.

But piracy does have its lighter moments. A thief who sailed a stolen yacht across the Bass Strait between Australia and Tasmania in February 2005 left an anonymous letter at Tasmania's *Examiner* newspaper, apologising to Melbourne businessman Philip Murphy whose $350,000 yacht he had stolen from the Blairgowrie marina on 31 January. In it the thief said he was 'no Captain Jack Sparrow', a reference to the character played by Johnny Depp in the movie *Pirates of the Caribbean*.

The man said he had not intended to sail to Tasmania, but with no fuel, radio, charts or navigation aids to get back to Melbourne, it was the only place he knew he could sail in to anchor. 'Of a lot of bad ideas, this was the best and I believe it saved my life,' he wrote. 'I don't expect you to forgive me but unless you have been through it you can't possibly understand. Maybe one day we can sit down and have a beer and I will tell you.'

The yacht was found abandoned off Tasmania's northwest coast on 2 February. It seems the thief had sailed across a stormy Bass Strait, where the waters of the Pacific and the Indian Oceans meet, accompanied only by his Alsatian dog. The police found the vessel's dinghy in a forest reserve south of Devonport on the north side of the island on 7 February, after being supplied with details of its location by the thief in his letter.

Acting Detective Inspector Darren Hopkins said, 'He's certainly doing all the right things at the moment and the next step is to turn himself in. We are asking the person responsible for taking the yacht from Melbourne to contact Devonport CIB so the matter can be resolved quickly, as a significant number of police resources are being used on this investigation.'

Now you can buy any of these other books by
Nigel Cawthorne from your bookshop or direct
from the publisher.

Free P+P and UK Delivery
(Abroad £3.00 per book)

HOUSE OF HORRORS
ISBN 978-1-84454-696-1   PB   £7.99

ON THE FRONTLINE
ISBN 978-1-84454-733-3   PB   £7.99

THE WORLD'S TEN MOST EVIL MEN
ISBN 978-1-84454-745-6   PB   £9.99

SPECIAL FORCES WAR ON TERROR
ISBN 978-1-84454-782-1   PB   £11.99

HEROES
ISBN 978-1-84454-470-7   PB   £7.99

TO ORDER SIMPLY CALL THIS NUMBER
+ 44 (0) 207 381 0666

Or visit our website
www.johnblakepublishing.co.uk

Marshall County Public Library
1003 Poplar Street
Benton, KY 42025